THE ANTHROPOLOGY OF FOOD AND NUTRITION

General Editor: *Helen Macbeth*

Recent titles:

For a full volume listing, please see the series page on our website:
https://www.berghahnbooks.com/series/anthropology-of-food-and-nutrition

PURE FOOD

Theoretical and Cross-Cultural Perspectives

....

Edited by

Paul Collinson and Helen Macbeth

berghahn
NEW YORK · OXFORD
www.berghahnbooks.com

First published in 2023 by
Berghahn Books
www.berghahnbooks.com

© 2023 Paul Collinson and Helen Macbeth

Library of Congress Cataloging-in-Publication Data
Names: Collinson, Paul, 1969- editor. | Macbeth, Helen M., editor.
Title: Pure food : theoretical and cross-cultural perspectives / edited by
  Paul Collinson and Helen Macbeth.
Description: New York : Berghahn Books, 2023. | Series: The anthropology of
food & nutrition ; volume 12 | Includes bibliographical references and index.
Identifiers: LCCN 2023000741 (print) | LCCN 2023000742 (ebook) | ISBN
  9781805390183 (hardback) | ISBN 9781805390190 (ebook)
Subjects: LCSH: Food habits. | Food adulteration and inspection. |
  Food--Quality. | Nutritional anthropology.
Classification: LCC GT2860 .P87 2023 (print) | LCC GT2860 (ebook) | DDC
  394.1/2--dc23/eng/20230412
LC record available at https://lccn.loc.gov/2023000741
LC ebook record available at https://lccn.loc.gov/2023000742

British Library Cataloguing in Publication Data
A catalogue record for this book is available from the British Library

ISBN 978-1-80539-018-3 hardback
ISBN 978-1-80539-019-0 ebook

https://doi.org/10.3167/9781805390183

CONTENTS

ILLUSTRATIONS

Figures

Table

PREFACE

Paul Collinson and Helen Macbeth

This book is another in the Berghahn Books series *The Anthropology of Food and Nutrition*, which follows the aims of the International Commission on the Anthropology of Food and Nutrition (ICAF) in its pursuit of cross-disciplinary communication on issues concerning human food. Anthropology is a broad subject encompassing all aspects of the human condition past and present, and itself involves many subdisciplines specialising in different perspectives on humanity. In our view, bringing a range of insights to bear is central to the study of food, an endeavour that necessitates communicating not only across the subdisciplines within anthropology, but also with scholars from different disciplines and with practitioners engaged with food in some way in their professional lives.

In this volume, the focus is on pure food, something that has many interpretations and is by no means immutable, an observation explored in a number of different chapters. The contributions each shed light on specific areas, tackling issues as diverse as pure food in ancient Greece and Rome, the changing meaning of purity through the ages, the sociocultural basis of pure food and disgust, the psychological efficacy of purity and food, the use of blood as food, food purity and tourism, pure food in public institutions, and attitudes towards food safety, organic food and farming, among many others. Taken together, they demonstrate that pure food is a common issue for humanity, whatever the society, whatever the era. Each chapter could be read on its own for the material it presents, but in the juxtaposition of these perspectives, the book seeks to provide a holistic insight into what is a profoundly diverse and complex topic. Although no one volume can encompass all the many perspectives on pure food, the Introduction and the Epilogue link the chapters within a theme that is at once theoretical and empirical, grounded in observations of the significance of pure food across different societies and cultural contexts.

The editors and contributors to this volume benefited from multidisciplinary discussions hosted by the Hanse-Wissenschaftskolleg Institute for Advanced Study, Delmenhorst, Germany, and from further discussions through Oxford Brookes University, United Kingdom and the Max-Planck-Institut, Starnberg-Seewiesen, Germany. Professor Dr Wulf Schiefenhövel in particular is thanked for his role in these and subsequent discussions. Finally the editors would like to thank all the contributors to this volume, the anonymous reviewers for their helpful insights on the draft manuscript, and everyone at the publishers, Berghahn Books, for making this book possible.

Paul Collinson
Helen Macbeth

INTRODUCTION
PURE FOOD: THEORETICAL AND CROSS-CULTURAL PERSPECTIVES

Paul Collinson and Helen Macbeth

A quest for eating healthily has become one of the defining features of food consumption habits in the Western world in the twenty-first century. Awareness of and concern about the origins of food, the nature of its production, its constituent ingredients and, fundamentally, the relationship between what we eat and who we are has grown markedly and permeates many different aspects of popular culture and day-to-day living. This is manifested in innumerable different ways, from food labelling to diet books, from organic farming to guerrilla gardening,[1] and has profoundly influenced the way in which food is produced, distributed, bought, consumed and recycled today. It is associated with other interrelated attitudinal and behavioural trends, including: a greater concern with issues surrounding the environment and sustainability; the rise of consumer activism and green politics, anti-globalisation, localism and communitarianism; the emergence of the 'risk society'; and more awareness of issues surrounding the relationship between physical and mental health, along with movements such as 'gym culture'.

The quest often involves a striving for a biological or quasi-biological concept of 'purity'. But what does 'food purity' mean? Why is purity itself regarded in such a positive way? How do notions of food purity vary cross-culturally? What implications does food purity have for food production and consumption? And how do concepts of food purity link with our own sense of psychological wellbeing? This book seeks to answer some of these questions. It collects together contributions from anthropologists and scholars from other disciplines, as well as practitioners, who examine different aspects of pure food from theoretical and empirical standpoints. Some chapters focus on the historical and theoretical dimensions of notions of purity as related to food, whereas others provide examples of the importance of pure food in different cultures, drawing primarily upon ethnographic research conducted variously in Latin America, Melanesia and Western Europe, along with practitioner experiences of food-related issues of significance in contemporary societies. The objective of the book is to shed light on variations in practices, behaviours and cultural beliefs in different places in relation to pure food, while also highlighting some of the similarities between them.

This Introduction will set out the main themes of the book and the chapters that follow, which are described at appropriate points in the discussion. It begins with an examination of purity itself, the origins of the term and what purity means when applied to food. This leads into an exploration of anthropological concepts of purity, drawing on theories of classification and ideas surrounding dirt, disgust and pollution, and noting how notions of food purity form a central component of religious and social ideology in a number of societies. We then discuss the associations between pure food and health, examining issues surrounding food hygiene, safety, regulation and risk, health foods and food labelling, in terms of the listing of ingredients, additives and nutritional information, as well as new forms of labelling that consider environmental impacts and fairtrade, among other issues. We go on to consider the rise of vegetarianism and veganism in relation to pure food, as well as the recent emergence of dietary regimes in which the quest for food purity is the key goal. The rise of organic farming and food is the focus of the next section, which also examines how food is promoted and marketed. Motivations for dietary choices are then explored in the context of the important relationships between the factors underpinning food choices and pure food itself. We finish by drawing the discussion together and offering some tentative conclusions.

What Is Purity?

According to the online etymological dictionary *etymonline*,[2] the word 'pure' is derived from the Latin term *purus*, which means 'clean, clear, unmixed, unadorned, chaste and undefiled'. The same source claims that the English word 'impure' was in common use in the early sixteenth century as meaning 'earthy, mundane, not spiritual'. It goes on to explain that during the course of the 1500s, the meaning of 'impure' expanded to encompass people and activities that were considered 'obscene, lewd, unchaste and immoral' and then, by the 1590s, the word conveys anything 'mixed with offensive matter, tainted'. Thus, the positive moral association of purity and the negative association of its antonym were there from the early usage of the words in English and are reflected in the way in which the terms are frequently viewed today (for a further exploration of these concepts, see Lejavitzer and the Epilogue, this volume).

Notions of purity and impurity – and pollution – are interwoven throughout social and cultural life across all societies, and anthropologists and other social and behavioural scientists have exhaustively documented the numerous different ways in which the concepts are manifested (Duschinsky 2016). The body is a key locus for these ideas. The potential polluting effects of bodily secretions are, as far as is known, a cultural universal, albeit a highly variable one, and are reified in the form of a welter of different taboos from, for example, the consumption of nasal mucus (e.g. Portalatín 2007) to the ritualised seclusion of menstruating women. Whereas purity is commonly associated with chastity and virginity, anything deemed sexually transgressive is often labelled as 'dirty'. Many religions have complex ideas concerning ritual pollution, with blood being particularly marked out. On another level, it is no coincidence that the etymologies of *holy* and *whole* are closely linked; to be complete (and pure) has long been associated with being sacred. The contemporary resonance of 'whole' when used as a prefix in relation to certain types of (pure) food – viz wholefoods, wholegrains, wholewheat, etc. – is almost certainly related to this association as well.

These days, discourses surrounding the environment are frequently imbued with notions of purity and pristine(ness), whilst the popular understanding of the term 'pollution' now largely implies the contamination of the environment to the exclusion of virtually all other meanings. The boundaries between communities, societies and nations themselves may sometimes also be drawn with reference to highly contentious ideas surrounding cultural and racial 'purity'. Even space in the home is organised with reference to culturally proscribed ideas about correct layout and the possible polluting effect of cross-contamination, such as, to take a classic example, shoes being placed on a dining table (Douglas 1966: 44). Finally, and most importantly for our topic, the purity or otherwise of what we eat has become a dominant motif, manifested and transmitted through a myriad of cultural forms, in shaping the social significance of food and foodscapes in the modern world.

In Chapter 1 of this book, the social anthropologist Jeremy MacClancy writes about the notions of purity and impurity in different periods of time. He discusses how, as the distance widened between producers and consumers from the late eighteenth century onwards, concerns grew about the ingredients in food sold commercially. This led to various pieces of legislation being passed in the United Kingdom and the United States that started to regulate additives in food. Whilst noting the apparently universal association of purity with the positive, something also explored by the human ethologist Wulf Schiefenhövel in the following chapter, MacClancy emphasises the fact that, when it comes to food, 'purity' is also a contested concept, its definition changeable according to time and social context. He also poses the question as to why, fundamentally, purity is viewed positively – and, as he points out, answering this is not at all straightforward. However, probably the best starting point is structuralism, a prominent theoretical paradigm across the social sciences and humanities in the latter half of the twentieth century.

Purity and Systems of Classification

That human beings need to classify the world in which they live, with systems of classification being socially determined and varying cross-culturally, is something that all students of social and cultural anthropology learn early in their education. It is one of the most fundamental concepts in the discipline and was articulated initially in 1903 by Emile Durkheim and Marcel Mauss in their book *Primitive Classification*. Their direct intellectual descendant, the renowned French anthropologist Claude Lévi-Strauss, was the great pioneer of structuralist thought in the last century and his ideas helped steer the development of social anthropology during the 1950s and 1960s and beyond. In books such as *Le Totémisme Aujourd'hui* (1962, published in English as *Totemism* in 1963) and *Mythologiques 1: Le Cru et le Cuit* (1964, published in English as *The Raw and the Cooked* in 1966), as well as numerous articles, he demonstrated the importance of food for the understanding of social life; his often quoted assertion that 'natural species are chosen not because they are "good to eat" but because they are "good to think"' (1963: 89) has resonated down the ages. The ideas of Lévi-Strauss were imported into British social anthropology through the work of several influential figures, including Edmund Leach, Rodney Needham and Mary Douglas (Kuper 1973: 206).

Douglas' work pushed the concept of purity to the centre of the discipline through the publication of *Purity and Danger* in 1966. Her ideas were formulated and illustrated partly through reference to food and food taboos, in showing how what we eat and what we don't eat are derived from systems of classification that reflect how societies view the world. In the famous third chapter of the book *The Abominations of Leviticus*, Douglas comprehensively debunked the functionalist and 'medical materialist'[3] view of food taboos, which held that they stemmed primarily from hygiene and environmental considerations. Instead, she showed, through a detailed analysis of the Book of Leviticus from the Old Testament, how they derived instead from societally based systems concerning the classification of animals. Some animals were considered unclean not because they were dangerous to health, but because they did not conform to the expected characteristics of the major categories of animal as they were understood in ancient Hebrew society. They therefore had to be 'marked out' in some way, by being tabooed.[4]

The overarching dictum of *Purity and Danger* that 'dirt is matter out of place' (Douglas 1966: 36) was not actually coined by Douglas – its first use has been attributed to the then future British Prime Minister Lord Palmerstone in a speech made in 1853 (Fardon 2013) – and yet it remains one of the most influential insights ever to emerge from social anthropology. By drawing on cognitive science, Douglas' ideas emphasised the fact that systems of classification work on a psychological as well as a societal level by removing 'mess', enabling human beings to make sense of their disordered, chaotic world. Dirt, for Douglas, 'exists in the eye of the beholder' (1966: 2). Classes of things rely on maintaining boundaries between them and this is achieved by separating out those things considered anomalous. In relation to food types, those that are viewed as disgusting are (usually), she argued, held to be so because they are seen as not conforming to a particular set of alimentary rules – examples of course abound, from the eating of pork in Muslim communities to insect consumption in many Western countries (e.g. Schiefenhövel and Blum 2007). As Marvin Harris (1985) famously said, some foods are dirty and disgusting because we don't want to eat them, not the other way round.

In Chapter 2, Wulf Schiefenhövel provides a comprehensive treatise on the nature of disgust cross-culturally from an ethological standpoint. Schiefenhövel stresses the dichotomy of food as being either pure or impure, and the association of 'pure' with 'proper' and 'impure' with 'improper'. He emphasises the primarily social basis of dietary laws around the world and demonstrates that these can have a physical manifestation in terms of the disgust reaction. His chapter also reminds us that categories can change over time as well as space, so that what may have once been considered disgusting can be transformed into a delicacy in another era. Schiefenhövel demonstrates his theme through a survey among students in Indonesia, the results of which underline the social basis of attitudes towards pure and impure foods. He also makes the point that the relationship between the physiological reaction of disgust, including nausea and vomiting, and the social classification of food is not a simple one, something to which we return below. Although dynamic and fluid in nature, the key message is that socially determined categories exist in all societies and serve a fundamental human need for order.

How fundamental this is can be illustrated by recent developments in neuroscience, particularly the Bayesian Brain theory, as outlined by the psychotherapist Mark Carter in Chapter 3. Carter draws together concepts developed in anthropology, psychoanalysis and neuroscience that emphasise that the need to understand and classify the world, to make it more ordered, has been shown to be critical for survival. In taking Douglas' (1966) work as a starting point, he shows how her ideas dovetail well with recent ideas on how the brain regulates emotions and survival mechanisms. He describes a clinical example from his own work, in which a young boy uses a 'pure' food in the story of The Gingerbread Man as a metaphor for his emotional and psychological state. Carter uses this to reflect the wider themes of his chapter, with the purity of form of the gingerbread man at the start of the story and its messy end when it is eaten, reflecting, in microcosm, overarching ideas concerning the importance of 'order' to human psychological wellbeing.

Although Douglas' ideas changed over the years and she revised some of her 1960s insights later in life, *Purity and Danger* undoubtedly left an inestimable and lasting legacy on scholarship, something explored in the collection

Purity and Danger Now (Duschinsky et al. 2016). According to an article published in *The Times Literary Supplement* (1995), it was one of the 100 most influential books in any sphere written since the Second World War. As well as being referred to in many of the following chapters, Mary Douglas also has an indirect connection with this book, as she was one of the founding members of the International Commission on the Anthropology of Food and Nutrition (ICAF), the organisation that gives its name to the series in which this volume forms the latest part.

Food Purity: A South Asian Example

In many societies around the world, ideas about purity and pollution are much more central to everyday life than in others, and often form part of a complex cosmology within which food plays a central role. We find their fullest expression, perhaps, among South Asian communities. In Hinduism, for example, food is an intrinsic component of the social and moral order of society, as well as being intimately connected to psychological wellbeing. That the purity of mind depends on the purity of food is something emphasised throughout the Vedas, the Hindu sacred texts. The Chandogya Upanishad states:

> The earth (food) when eaten becomes threefold; its grossest portion becomes faeces, its middle portion flesh, its subtlest portion mind. (6.5.1) (Max-Müller 2000: 188)

Effectively, 'you are what you eat'. Hindu teachings divide food into three categories: Tamasic, Rajasic and Sattvic. Tamasic foods are considered impure and include categories such as leftovers or spoiled food; they are associated with negative emotions such as anger, jealousy and greed. Rajasic foods include meat, eggs, fish and spicy foods, and are considered to produce strong emotions and passions as well as psychological restlessness. Sattvic foods, which include fruit, vegetables, wholegrains and nuts, are held to be the purest form of food and the most desirable, promoting stability, calmness and wellbeing (e.g. Dhanya et al. 2019).

Notions of food purity and pollution are part of a complex belief system that underpins how food should be procured, prepared and consumed (e.g. Sen 2004: 30)[5] – as well as reinforcing social hierarchies between different communities and castes. The latter connection was explored by Louis Dumont in his famous structuralist study, *Homo Hierarchicus: The Caste System and Its Implications* (1980 [1966]), which was published in the same year as *Purity and Danger* and became another anthropological 'classic'. Debate has since raged about Dumont's thesis on the importance of purity and pollution in the creation and maintenance of the caste system, which is well beyond the scope of this chapter. What is clear, however, is that these concepts remain important in shaping ideas about the purity of food in South Asia and among South Asian diaspora communities globally.

Ethnographic evidence abounds on how this is manifested.[6] In relation to food preparation and handling, space constraints restrict us to a few basic highlights. In orthodox Hindu households, the kitchen is often seen as a sanctified space akin to the inner sanctum of a temple. Cooking is generally performed by a senior female within the household, who must not be menstruating and must wash thoroughly and wear fresh clothes before entering the kitchen. Non-Sattvic foods such as onions, garlic, chicken and eggs are sometimes prepared using separate sets of utensils from those used to cook traditional foods; some affluent households may have secondary cooking areas or even additional kitchens for preparing different categories of food. A plate that has been used is considered as defiled by the eater's saliva and polluting to the person who washes it up. Sharing food is defiling, as it may also have been contaminated by saliva. The cooking process itself is a potential source of pollution, through possible contamination by the chef's saliva or sweat. Food should never be tasted during cooking, with readiness determined by odour and appearance alone. Food cooked by members of a lower caste is considered defiling for those of an upper caste. Food is always eaten with the right hand, with the left believed to be unclean.

An illustration of just how powerful these cultural beliefs can be comes from an orthodox Hindu family in London known to one of the authors of this chapter. The household is strictly vegan. There is a small temple in the house in which separate sets of plates, bowls and cups are used to offer food to God prior to a family meal. Once an offering is made, the food is added to the saucepans in the kitchen and incorporated with the rest of the food being prepared, in order to bless and purify it. On one occasion, a male acquaintance of the family, who was known not to follow Hindu strictures closely and to eat meat, fish and eggs, visited the house. He was served tea using an old set of crockery that the female head of the household had at the back of the cupboard; when he was gone, these were thrown away.

It is clear from the anthropological record that, in a South Asian context at least, food purity and the cultural imperative to maintain it are associated with far more than the avoidance of infection and disease, being absolutely intrinsic to familial and social life in both the subcontinent and in the diaspora. This echoes Douglas' thesis. The deep links between religious ethics, systems of classification, societal mores, and familial and social organisation in South Asian communities are articulated by and through food, which forms a complex language of symbolic and cultural expression.[7] The same could be said, with varying degrees of emphasis along the relational axes, of food the world over, except that these connections may not be as obvious or as pronounced – or studied in such depth (cf. Messer 2007).

Pure Food and Personal Purity

In a Western cultural context, Chapter 4 by Amalia Lejavitzer, a scholar of classical Greek and Roman philosophy, explores the relationship between pure food and diet in Greco-Roman belief systems in terms of the therapeutic, health and spiritual associations of different types of food. Against the background of the wider meanings of 'diet', as in δίαιτα in ancient Greek and diæta in Latin, both concerned with lifestyle[8] (Medina and Macbeth 2021), she refers not just to healthy eating but also to exercise and rest, baths and purges as elements related to concepts of purity and 'paths to purification'. She describes how honey and olive oil were seen as divine gifts, which, as well as stemming from their health-giving properties, rendered them purer forms of food. She then goes on to discuss vegetarianism and dietary frugality, and their links with ancient medicine in the works of Porphyry and Hippocrates. In concluding, she makes the important point that pure and impure foods 'represent a complex universe of meanings' and a 'system of symbols that have deep spiritual, moral and, above all, identity implications'. In summary, there is a strong sense of interaction, even unity, between the purity of the foods eaten and the personal purity, hygiene and health of the ancient peoples she is describing.

A noteworthy modern parallel to the Greco-Roman integration of food choices, lifestyle and the 'purity' of the body is found in Chapter 5 by the social anthropologists Lorenzo Mariano and Xavier Medina. This is based on ethnographic research into the culture of adherents to an 'Eat-Clean' fitness regime in Spain, concentrating particularly on the detailed attention paid to the types of food and drink that their informants consume. The authors argue that the intense control of consumption and culinary practices by members of this community is a central element of their self-identity, ideology and culture. Their informants' use of the phrase 'eating clean' describes a concept similar to those used in other cultures to classify different types of food as pure, impure or tabooed. Furthermore, rules surrounding alimentary transgressions are very strictly defined, with self-punishments administered for deviations from the pure dietary path. In this way, their system implies a complete separation between what is considered 'pure' or 'impure' in what they consume, which is employed in order to maximise their fitness. Members of the community share information with each other, surf the internet to become experts, and learn to be precise over the amount and type of ingredients included in every portion of food that they eat, while neither pleasure nor price is significant in their dietary choices.

These last examples fit well into Douglas' thesis. They highlight a unity between the purity of the food, body and mind, with social rules playing a critical role in directing behaviour. We now change tack somewhat to examine some of the wider and more everyday relationships between pure food and health – and, in so doing, highlight some drawbacks of Douglas' ideas.

'Medical Materialism', Pure Food and Health

Safety, Regulation and Risk

As Douglas herself acknowledged later (2004), the somewhat rigid, mono-lithic and overly deterministic schema Douglas outlined in *Purity and Danger* has significant limitations (Macfarlane 2006), and for these her work has been extensively criticised (e.g. Hetherington 2004; Navaro-Yashin 2009). These shortcomings are evident in relation to her outright rejection of what she termed the 'medical materialist' perspective.

For most people today, hygiene is a significant consideration for the way in which food is handled, prepared and consumed, and is very much linked to concepts of cleanliness and therefore purity. Most of us are familiar with the reasons behind practices such as washing hands before cooking, sterilising food preparation areas, using separate utensils for cutting raw meat and other foods, taking care over the handling of raw poultry, etc.[9] Our desire to wash, to scrub, to disinfect, to *avoid dirt* is seemingly driven, in modern complex societies at least, from what we have been told about pathogens and infec-tions. However, Douglas had argued that this is essentially superficial and what is really going on springs from a much deeper and more fundamental desire for order; the South Asian examples cited above would appear to back this up. Although this is a compelling argument, a central criticism levelled at this model, and at the way it has been applied by some of her intellectual descendants, is that dirt is not *simply* matter out of place; dirt can also be a source of pathogenic infection. Dirt therefore does in fact exist as a risk to health, *pace* Douglas (1966: 2), and in an absolute form (see, for example, Curtis and Biran 2001; Curtis 2007; Rozin et al. 2010). The disgust reaction is germane here: evolutionary mechanisms may also be important in the asso-ciation of disgust with certain things almost universally seen as inedible, such as soil and faeces, in order to avoid infection and disease.[10]

In the public sphere, news reports about people becoming ill or dying after being served 'dangerous' food are commonplace, and are often related to the use of food additives or artificial chemicals, either introduced intentionally or otherwise. Some of the more high-profile food scandals have included: the bovine spongiform encephalopathy (BSE) or 'mad cow disease' crisis in the 1990s in the United Kingdom (discussed by Macbeth in Chapter 10 in this volume); the deliberate contamination of infant milk powder in China in 2008–9, in which a chemical (melamine) was added in order to raise the protein content, which killed at least six children and affected thousands of others (Xiu and Klein 2010; Watson and Klein 2019: 13); the discovery of the illegal use of clenbuterol in pig feed in China in 2011 and in cattle feed in Mexico in 2001 (discussed by Deraga in Chapter 9 in this volume); the horse-meat scandal in Europe in 2013, in which significant amounts of horsemeat were found in meat products being sold as beef; and the chlorfenapyr scandal

in Punjab in India in 2016, when baked confectionary products were deliberately laced with insecticide, reportedly as a result of a family argument,
killing thirty-three people. There are also the controversies over genetically
modified organisms (GMOs) in Europe, the United States and elsewhere
from the 1990s onwards.

As we were completing this Introduction, an alert was issued by the
World Health Organization in October 2022 that said that the deaths of
sixty-six children in The Gambia could be potentially linked to contaminated children's cough syrup, which contained 'unacceptable amounts of
diethylene glycol and ethylene glycol'. The substances can apparently cause
acute kidney injury and, according to local medical authorities, there was an
increase of this condition among children under five detected in the country
in July 2022.[11] Also at the time of writing, media reports emerged drawing
on a newly published George Washington University study, which found that
almost one in three Americans had detectable levels of a toxic herbicide,
2,4-Dichlorophenoxyacetic (2,4-D) acid, in their urine, which has been linked
in high doses to birth defects, reproduction problems and some cancers. The
implication was that this was being ingested with agricultural products. 2,4-D
was also a key ingredient in the notorious Agent Orange used as a defoliant
during the Vietnam War (Freisthler et al. 2022; Lakhani 2022).

With a widening gap between production and consumption of food, such
scandals and controversies about food purity have emerged with increasing
regularity over recent decades. As Inglis (2015: 475–78) has pointed out, food
has never been more regulated than it is today – and with more regulation has
come a greater propensity to uncover issues over 'food purity' that need to be
addressed. However, given that there are so many different bodies involved
in the regulatory processes and many of the most serious food controversies
transcend national borders, their practical resolution becomes increasingly
complex and problematic.

The issue here is that such food controversies reflect real biological and
medical problems understood in materialist terms. However, not all cases of
food-borne illnesses are so dramatic. In the United States, it is estimated that
there are around 48 million cases of foodborne illness annually, equating to
one in six of the country's population, resulting in 128,000 hospitalisations
and 3,000 deaths (US Food and Drug Administration 2022a). Research by
the UK's Food Standards Agency (2020) estimated the number of food-
borne illnesses each year in the country at 2.4 million, up from one million in
2009. Partly as a result of the latter finding, a standardised system of hygiene
ratings, the Food Hygiene Rating Scheme, for public businesses and catering establishments serving food was introduced by the UK government in
England, Wales and Northern Ireland in 2011.[12] Through regular inspections,
outlets are rated according to a five-point scale, which they are encouraged to
(in England) or have to (in Wales and Northern Ireland) display on the premises. Surveys suggest that the ratings are an important consideration used

by consumers in deciding which outlets to choose (e.g. Benson et al. 2019; Armstrong et al. 2021). Other countries have introduced similar schemes that have also become relevant for consumers when making decisions about where to eat, in some cases even more so than in the United Kingdom (e.g. Aik et al. (2018) for Singapore and Vainio et al. (2020) for Finland).

So, returning to our earlier definitions of purity, it is important to acknowledge that these regulations are a response to a 'medical materialist' perspective on hygiene and food safety, or at least a popularised version of it. It follows that our care with hygiene and avoiding harmful food impurities stems not *only* from what scientists and educators tell us about germs and pathogens, nor is this *all* down to a psychological desire for order or the need to maintain cultural categories. It also emerges from day-to-day human experiences as well as from reports in the media – and chapters in academic books(!) – of the consequences of not being careful and consuming potentially dangerous substances, whether seen or unseen (cf. Curtis 2007, 2011; Paxson 2019). Overall, it seems clear that for most people today, food hygiene and safety are important both inside the home and outside it, and the reasons they would give for this are drawn from the medical sciences, even if these reasons are sometimes filtered and popularised through the media and social communication.

Contemporary concerns over food safety, as well as healthy eating, have led many commentators to conclude that we are currently living in an 'age of anxiety' in relation to food, especially in Western countries (e.g. Coveney 2006; Jackson 2010). Anxiety has undoubtedly been heightened by the global COVID-19 pandemic, with some research suggesting that this has led to a change in consumption patterns in some countries. This dovetails with wider societal trends associated with the emergence of the 'risk society', a term most closely associated with the German sociologist Ulrich Beck (1992). The concept takes as its starting point the observation that everyday life in modern, complex, industrialised countries (and increasingly in less industrialised countries as well) has become increasingly focused on identifying, managing and mitigating risk at both an individual level and in relation to whole communities and populations. Modernity has led to a bewildering variety of potential risks, and sometimes these are very real and responses are entirely reasonable and proportionate. Beck himself was particularly concerned with ecological and environmental risks, viewing these as the main consequence of industrialisation. However, sometimes they are based on fallacies in which perceived risk in the popular imagination balloons out of all proportion to the risk that is actually present. In this case, it is often the media (especially social media) that act as an echo chamber and loud-hailer, amplifying single, often very rare events to the status of an everyday occurrence, usually by simply not mentioning their rarity – with the implicit message that 'this could easily happen to you'. (The same principle applies to the marketing of lottery games!)

In relation to food, perceived and actual risks vary on a case-by-case basis; in some instances, they may be entirely in accordance, while in others, the gap may be very large indeed. One current issue relating to 'best before' and 'use by' dates on food products illustrates this well and encapsulates the meta-debate over the role of risk in modern society. Food manufacturers err on the side of caution in calculating 'best before' dates, building in sufficient elasticity to guarantee food quality, minimise the risk to consumers and ensure that the latter will continue to buy their products (e.g. Vågsholm et al. 2020). Consumers, meanwhile, often fail to distinguish sufficiently between 'best before' and 'use by' dates (e.g. van Boxstael et al. 2014; Aschemann-Witzel et al. 2015; Tiwari 2016; Toma et al. 2020), with the latter carrying a much more serious risk of illness if ignored. From the perspective of campaigners, the approach of the manufacturers combined with the risk aversion of consumers contributes significantly to food waste, with millions of tonnes of perfectly edible food being thrown away each year.[13]

Globally, the UN's Food Waste Index estimates that around 17 percent of all food that entered the food chain in 2019 was wasted, equating to 931 million tonnes (UN Environment Programme 2021: 8). This excludes losses from food production, transport, storage and processing, which were estimated at 13.3 percent globally in 2020 (Food and Agriculture Organization of the UN 2023). In the United Kingdom, it has been estimated that around 22 percent of all food that enters the food chain is wasted, worth a total of £19 billion per year (WRAP 2022). In the United States, the equivalent figures are a staggering 31 percent and US$161 billion (UN Environment Programme 2022; US Department of Agriculture 2022; US Food and Drug Administration 2022b). While comparable statistics for the European Union (EU) are difficult to come by, EU countries reportedly waste 88 million tonnes of food annually.[14]

In this case, then, a striving for food purity in the sense of avoiding pathogens reflects the wider risk-avoidance culture that is an increasingly important feature of modern life in the industrialised world – and something that has serious implications for the future sustainability of food production. In many Western countries, there is a developing movement to reduce food waste by encouraging people to consume rather than dispose of food that has gone past its 'best before' date – or to scrap the latter guide altogether. Several major UK supermarkets have already removed such dates from major product lines in recent years,[15] while the European Commission is, at the time of writing, reportedly planning a change to its rules.[16] Given their potential impact on reducing food waste, it is to be hoped that these efforts will achieve their desired aim and elevate the bar of perceived risk for the average food consumer. However, this will be challenging, given the rise in food-borne illnesses, as noted above, as well as pushing against wider societal trends that are moving in the opposite direction.

We can debate almost endlessly about where to draw the boundaries between materialist, functionalist and structuralist interpretations of the origin of ideas of purity and pollution – as indeed many people have. There is probably no one definitive answer to be found here, and for now it is enough to note that there is more to the quest for pure food than meets the eye (or mouth!), as we will hope to demonstrate in the rest of this chapter and book.

Health Foods, Purity and Labelling

It is evident that a striving for healthier, less processed and 'purer' types of food has been driven largely by a far greater popular awareness today of the links between diet and health.[17] This derives not only from a desire to avoid the dangers of pathogens, as discussed above, but also due to a recent emphasis in popular discourse on the dangers of the modern 'Western diet', containing high amounts of processed foods, fats and sugars – and probably about as far away from the teachings of the Vedas as it is possible to get. Levels of obesity in many countries (and not only in the West) have risen significantly in recent years, particularly among children, placing additional burdens on public healthcare services.[18] Worldwide, governments, health authorities and other public bodies spend vast sums of money on information campaigns about healthy eating, a reflection of the significant costs to the public purse of treating diet-related disorders (which include diabetes, cardiovascular diseases, cancers, neurodegenerative disorders and autoimmune conditions) in industrialised nations.[19]

As so-called 'health foods' have recently moved from specialist shops into mainstream supermarkets, they are sold alongside 'ordinary' foods, albeit usually for a higher price.[20] Information relevant to certain dietary restrictions may also be shown on labels. Whilst some health foods claim to be 'purer' and are bought as such, not all of them can be equated to pure food. Most, unsurprisingly, relate to dietary requirements as defined by medical and nutritional science, often with reference either to supplement(s) needed for some health conditions or to the absence of an ingredient to be avoided by certain groups of people, such as 'gluten free' for coeliacs and 'lactose free' for the lactase deficient. Other health foods are those sought by followers of different dietary regimes, which may have real, exaggerated or imaginary links to scientific nutritional advice and unclear links with 'purity', if any. This is a significant point, because the vast literature on nutrition and dietetics is almost entirely directed towards the relationship between dietary patterns and personal health, and is often focused on different individual health conditions rather than on different belief systems.

In recent years, the category of health foods has been supplemented by the rise of 'superfoods' – foods that are supposedly intrinsically imbued with enhanced health-giving properties. As well as their nutritional benefits, superfoods are also often viewed as 'purer' and are generally foods that have been subject to no or only minimal processing – wholefoods being a prime example.

Although what can be considered as a superfood varies widely, examples of those that are usually included in any lists or cookbooks include quinoa, kale, sweet potatoes, wholegrains, beetroot, wheat grass, pomegranate, acai, root ginger, ginseng, certain types of nuts (particularly almonds and walnuts), and ingredients for making drinks, such as rooibos, burdock and kombucha. As McDonell and Wilk point out, superfoods are at once a marketing device and a 'folk category' (2020: 2) for classifying foods, and are often believed to have 'magical' properties that have simultaneous physical, psychological and spiritual benefits. Loyer (2016) notes that superfoods have become a distinct sociocultural category in their own right, the production, distribution and consumption of which have important social and environmental implications (see also Reisman 2020 in relation to almonds), as well as 'social power' in view of their liminal and 'marked out' status (echoes of Douglas here as well). In the sense that purity is usually a defining characteristic of superfoods, they can also be considered pure foods – although this is potentially changing due to the proliferation of processed superfoods now available, often sold in the form of shakes, powders and tablets (e.g. LeBlanc 2020). We explore some of these points further in the next section, in relation to pure food and diet.

Another recent aspect of health foods is related to the growth in the consumption of 'traditional' foods, some of which may have been 'rediscovered' after having fallen out of favour – a trend likely to be motivated partly by the cognitive associations in the public imagination between 'traditional', 'healthy' and 'pure'. Seaweed and arugula (rocket), both pure foods *par excellence*, are two examples, with consumption growing significantly in recent years in Europe and the United States. Cultivation of arugula was apparently prohibited in the Middle Ages in Europe due to its reputation as an aphrodisiac, and it became a marginal food in consequence, only being rediscovered in the early years of the twentieth century in Italy and southern France.[21] Another example is the Icelandic yoghurt Skyr, which is now eaten in many European countries and the United States, and is marketed as a more healthy alternative to other yoghurts, being free of artificial additives and lower in fat. According to a manufacturer's website:

> Skyr had long been one of the food world's best-kept food secrets, until recently that is. Arla has now brought the Icelandic-style yogurt to the UK, bringing a little taste of Arctic serenity to those who long to embrace the Nordic way of life.[22]

The importance of food origin in the marketing of certain types of foods, as suggested by this quote, is a point we shall address further below. Foraging, another significant aspect of recent popular food trends, is also germane here – with the idea that entire steps in the food chain can be bypassed by simply collecting food directly from the forest or seashore, etc., greatly enhancing the perceived healthiness and purity of the foods that are gathered.

In the United Kingdom there has been a huge push in recent years to introduce healthier food into public institutions, such as schools and hospitals, with greater attention paid to its purity in the sense of origin and processing. High-profile public campaigns, such as that mounted by the British 'celebrity chef' Jamie Oliver over food in schools, have had a marked effect. An example of the results of such a campaign is described by the food consultant, researcher and campaigner Lucy Antal in Chapter 6 in relation to institutions in the city of Liverpool. Her chapter is focused on how local community groups have worked with public bodies to develop ways of ensuring that the food that is served in public buildings conforms with the latest guidance on healthy eating. She uses two case studies, one relating to the Royal Liverpool University Hospital and one focused on schools in the city, to show how, despite various challenges and barriers, such a partnership has greatly improved the wholesomeness and nutritional value of the food served to hospital patients and to young people in Liverpool. She concludes by suggesting that recognition of the importance of healthier and purer forms of food by at least some public bodies in the United Kingdom is a source of hope for the future.

Following high-profile controversies about what it is that we are eating, which have underlined the uncertainties that occupy the gap between 'farm and fork', nutritional labelling – listing all ingredients – has become enforced in law and is a central aspect of the way in which food is sold and consumed in many countries today. In the United Kingdom, labels publicise ingredients and admixtures in products for human consumption as well as emphasising their purportedly health-giving properties, as exemplified in Figure 0.1.

Various pieces of legislation related to food were implemented in the late nineteenth and early twentieth centuries in both Britain and the United States, a response to the huge rise in mislabelled and mis-sold food and medical products at the time (see MacClancy, Chapter 1 in this volume; Young 1989). In the United States in 1938, the Food, Drug and Cosmetic Act was passed, which stipulated that food manufacturers identify on the packaging any artificial colourings, flavourings or preservatives added to the food. The United Kingdom passed the Food and Drugs Act in the same year, which had similar provisions (Skrovan 2017). With the United Kingdom's accession to the then European Economic Community in 1973, UK legislation fell into line with European provisions, with various European Council Directives being incorporated into UK law and that of most Member States, which became progressively more comprehensive over subsequent years. Since the United Kingdom left the EU in 2020, UK labelling has so far remained in line with European standards.[23]

Food labelling is now central to the retail branding of food, with some consumers demanding increasingly detailed information on what it is they are eating. The UK government's stipulation in April 2022 that food outlets with over 250 employees must include calorific information about the food they are serving is a case in point. Some researchers have pointed out that

Figure 0.1. The historical roots of food labelling can be traced back at least a century. Nutritional and health labelling on the side of a cereal packet.
© Paul Collinson

the proliferation of labels can also cause confusion among consumers (e.g. Chrzan and Ricotta 2019: 2), who may stop paying attention to them and cease engaging with certification schemes as a result (Grunert et al. 2014; Gray 2016). Yet, this labelling does allow consumers who do (or perhaps have to) check ingredients to identify any that for them would be problematic. However, that admixture *for them* should not necessarily be called an impurity or pollutant *for all*. This highlights a distinction between different modern uses of the word 'pure' in relation to food, as to whether it means without *any* admixture or only without a *harmful* admixture.

As well as nutritional labelling, food products also increasingly come with other forms of labels to designate compliance with principles such as fairtrade, organic farming, sustainability and environmental benefits. In the United Kingdom, they include the LEAF (Linking Environment and Farming) mark, the Rainforest Alliance certification, the Marine Stewardship Council's Sustainable Seafood label, the Forestry Stewardship Council Mixed Sources mark and the Soil Association's Organic Standard label. All of these reflect the integration of concerns over the intrinsic qualities of food with other wider societal movements and trends – a relationship that has a long history and is becoming ever-closer, something that we consider below.

Pure Food and Diet

At a surface level in contemporary Western societies, there is apparently a significant divergence from ideas concerning the strong unity between personal and/or metaphysical purity and physical health found in ancient Greco-Latin and contemporary South Asian cultures described earlier. However, scratch below the surface, and these differences are not so obvious – and sometimes dissolve entirely. The gap also seems to be narrowing rapidly.

In *Risk and Blame*, a collection of Douglas' essays on cultural theory first published in 1992, she proposed a fourfold typology of urban culture, in which a 'city core' whose values and ideas stem from professional scientific knowledge is contrasted with 'individualist', 'isolate', and 'dissenting enclaves' (Douglas 2003: 104–8). In the latter, she argues that the values of the core group are regarded with suspicion, and alternative theories hold sway – and uses food to illustrate this. She cites the Arts and Crafts movement of the early 1900s in Britain, in which 'natural products and raw foods' were emphasised (2003: 108), as well as the Californian gay community in the 1980s, which apparently believed that a healthy diet and macrobiotic foods could prevent HIV infection (ibid.), as examples. Although still existing as social and cultural entities, one might argue that, in relation to food, the ideas of Douglas' 'dissenting enclave' are in the process of being absorbed into mainstream culture in many Western countries and are no longer seen as out of step with it in the way that they were in the early 1990s (and early 1900s).

The ever-closer intersection between pure food and diet illuminates this point and is the main focus of this section.

Vegetarianism and Veganism

Vegetarianism and veganism[24] are commonplace in many societies today, while a bewildering array of other dietary regimes have also emerged in recent years, some of which emphasise a 'purer' form of eating. The widespread adoption of these diets shows that Douglas' (1966) clear-cut division between 'medical materialism' and her structuralist interpretation of the ordering of 'pure' and 'impure' within a relevant belief system need not be such a dichotomy. One reason for this is that in most societies today, acceptance of a scientific materialism (or its popularisation) is part of their cosmology. The emergence of vegetarianism and veganism in different societies illustrates this observation well.

There is not necessarily an easy relationship between vegetarianism and veganism, and pure food. After all, there is no intrinsic, biological reason why fruit and vegetables should be considered 'purer' forms of food than fish and meat. However, the historical rise of these dietary regimes around the world was strongly linked to ideas of food purity, both in Western and non-Western societies, and remains so in some contexts – although quite different motivations are sometimes involved as well, as is discussed below. Both vegetarianism and veganism involve the elimination of certain types of foods from the diet, and reflecting on the motives for doing so reveals some that involve perspectives on food purity, whereas others are linked to different ideals.

The Vedic principles of food classification have already been mentioned in relation to South Asian communities, in which meat, fish and eggs are thought of as less pure (and potentially more polluting) forms of food than others. These ideas have had an important influence on the take-up of vegetarianism in the West, where they were combined with more general notions of purity (and puritanism!) relating to various social movements from the seventeenth century onwards. Whether followed for ideals of purity or not, vegetarianism and, especially, veganism are associated with healthier eating. This relationship has deep roots, but has become particularly emphasised in associated dietary regimes that have emerged more recently, in which the quest for purity often forms a central goal.

Although the English term 'vegetarianism' was only coined in the 1840s, the dietary choice has a long history (e.g. Stuart 2008). Pythagoras is often cited as being the first vegetarian (or vegan) and several famous historical figures such as Leonardo da Vinci, John Wesley, Leo Tolstoy, Mary Shelley, Franz Kafka and George Bernard Shaw, to name but a few, were also adherents. Motivations for their vegetarianism varied: for some, personal health and concern for animal welfare, for others religious conviction (Twigg 1979).

Religion has been highly significant in the adoption and spread of vegetarianism and veganism, with various religious movements through the ages espousing a meat-free diet as part of an overall philosophy that emphasises the importance of purity in various aspects of life – thought, behaviour and mode of living (e.g. Calvert 2012, 2018). Lejavitzer's chapter shows just how deep the historical origins are that unite metaphysical ideas with the purity of food and associated lifestyle regimes in Greco-Roman cultures. A separate history can also be traced in the case of Eastern religions, in which those doctrines incorporating the ancient Indian concept of *ahimsa* (meaning 'non-injury' in Sanskrit), the principle of not causing harm to any other living creature, have been especially influential. *Ahimsa* forms an important tenet in Buddhism, Hinduism, Sikhism and Jainism.[25]

Currently there are more vegetarians in India than in the rest of the world put together, with estimates from survey data ranging from 23 percent to 37 percent of the population – approximately 317 million to 511 million people (Natrajan and Jacob 2018: 56). However, vegetarianism varies between the four religious communities cited above, with incidence ranging from 22 percent in the case of Buddhists[26] to 98 percent for Jains,[27] according to survey data (National Sample Survey Office (NSSO) 2013, quoted in Natrajan and Jacob 2018: 57).

Modern dietary habits and cuisine in India have been shaped by these different religions but also by many, more recent political, social, economic and environmental factors, as well as external influences through exposure to other culinary traditions (cf. Banerjee-Dube 2021: 106). This observation can obviously be applied more generally worldwide as well (Inglis and Gimlin 2009; Moffat and Prowse 2010), and yet vegetarianism and veganism remain important to a significant proportion of the Indian population. Western dietary habits are also becoming more influential on the subcontinent, as testified by the success of the fast-food chain McDonald's,[28] albeit by tailoring its menu to suit local tastes and with a complete separation of vegetarian and 'non-vegetarian'[29] foods (Nandini 2014). This illustrates the important point, also made by Watson (2006) in relation to the rise of McDonald's in China, that the globalisation of food does not necessarily mean homogenisation, but the transfiguration of global foodways to suit local consumption traditions and habits. Nevertheless, in India, religion continues to be an important influence on determining people's dietary choices, with the connection between sacredness and purity being fundamental to this.[30] With ideas imported from abroad, modern scientific understanding has merged with the various cosmologies of a population as large and as socially diverse as in India to create new forms of alimentary ideologies and cultures.

In relation to the rise of the vegetarian movement in the West, Stuart (2008) shows how ideas imported from India from the early seventeenth century onwards had a marked effect on the rise of European vegetarianism, and were combined with ethical and proto-ecological concerns in the work of various influential advocates from the European elite of the time, including Jean-Jacques Rousseau, René Descartes, Pierre Gassendi, Francis Bacon, Voltaire and Benjamin Franklin. For these early adopters, to take up vegetarianism was to subscribe to a purer form of living, something that, in its most extreme form, became associated with Puritanism itself. Some of Oliver Cromwell's soldiers and followers during the English Civil War, for example, apparently called for the creation of a 'slaughter-free society of equality' (ibid.: 3). These sentiments were echoed later in the Victorian era in Britain, when vegetarianism was linked to powerful notions surrounding the importance of individual self-restraint and often went hand in hand with other nineteenth-century political and social movements, including socialism, teetotalism, spiritualism, naturism and the campaign for women's suffrage (Gregory 2007; Schweers 2021). An integration of such food consumption patterns with wider patterns of social ideals fits well with Douglas' model, and it is notable that the word 'puritanical' is still used today in relation to veganism (as well as other supposedly strict forms of behaviour), both as a badge of honour for its adherents and also, more usually, as a means to castigate them by its detractors.[31]

The rise of vegetarianism and latterly veganism has been a major aspect of food trends in the Western world since the 1960s and has gone hand in hand with the emergence of wider social movements and attitudinal changes (Wright 2021). Bestselling books such as Frances Moore Lappé's *Diet for a Small Planet* (1971), Mollie Katzen's *Moosewood Cookbook* (1974) and Peter Singer's *Animal Liberation* (1975) were highly influential in giving impetus to the take-up of meat-free diets. Data concerning incidence of vegetarianism and veganism today abound, but they can be highly contradictory and sometimes of questionable validity. However, there appears to be a significant rising trend among millennials (and their successors, Generation Z, as they are sometimes called) in the United States, with, according to surveys, 22 percent of them having tried a vegetarian diet at some point (Jacimovic 2021). In the United Kingdom, the adoption of these diets also appears to have risen more quickly than in the United States in the last few years.[32]

Recent research by a UK supermarket chain noted that half of those who said they were vegetarian or vegan also eat meat 'at weekends', 'occasionally' or 'on special occasions' (Waitrose and Partners 2018: 6). This survey demonstrates that – as with pure food itself – such categories are not absolutes, but are, in essence, social constructions and incorporate a certain latitude for flexibility. The rise of the term 'flexitarian', defined as having a semi-vegetarian, or meat-reduced diet, in recent years is an obvious manifestation of this. Thus, although people might be aspiring to adopt a 'purer' diet by *attempting* to eliminate meat, fish or all animal-based products, the reality for many is, literally, more mixed. It is also interesting that the survey revealed that meat is eaten on occasions that are 'marked out' in some way as 'special'; Douglas would certainly have had something to say about that.

A variation on this theme is explored in Chapter 7, in which the anthropologists Gabriel Saucedo, Claudia Mercado and Paul Collinson review the use of blood as food in different societies around the world. Self-evidently, to adopt a diet free from the consumption of animals and animal-derived products is to eliminate the consumption of blood, but some, who do not avoid all meat, may have specific views about consuming blood products. The authors describe the social and cultural contradictions in the ways in which blood is used as food (by whom, whether it is cooked or consumed raw, etc.) and contrast these examples with other contexts in which blood is considered dirty, dangerous and polluting. These instances are then reconsidered in terms of health and nutrition by comparing the chemical constituents in the blood of different species reared for their meat. The authors use an ethnographic example to draw attention to the social significance of blood consumption as part of a traditional ritual in rural Mexico. The chapter also serves to highlight the significance of blood consumption down the ages in religious and spiritual practices derived partly from its ambiguous status as an intrinsically pure food on the one hand and yet potentially a source of danger and defilement on the other.

New Dietary Regimes

In the 'Lisa the Tree Hugger' episode of *The Simpsons*, Lisa's friend Jesse states that he is a 'Level Five Vegan' and 'won't eat anything that casts a shadow'.[33] Life imitates art and apparently the term has since caught on in vegan circles to refer, with tongues slightly in cheeks, to anyone who refuses to make any sort of compromise with their dietary strictures (Vegan.com 2022). Whilst obviously not going to Jesse-like extremes, some of the diets that have emerged in recent years – many of which are variations on veganism – can be dauntingly prescriptive in what they advocate for their followers, and we now turn our attention to some of them.

In recent years in the West, vegetarianism and veganism have morphed into – and to a certain extent have been replaced by – several sub-branches, and are now accompanied by a new emphasis on 'clean eating' through the consumption of 'purer' forms of food (or 'superfoods'). Most restaurants and fast-food chains are now offering vegan alternatives,[34] while a whole movement has emerged around 'cooking clean' at home. Detox diets have risen to prominence in many Western countries in recent years and are based on the idea that so many foods now contain unnecessary ingredients and contaminants (pesticides, artificial flavourings, colourings, etc.) that are considered harmful for the body and should be removed from the diet in favour of supposedly 'detoxifying' foods such as plant-based juices and foods high in fibre. Raw Foodism (also known as Raw Veganism), whereby at least three-quarters of a person's food intake consists of uncooked food – or, in the strictest versions, the elimination of all foods that have been cooked, pasteurised or heated above 118°F (Cunningham 2004) – is also becoming more popular (Raba et al. 2019: 49).

Although not a vegan diet, the Paleo Diet specifies a dietary regime supposedly modelled on that of our hunter-gather ancestors during the Palaeolithic era. Lean meat, fish, eggs, fruits, vegetables, nuts, seeds, and healthy fats and oils – all of which are held by the diet's advocates to be 'purer' forms of food – feature heavily in this regime (Newman 2017; Mayo Clinic 2020), whereas processed foods, grains, most dairy products, sugar, legumes and any food containing additional ingredients or 'looks like it was made in a factory' (Gunnars 2018) are eliminated.

As well as all these, a host of mostly female celebrities around the world – echoing the role of the influencers of the seventeenth century – have promoted their own personal 'pure' dietary regimes, drawing on their invariably huge followings on social media.[35] The internet is also awash with sites devoted to the supposedly transformational effects of pure food. In the case of Buzzfeed.com's 'Clean Eating Challenge', for example, the claim is that 'you'll learn to eat healthily, feel awesome, and stay that way' by detoxing and eating 'real food' for two weeks (Buzzfeed.com 2022). In 2014, with the launch of a scheme by a husband-and-wife team through crowdfunding in the United Kingdom, January became 'Veganuary'; a reported 620,000 people from 220 countries signed up in 2022 (compared to 4,000 in 2014) (Veganuary.com 2023). Sugar-free bakeries have also sprung up all over the place.

A preview on Amazon.com for a recent book called *The Naked Diet* by the food consultant Tess Ward encapsulates these trends:

> The Naked Diet is all about changing your way of eating for the better, making you feel cleaner and purer. It takes a stripped back approach to the food that you eat, that will give you more energy, help you lose weight and cleanse your body... It isn't about dieting, it's about changing your mindset, so that you eat less processed, cleaner and simpler foods that restore and nourish your body back to its naked and pure state.[36]

The chapter headings of this book — 'Pure', 'Raw', 'Stripped', 'Bare', 'Undressed', 'Nude', 'Clean' and 'Detox' – invoke a liberating, almost quasi-sexual view of clean eating, with the cleansing of body and mind the ultimate goal. The parallels here with the Vedic principles and Greco-Roman practices discussed earlier are manifest. The shelves of bookshops in Western countries are now heaving with similar titles[37] (Waterstones.com, a UK online bookseller, listed over 10,000 books that included 'vegan' in the title or as a keyword in 2022),[38] underlining the apparently insatiable demand that has emerged for guides to how to eat more purely. MacClancy's chapter in this volume provides similar examples.

Today, as at the time Douglas was writing *Purity and Danger*, contemporary 'Western' medicine is based on scientific research, such as biochemical analyses, physiological measurements and random controlled trials. A significant difference in this from other, traditional, belief systems is that the latest scientific research is always questioning or reanalysing earlier research conclusions, sometimes to prove or sometimes to disprove them. Results accepted and published in refereed journals then become the foundation of our understanding or, at the very least, become the subject of further research. This is also the case for the scientific approach to nutrition and health. Whereas in several cases popularised health food beliefs are supported by evidence from such scientific trials, the claims made for some of the other diets to emerge in recent years are far less certain and, in some cases, may even be harmful.[39]

To condemn entire food groups metaphorically to the dustbin as 'impure' (and therefore 'dirty') potentially invites an '*un*healthy' relationship with food. For example, from a scientific perspective, there are particular concerns about the take-up of plant-based diets among young people, with the discovery of a rise in micronutrient deficiencies among teenagers in the United Kingdom in the last decade or so being described as a 'crisis' (Derbyshire 2018; Derbyshire et al. 2020). Especially worrying is research showing that the iron intake of more than half of teenage girls in the United Kingdom is below the recommended level (cited in Derbyshire et al. 2020). Others have argued that 'fast' vegan foods may be worse for health than meat-based products, since, as well as not providing the same levels of essential nutrients, they may contain higher levels of fat, sugar and salt (Park 2020). So, in attempting to adopt a 'purer' diet, people may actually be doing the opposite by consuming 'impurer' forms of food (in their own understanding of the term), which contain potentially *more* additives and highly processed ingredients than those foods that have been rejected. In his chapter, MacClancy also refers to orthorexia, defined as an obsession with eating only foods considered 'pure and perfect', something that could also have severe implications for health if followed too rigorously. (The condition is also mentioned in Mariano and Medina's chapter.) All of this emphasises the point stressed throughout this chapter and book concerning the malleability of the concept of food purity.

These concerns aside, the crucial issue for our purposes is that most modern dietary regimes serve to satisfy a quest to consume less adulterated, less processed, less 'complex' – fundamentally 'purer' – forms of food. Along with the intrinsic qualities of food itself and what constitutes a healthy diet, issues surrounding the way in which food is produced, distributed and sold have become central to consumer concerns over contemporary food systems and industrialised food production. These are all important factors in the rise of the organic sector in recent years, an issue to which we now turn.

Organic Farming and Food

For many, reducing the physical and/or perceived distance between field and fork, with hopefully a minimum of human interference both in the field and in processing, has become a key goal in determining food choices and ensuring that what is on the fork is as unadulterated and 'pure' as possible. For those adhering to the types of 'clean eating' diets described above, foods that have been combined with other ingredients, altered or in any way interfered with during production and processing are considered less 'pure' and inherently less trustworthy. This idea has been fuelled further by controversies over food safety, in relation to many of the ways that food is produced, handled, prepared and processed, as well as the contaminating effects of chemical weedkillers, hormones and other therapies used on livestock.

Consumers' declining confidence in food as well as health considerations – their own, that of their family and that of the environment too – have been important factors driving an exponential growth in organic farming and food in recent years (Monier-Dilhan and Bergès 2016; Macbeth, this volume). Global sales rose from US$18 billion in 2000 to US$106 billion in 2019 (Wunsch 2021), with the total value of the sector predicted to expand from US$165.52 billion in 2018 to US$679.81 billion by 2027 (Wunsch 2020). Eleven European countries[40] had more than 10 percent of their agricultural land under organic production in 2020 (Eurostat 2022).

Organic farming has a long history in the West, its origins tracing back to at least the early years of the twentieth century and a particular rural revivalist agenda. Advocates and writers such as Albert Howard (who introduced Indian ideas on composting to a Western audience), Lord Northbourne[41] (to whom the term 'organic farming' is generally attributed) and Eve Balfour (who founded the UK's Soil Association, which today certifies 70 percent of all of the United Kingdom's organic food)[42] in the United Kingdom; Ehrenfried Pfeiffer and Rudolph Steiner (who both promoted 'biodynamic farming') in continental Europe; and Jerome Rodale (founder of the Rodale Institute, which remains one of the leading organic farming training institutions in North America) in the United States were highly influential in the growth of the movement worldwide.[43] Most of their books are still in print.[44] In believing, to quote Howard, that 'the health of soil, plant, animal and man is one and indivisible',[45] they also anticipated, and indeed shaped, the subsequent environmental movement by calling for a relationship between humanity and the environment based on nurture rather than domination (e.g. Delate and Turnball 2019).[46]

Organic farming and food are by no means only a Western phenomenon. For example, of the 3.1 million total number of producers worldwide in 2019, 1.37 million were in India (Willer et al. 2021: 20). India and China have their own certification schemes, as do many other countries in Asia, Latin America and Africa. Whilst the criteria vary considerably and levels of enforcement may be questionable in some cases, it is clear that support for the organic sector is expanding rapidly to encompass most of the world's countries. And of course, for many small-scale and subsistence farmers in the Global South, organic farming is something that they have practised for millennia anyway – as Albert Howard (2011 [1931]) demonstrated almost a century ago.

Strong links can therefore be traced in the ideas of the early organicists, as they came to be known, between the purity of food, the purity of land and the purity of those who live upon it, and the philosophies of the Greco-Roman and Indian traditions discussed earlier in this chapter. Their ideas are also, if anything, more relevant to contemporary consumers than they were at the time they were writing in the first half of the twentieth century. In Western societies today, two concepts in support of organic farming seem to have run in parallel. Both result from distrust of some recent food production and processing methods; the first is based on the belief that, in avoiding these, earlier 'traditional' methods were purer; the second follows scientific analyses of harmful residues found in modern foods and the demonstration of how these enter the food chain. Having pointed to these two perspectives, Macbeth (this volume) describes a situation where they diverge.

Exploring Motivations behind Dietary and Consumer Choices

The concerns of consumers over what it is that they are eating have become central considerations in the way in which producers and retailers promote and market food. The result is that some types of foods and dietary regimes may be regarded by some consumers as 'purer' because of how they are promoted. An example of this is in the use of descriptive words, such as *extra virgin* olive oil, *wild-caught* salmon or *line-caught* tuna, or in the publicised association of a food with a specific place from which it originates, such as *King Island* Cloud Juice[47] or *Galway Bay* Gourmet Oysters;[48] this is also a concept underpinning uses of the French word *terroir*. Some foods are not linked precisely to a specific geographical place name, but to a region that is often considered 'purer' than the places in which the products are being sold; examples include Milka's *Alpine* milk chocolate,[49] Korpihunaja's *Arctic* (or *Polar*, depending on the language used) honey[50] and *North Atlantic* langoustines.[51] Promoting foods in this way is aimed at generating a more positive image by virtue of their being linked with particular environments, cultural traditions or lifestyles, something that imbues them with a heightened sense of 'purity' in comparison to other, nonautochthonous foods. The spread of the 'Mediterranean Diet' – modelled on what has become a popular concept, well beyond its geographical origins, of a 'typical diet' of the peoples of the Mediterranean region (Medina and Macbeth 2021), with its emphasis on fruit, vegetables, beans, fish, nuts and olive oil – has been another significant feature of recent food trends and is a case in point. Whilst not based on pure foods intrinsically, it is typically held to be a 'purer' dietary regime by many of its adherents from outside the region itself (see, for example, the numerous articles on the Mediterranean Diet in the magazine *Clean Eating*).[52] There is an obvious element of 'invented tradition' in this (cf. Hobsbawm and Ranger 2012), something that, at a stretch, could potentially be applied to the Paleo Diet too.

Relatedly, the connections between cultural and culinary authenticity have also been successfully harnessed by the tourism industry in recent years in promoting food and environmental tourism. In Chapter 8, social anthropologist Paul Collinson discusses the ways in which the culture of western Ireland has been mythologised through the ages and is now utilised by the tourist industry to promote food and environmental tourism. Drawing from content analysis of various tourism websites as well as ethnographic observations, he demonstrates how the 'pristineness' of the rural culture and environment is explicitly associated with the purity of food for marketing purposes. From an anthropological perspective, the reasons for this stem from the observation that 'purity' represents a manifestation of postmodern social forms, in which the ideas of 'unadulterated', 'uncorrupted' and 'authentic' represent valuable cultural assets, and are contrasted with everyday experience in 'modern' industrialised societies.

There exists a reciprocal and mutually reinforcing link between the marketing and the consumption of foods, with marketeers studying motives and incorporating them into their ideas for publicity, and consumer choices being driven, at least to a certain extent, by the wording of advertising and other means of promotion. A key issue of relevance to this book lies in people's motivation for their dietary choices. In this respect, a distinction is often made in the literature between altruistic concerns (e.g. for the environment) and egoist concerns (e.g. related to the health benefits for oneself and one's family). Hjelmar (2011) also distinguishes between 'automatic' and 'reflective' consumers, with the former mainly concerned with practical considerations such as labelling and price, and the latter who think more carefully about their purchasing habits based on concern for the environment, animal welfare and the purity of food. Marketing and retailing affect these in different ways and to varying extents.

According to survey data, among vegetarians and vegans, several motivational drivers are usually at play in determining consumer choices,[53] although some may be more important than others according to the context. Health benefits and concerns for animal welfare and the environment feature prominently among Western respondents, whereas other factors such as those stemming from religious ethics and social mores are likely to play a greater role in non-Western societies. In a comparative study of vegetarians in the United States and India, for example, Ruby et al. (2013) noted that concerns for animal welfare and the environment are more prevalent among western vegetarians than among their Indian counterparts, whose motivations show a greater concern with notions of pollution and purity. In the Waitrose survey mentioned above (Waitrose and Partners 2018), people cited a variety of reasons for becoming vegetarian or vegan, with animal welfare and health being the prime motivating factors.[54]

In relation to the purchase of organic food, 'altruistic' and 'reflective' motivations include: supporting small, local producers; participating in the development of more environmentally food systems;[55] emotional responses engendered through direct interaction with producers;[56] and traceability.[57] Importantly for our purposes, the intrinsic qualities of organic food in the context of its perceived purity and concerns around food safety also emerge strongly from the evidence base.[58] From studies conducted in Sweden, Magnusson et al. (2001) and Magnusson et al. (2003) found that supposed health benefits associated with organic food outweighed environmental concerns, concluding that 'egoistic motives seem to be stronger than altruistic motives' (Magnusson et al. 2003: 115). According to Nagy-Pércsi and Fogarassy: 'The reduced consumption of chemicals in organic farming is the main criterion for which the consumers choose products' (2019: 6075). Similar conclusions have been drawn by Kapuge (2016), Lee and Yun (2015), and Padel and Foster (2005), among many others. Motivation is also discussed by Macbeth in Chapter 10 in relation to why consumers of organic foods are willing to pay premium prices for these products. Although health benefits are most commonly mentioned, other issues that can be considered ethical, primarily in relation to avoiding pollution of the wider environment, are also important. One can argue that in either case, concepts of purity are involved.

In summary, despite altruistic and ethical motivations, it can be said with some certainty that egoist concerns surrounding the potential deleterious effects of additional chemical inputs in the growing of food and rearing of animals (pesticides, herbicides, insecticides, artificial fertilisers, hormones, antibiotics and so on) are a prime motivational factor driving the growth of the organic food sector worldwide, although other pragmatic issues are also clearly important – including, of course, price.

What one finds, then, is that when dietary and consumer choices are not derived from religious rules, they can be, to varying extents, linked to the social attitudes of individuals – an association that probably arose in most Western societies during the nineteenth century. 'To varying extents' means that there is a continuum, not a separation, between Douglas' categories, at least in contemporary societies. However, whilst that continuum exists across a whole population, each individual is likely to have more clear-cut views.

Ethnographic Approaches

Much of the literature cited above is drawn from survey-based research of consumer attitudes and behaviour. Significant value can be added by qualitative and ethnographically based approaches that provide more detailed explorations of the attitudes surrounding organic food and how they vary cross-culturally.[59]

Being interested in how modern technological advances are perceived by the general population in West Mexico, Daria Deraga, a biosocial anthropologist, presents in Chapter 9 the results of a bioethical study of consumer attitudes to different forms of agriculture and food production. Her study is based on interviews, conducted variously among low- to middle-income adults in a rural area, at an elite farmers' market, at an artisanal fair in Guadalajara and with university students; individuals of different age groups and gender and at varying socioeconomic levels were included. She asked about food that they considered safe to eat and their criticisms where that they perceived that safety to be compromised. She included questions about genetically modified organisms, cultured meat, vegetarianism and organic foods, and in this chapter relates the responses to concepts of purity or danger. She found that 'most were opinionated on their choices of food they consumed' (p. 175), but that there were interesting differences with socioeconomic status, educational level and age. From her results, she discerns an attitudinal change towards concerns about available foods and their production methods, driven principally by younger consumers.

The main theme in Chapter 10 by biosocial anthropologist Helen Macbeth is an exploration of the perception that food labelled 'organic' is also 'pure'. After a critical discussion of the meaning of the word 'organic' within scientific communities, as concerning all living or once living matter, or in chemical terms associated with carbon atoms, the author presents an ethnographic study conducted over several years of one beef farm in Oxfordshire, England, and describes all the activities essential for the beef produced to qualify for the label 'organic'. What is intriguing is how the chapter ends with the farmer giving up the activities for the right to use the 'organic' label in order to pursue other methods to ensure better health for the cattle and a better quality of the beef. Macbeth's chapter highlights the stringent standards for organic farming in the United Kingdom, despite the variability between certifying organisations, which has led some farmers, as in the case she studied, to decide to withdraw from the scheme. However, this has apparently not held back the organic sector greatly, as is evidenced by its continued expansion detailed earlier.

The chapters by Macbeth and Deraga as well as several chapters by other authors in this volume (including Schiefenhövel, Mariano and Medina, and Saucedo, Mercado and Collinson) are the latest examples of the insights that ethnographic research can bring to bear into understanding food choices – and indeed into food studies generally. This is a key message of this book and a good point to draw together this review and present some concluding remarks.

Conclusion: Towards a Unified View of Pure Food

In this Introduction, we have considered the meaning and contemporary significance of 'pure food' across a range of different societies and contexts. The
structuralist schema outlined by Douglas (1966) has been a significant thread,
telegraphing its inclusion in the first three chapters of this volume. We have
noted its explanatory power in relation to the social classification of foods and
culturally proscribed ideas of food purity, as well as the relationship between
purity and psychological health, as described in Carter's chapter. However, we
have also noted how the 'medical materialist' approach, effectively rejected
by Douglas in *Purity and Danger* (1966), does have value in relation to the
links between pure food and personal health, dietary regimes and notions of
food safety.

A quest for pure food also dovetails with observations of wider societal
trends concerning the perception, management and mitigation of risk. The
rise of modernity has brought with it an increasing variety of real and imagined risks manifested, for example, by concerns over the safety of food and
the plethora of regulatory interventions that now govern its movement from
field to fork. Additionally, in the risk society, perceptions of some risks are
often amplified significantly, with 'best before' dates an example we highlighted in relation to food. But equally, risks to the environment, climate and
sustainability from the ways in which food is now produced, distributed, consumed and wasted constitute real threats to the future of humanity and the
planet itself, considerations that are partly driving the rise in the 'rediscovery'
of certain types of foods, new forms of 'traditional' and artisanal processing,
contemporary dietary regimes and organic farming (among other trends), all
of which are strongly linked to the desire to eat (and live) more purely.

Another theme in this Introduction has been the strong relationship
between pure food and purification of the body and mind, as described by
Lejavitzer in relation to ancient Greece and Rome. In contemporary Western
societies, for many people the pursuit of personal health is often entirely
divorced from the pursuit of purity, and therefore from pure food. However,
the South Asian examples cited here as well as the fitness culture described
by Mariano and Medina remind us that, in some contexts, parallels with
Greco-Roman ideas remain. Similarities are also evident in the latest dietary
regimes surrounding the 'detoxing' of the body, which also place a strong
emphasis on the links between pure food, bodily purity and mental wellbeing.

We have also considered the motivations for adopting certain diets that
involve the *elimination* of foods, particularly meat. Whilst for many of their
adherents, the pursuit of purity may not be an obvious driver for their dietary
choices, by teasing these motivations out a little, we can see how they are
often intrinsically related to pure food. As well as the perceived deleterious
effects of contemporary systems of food production and processing on personal health, altruistic motivations concerning environmental pollution and

sustainability are also important factors. Dietary choices that focus on reducing or eliminating the perceived harmful effects of additives to food and the environment, either from the human diet or from production and processing, or more usually both, can be viewed as being motivated by a quest for purity. The relationship between the health (for this read purity) of the land, soil and community described by Albert Howard is manifest here, and it is this recognition on the part of contemporary producers and consumers that is driving the growth of the organic sector worldwide, despite the challenges inherent in the endeavour, as detailed by Macbeth in Chapter 10.

One key point that we would like to emphasise – and one that should be obvious from the foregoing discussion – is that pure food, as with purity itself, is not a monolithic category and is by no means immutable. This is a point also picked up in a number of the following chapters, especially the one by MacClancy. Rather, it is always and everywhere a contested social phenomenon, whose meaning and significance can (and does) alter, sometimes radically, over time and space. This can engender significant debate and controversy, both in the academy and outside, some of which we have noted here.

This latter observation is emphasised in the Epilogue to this volume, in which we expand upon the meanings and etymology of the word 'pure' drawn from various dictionary sources, before considering the different approaches to pure food used by the contributors, drawing out some of the links between them. In so doing, we explore notions of objective and subjective purity, and discuss the ways in which the purity of food dovetails with concepts surrounding the purification of the individual, physically, psychologically and spiritually, and even to ideas of improving the environment. A concluding section looks at the future of pure food. Here we extrapolate from the observations made in this chapter concerning the strong relationship between pure food and lifestyle, arguing that this is highly likely to deepen in Western countries over the coming decades. The emphasis on food safety and regulation is also likely to become increasingly central to food production, distribution, consumption and disposal. However, one crucial observation we make in the Epilogue, picking up a point made in some of the other chapters, is that for far too many people in the world today who do not have enough to eat, pure food is likely to be viewed as 'an indulgent luxury with little meaning in their everyday lives' (p. 208).

This chapter has in many ways only just scratched the surface of what is a vast topic, and we are conscious that there are some areas in which we could have gone into a lot more detail and some issues that we have failed to address at all. However, what comes across strongly from this review are the benefits of adopting a cross-disciplinary approach. This is a principle that ICAF has always championed through its conferences and publications, and is something that we have attempted to uphold in compiling the current volume. Whilst many of the following chapters are written by anthropologists, the book includes a number of contributions from specialists in other disciplines, which, we believe, add important additional dimensions to the topic. There are certainly gaps in what we present on the following pages, but we hope that this volume adds value to the existing corpus of knowledge on pure food. Above all, we hope it is an interesting and enjoyable read.

Paul Collinson is a social anthropologist with interests in the anthropologies of food, conflict and development in Europe and Africa. He is a Visiting Research Fellow and former lecturer at Oxford Brookes University. He also works as a senior conflict analyst for the UK government.

Helen Macbeth is Honorary Research Fellow and retired Principal Lecturer in Anthropology at Oxford Brookes University. She is a former President of the International Commission on the Anthropology of Food and Nutrition with a strong interest in crossing the boundaries between traditional academic disciplines.

Notes

1. See http://www.guerrillagardening.org/ (last accessed 6 October 2022).
2. See https://www.etymonline.com/word/impure (last accessed 25 December 2021).
3. A term coined by Douglas herself concerning the origin of food taboos to describe a view that they stem from a need to protect humans from foodborne illnesses.
4. The classic example is the pig, which has a cloven hoof but does not chew the cud.
5. It is worth noting that the maintenance of cleanliness and hygiene was a central component in the Ayurvedic principles of medical knowledge that were laid down in India over 3,000 years ago (see e.g. Pushpangadan et al. 1987: 2; Sen 2004: 30).
6. The following section is largely drawn from Sen (2004) and Lüthi (2010), as well as the personal observations of Paul Collinson of Indian families in India and the United Kingdom.
7. Janeja's (2010) 'sensuous ethnography' of food in Bengali society, for example, demonstrates that both Hindu and Muslim notions of purity/impurity are fundamental to the ways in which food works in shaping social relationships and identity. Lüthi argues that from his observations in the town of Kottak in Tamil Nadu state in southern India, notions of food purity stem from a desire to achieve 'spiritual power' (2010: 65). Other examples abound.
8. The translation of the ancient Greek word δίαιτα involves many perspectives concerning ways of living, lifestyle, customs and culture; in some contexts it even refers to rules as the word 'diet' is used in the case of the 'Diet of Worms'.
9. A survey carried out by the UK's Food Standards Agency in 2018 found that 82 percent of people always washed their hands before handling and preparing food, and 85 percent did so immediately after handling raw meat, poultry or fish (Fuller et al. 2019: 45).
10. See e.g. Curtis and Biran 2001; Rozin et al. 2010; Curtis 2011; Sherman et al. 2012; Weinstein et al. 2018.
11. https://www.bbc.co.uk/news/world-africa-63150950 (last accessed 7 October 2022).

12. A separate scheme operates in Scotland.
13. An example is the UK nongovernmental organisation WRAP's 'label better, less waste' campaign (WRAP 2020).
14. https://www.euronews.com/green/2022/08/01/waitrose-tesco-ms-which-uk-supermarkets-are-ditching-best-before-dates-and-why (last accessed 31 August 2022).
15. https://www.bbc.co.uk/news/uk-62658965 (last accessed 30 August 2022).
16. https://www.euronews.com/green/2022/08/01/waitrose-tesco-ms-which-uk-supermarkets-are-ditching-best-before-dates-and-why (last accessed 31 August 2022).
17. In the US context, Wartella et al. (2010) date this back to 1973, and the introduction of regulations for the nutritional labelling of food.
18. For insights from social science on these issues, see e.g. Castro and Fabron (2019) for Argentina; Collinson (2013) for Ireland; Gogol and Singh (2021) for India; Hatch (2016) for the United States; Katzmarzyk (2010) for the United States and Canada; Mendenhall (2019), Moffat and Prouse (2010), Poulain (2017: Chapter 5) and Weaver (2018) for India; Yates-Doerr (2015) for Guatemala; and Zivkovic (2018) for Australia.
19. A stark example of this can be seen in the United Kingdom, whose National Health Service (NHS) reportedly spent 10 percent of its overall hospital budget, a total of £5.5 billion, in the 2017–18 financial year treating diabetes. Given that 90 percent of people with diabetes in the UK suffer from Type 2, which is linked to poor diet, a large proportion of these costs are preventable. It is estimated that, for the year 2017, over 950,000 deaths and over 16 million years of life were lost in Europe due to unhealthy diets (*The Lancet* 2018; also see Antal, this volume).
20. Bostan et al. (2019) cite the price premiums for organic food for various European countries: Switzerland 10–20 percent, Denmark 20–30 percent, Sweden 20–40 percent, Austria 25–30 percent, the United Kingdom 30–50 percent.
21. https://www.nutritionandinnovation.com/arugula/ (date accessed 31 August 2022).
22. https://www.arlafoods.co.uk/brands/arla-skyr/what-is-skyr/ (date accessed 31 August 2022).
23. https://www.food.gov.uk/business-guidance/packaging-and-labelling (date accessed 25 December 2021).
24. Vegetarian is defined as never eating meat, poultry, fish or seafood; vegan is defined as never eating meat, fish, seafood, poultry, dairy or eggs.
25. Jainism is often cited as mandating the strictest prohibitions on the consumption of animal-derived foods of any world religion, with *ahmisa* a fundamental element of Jain philosophy and something that goes beyond traditional veganism in its strong connections to ideas about the purity and liberation (*moksha*) of the soul (Evans 2012: 5; Miller and Dickstein 2021). In light of this and other aspects of Jainism, some authors have argued that its worldview could be viewed as a 'blueprint' for environmental sustainability in the modern world (e.g. Otterbine 2014; Rankin 2018; Shah 2018; Jain 2021).
26. Despite the fact that *ahimsa* forms an important tenet in Buddhism, in which it is one of the Five Precepts and a means of attaining 'merit' for rebirth, vegetarianism is not advocated in the Pali canon (the teachings of Buddha, followed most closely by the Theravada school) and observance varies widely between different Buddhist traditions (Stewart 2015). Most Indian Buddhists are members of the

Theravada and Vajrayana schools, which tend to allow meat-eating (Kieschnick 2005; Schmidt 2018; Ngo Dinh Bao and Mahathanadull 2019). Practices also vary widely in Western countries (Kaza 2005), although apparently most contemporary Buddhists worldwide are not vegetarian (Stewart 2010, 2015).

27. The incidence of vegetarianism among Christian and Muslim communities in India is lower still, at around 7 percent according to the NSSO survey (Natrajan and Jacob 2018: 57).

28. McDonald's opened its first Indian outlet in Delhi in 1996. According to Goyal (2021), India now has around 480 outlets.

29. As Arunima (2014) points out, India is perhaps the only country in the world where meat is not described by its name.

30. The close relationship between vegetarian observance and religious adherence in India is starkly illustrated by the survey data cited here, ranging from 6.71 percent among Christians to 98 percent among Jains (Natrajan and Jacob 2018: 57).

31. An opinion piece in *The Times* newspaper from December 2021, which claimed that an English county council had banned meat and dairy products from official events, entitled 'Puritanical Vegan Hectoring Should Be Kept off the Menu', is a typical example (Iqbal 2021).

32. A Gallup poll in 2018 found that there had been little change in the incidence of either vegetarianism or veganism in the United States from 2012, with 5 percent and 3 percent of the population respectively adhering to such diets – in 2012, the figures were 6 percent and 2 percent (Reinhart 2018). A survey carried out in 2019 among adults aged eighteen and over by the Harris Poll recorded similar figures to Gallup of 4 percent and 2 percent (Stahler 2021). One survey claimed that the number of vegans in the United Kingdom had climbed from 1.1 million in 2020 to 1.5 million in 2021, equivalent to 2.2 percent of the population. This was potentially as a result of the COVID-19 pandemic, with people wishing to adopt healthier diets and spending more time cooking at home (Plant Based News.org 2021; see also Filimonau et al. 2021). According to a UK supermarket chain in 2018, almost 13 percent of the UK population identified as vegetarian or vegan based on their own research sample, with a further 23 percent identifying as 'flexitarian', defined as having a semi-vegetarian or meat-reduced diet (Waitrose and Partners 2018: 6).

33. *The Simpsons* (Fox), Season 12, Episode 4.

34. Three notable recent examples are McDonald's McPlant burger, Wagamama's vegan 'fish and chips' and Chipotle's sofritas (an organic, shredded tofu dish made with chillies, roasted poblanos and spices).

35. Examples include Fearne Cotton, Ariana Grande, Lewis Hamilton, Kim Kardashian, Serena Williams and Moby, all of whom are vegan: https://vegworldmag.com/the-vegan-revolution-how-plant-based-foods-are-set-to-dominate-the-economy/ (date accessed 14 March 2022). An insight into just how influential they are comes from a glance at the followers of Ariana Grande and Kim Kardashian on Instagram – 293 and 283 million respectively (search performed on 30 January 2022).

36. Preview of *The Naked Diet* by Tess Ward on Amazon.co.uk: https://www.amazon.co.uk/Naked-Diet-Tess-Ward/dp/1849496048 (date accessed 30 January 2022).

37. A good example is a recent self-help book published in the United Kingdom: *Bosh! How to Live Vegan, Save the Planet and Feel Amazing.* (Firth and Theasby 2019)

38. https://www.waterstones.com/. Search conducted on 29 January 2022.

39. See e.g. Carmody and Wrangham 2009; Katz and Meller 2014; Koebnick et al. 1999; Barad et al. 2020, among numerous other studies.
40. Namely Austria, the Czech Republic, Denmark, Estonia, Finland, Greece, Italy, Latvia, Slovakia, Slovenia and Sweden.
41. Born Christopher James Northbourne, who wrote under his hereditary title.
42. Soil Association 2021.
43. See e.g. Scofield 1986; James and Fitzgerald 2008; Paull 2006; Paull 2014: 34, 42.
44. See Pfeiffer 1938; Northbourne 2003 [1940]; Balfour 2006 [1943]; Howard 2011 [1945]; Howard and Ward 2011 [1931]; 2014 [1940]; Steiner 2020 [1924].
45. See e.g. https://www.thelandgardeners.com/siralbert (date accessed 24 December 2022).
46. For example, Northbourne apparently had a significant influence on E.F Schumacher (James 2008: xxii; McKanan 2017: 187), who was widely regarded as the 'father' of modern environmentalism and the author of *Small Is Beautiful: A Study of Economics as if People Mattered* (1973), one of the most influential works in the history of ecology and environmentalism. According to James, Northbourne and Schumacher organised a conference (presumably in the 1960s) on the revival of family farms in the United Kingdom (James 2008: xxii).
47. https://www.cloudjuice.com.au/ (date accessed 16 April 2022).
48. http://www.galwayoysters.com (date accessed 30 August 2022).
49. https://www.milka.com (date accessed 16 April 2022).
50. https://www.polar-honey.com/shop/en/finnish-natural-honey/20-arctic-honey-115g.html (date accessed 24 December 2022).
51. See e.g. https://www.faroeseseafood.com/species/langoustine/ (date accessed 24 December 2022).
52. https://www.cleaneatingmag.com/ (date accessed 19 February 2022).
53. See e.g. Dimitri and Lohr 2007; Wojciechowska-Solis and Soroka 2017; Bosona and Gebresenbet 2018; Petrescu et al. 2020.
54. The survey results were as follows: 55 percent citing animal welfare concerns, 45 percent health reasons, 38 percent environmental issues, 33 percent saying they don't like meat, 24 percent citing taste and 2 percent saying it is fashionable.
55. See e.g. Durham (2007), Hashem et al. (2014) and Seyfang (2006) for the United Kingdom; Monier-Dilhan and Bergès (2016) for France; Scalvedi and Saba (2018) for Italy; and Tobler et al. (2011) for Switzerland.
56. See e.g. Scuderi et al. (2019) for Italy.
57. See e.g. Mattevi and Jones (2016) for the United Kingdom; Tessitore et al. (2020) for Italy; Wier et al. (2008) for the United Kingdom and Denmark; and Yuan et al. (2020) for China.
58. See e.g. Kamenidou et al. (2020) for Greece; Kamenidou et al. (2017) and Pham (2020) for Vietnam; Rahman et al. (2021) and Thomas and Gunden (2012) for the United States; and van Loo et al. (2013) for Belgium.
59. For example, Adams' (2016) study of the 'fascination' with local food in the Brooklyn area of New York shows how people draw from a constellation of various different issues, including anti-capitalism and anti-globalisation, concerns with food production practices as well as a quest for better nutrition, in creating new foodways relating to pure food in the city. Jordan (2012) provides an autoethnographic account of shopping for organic foods in Vienna and Paris, where she finds that 'local food cultures' are often elusive. Instead, she highlights

the important point that producers and retailers who sell at local markets are usually operating within networks of production, distribution and preservation that may be obscured by a focus on the 'traditional' and supposedly 'purer' aspects of the foods that are being sold.

References

Adams, R.T. (2016) Local and Organic Food Movements. In Kopnina, H. and Shoreman-Ouimet (eds) *Routledge Handbook of Environmental Anthropology*, Routledge, Abingdon and New York, pp. 329–43.

Aik, J., Newall, A.T., Ng, L-C., Kirk, M.D. and Heywood, A.E. (2018) Use of the Letter-Based Grading Information Disclosure System and Its Influence on Dining Establishment Choice in Singapore: A Cross-Sectional Study, *Food Control*, 90: 105–12.

Armstrong, B., King, L., Clifford, R. and Jitlal, M. (2021) *Food and You 2: Wave 2 Key Findings*, Food Standards Agency, London. Published at: https://www.food.gov.uk/sites/default/files/media/document/fy2-w2-key-findings_review_final_0.pdf. Accessed on 15 January 2022.

Arunima G. (2014) Being Vegetarian, the Hindu Way. *Economic and Political Weekly*, 18 April. Published at: https://www.epw.in/blog/g-arunima/being-vegetarian-hindu-way.html. Accessed on 21 January 2022.

Aschemann-Witzel, J., Hooge, I. de, Amani, P., Bech-Larsen, T. and Oostindjer, M. (2015) Consumer-Related Food Waste: Causes and Potential for Action, *Sustainability* 7(6): 6457–77.

Balfour, E. (2006 [1943]) *The Living Soil*, Soil Association, Bristol.

Banerjee-Dube, I. (2021) Fetid Flesh and Fragrant Fare. In Ayora-Diaz, S.I. (ed.) *The Cultural Politics of Food, Taste, and Identity: A Global Perspective*, Bloomsbury, London, pp. 103–17.

Barad, A. Rivero-Mendoza, D. and Dahl, W (2020) Popular Diets: Raw Foods, University of Florida IFS Extension Document FSHN20-45. Published at: https://edis.ifas.ufl.edu/publication/FS404. Accessed on 5 December 2021.

Beck, U. (1992) *Risk Society: Towards a New Modernity*, Sage, London.

Benson, A., Irdam, D., Bulceag, I., Barber, T. and Draper, A. (2019) *Food and You Wave 5 Secondary Analysis*, Food Standards Agency, London. Published at: https://www.food.gov.uk/sites/default/files/media/document/food-and-you-wave-5-secondary-analysis-current-food-landscape.pdf. Accessed on 8 January 2022.

Bosona, T. and Gebresenbet, G. (2018) Swedish Consumers' Perception of Food Quality and Sustainability in Relation to Organic Food Production, *Foods*, 7(4): 54.

Bostan, I., Onofrei, M., Gavriluţă (Vatamanu), A.F., Toderacu, C. and Lazăr, C. M. (2019) An Integrated Approach to Current Trends in Organic Food in the EU, *Foods*, 8(5): 144.

Buzzfeed.com (2022) Clean Eating Challenge. Published at: https://www.buzzfeed.com/christinebyrne/clean-eating-challenge#.ubYlbDyB2. Accessed on 1 January 2022.

Calvert, S.J. (2012) Eden's Diet. Christianity and Vegetarianism 1809–2009, PhD thesis, University of Birmingham. Published at: http://etheses.bham.ac.uk/4575/. Accessed on 26 December 2021.

Calvert, S.J. (2018) Eden's Diet. Christianity and Vegetarianism. In Linzey, A. and Linzey, C. (eds) *The Routledge Handbook of Religion and Animal Ethics*, Routledge, Abingdon, pp. 223–31.

Carmody, R. and Wrangham, R. (2009) Cooking and the Human Commitment to a High-Quality Diet, *Cold Spring Harbor Symposia on Quantitative Biology*, 74: 427–34.

Castro, M. and Fabron, G. (2019) Food Knowledge and Migrant Families in Argentina, *Anthropology in Action. Journal for Applied Anthropology in Policy and Practice*, 26(3): 35–43.

Chrzan, J. and Ricotta, J.A. (2019) Organic Food, Farming and Culture: Introduction. In Chrzan, J. and Ricotta, J.A. (eds) *Organic Food, Farming and Culture: An Introduction*, Bloomsbury, London and New York, pp. 1–6.

Collinson, P.S. (2013) Food and the Economic Crisis in Ireland. In González Turmo, I. (ed.) *Respuestas Alimentarias a la Crisis Económica*, ICAF, Seville, n.p.

Coveney, J. (2006) *Food, Morals and Meaning: The Pleasure and Anxiety of Eating*, Routledge, Abingdon.

Cunningham, E. (2004) What Is a Raw Foods Diet and Are There Any Risks or Benefits Associated with It?, *Journal of the American Dietetic Association*, 104(10): 1623.

Curtis, V. (2007) Dirt, Disgust and Disease: A Natural History of Hygiene, *Journal of Epidemiology and Community Health*, 61: 660–4.

Curtis, V. (2011) Why Disgust Matters, *Philosophical Transactions of the Royal Society B*, 366: 3478–90.

Curtis, V. and Biran, A. (2001) Dirt, Disgust, and Disease: Is Hygiene in Our Genes? *Perspectives in Biology and Medicine*, 44(1): 17–31.

Delate, K. and Turnball, R. (2019) Organics and the Environmental Movement. In Chrzan, J. and Ricotta, J.A. (eds) *Organic Food, Farming and Culture: An Introduction*, Bloomsbury, London and New York, pp. 47–56.

Derbyshire, E. (2018) Micronutrient Intakes of British Adults across Mid-Life: A Secondary Analysis of the UK National Diet and Nutrition Survey, *Frontiers in Nutrition*, 5: 55.

Derbyshire, E., Mason, P. and Aslam, N. (2020) *Dietary Status of Teens and Young Adults in Micronutrient Crisis*, Health and Food Supplements Information Service, London. Published at: https://www.hsis.org/wp-content/uploads/2020/12/HSIS_Dietary-Status-of-Teens_report_web.pdf. Accessed on 22 February 2021.

Dhanya S., Ramesh N.V. and Mishra, A. (2019) Traditional Methods of Food Habits and Dietary Preparations in Ayurveda – the Indian System of Medicine, *Journal of Ethnic Foods*, 6(14): 1–9.

Dimitri, C. and Lohr, L. (2007) The US Consumer Perspective on Organic Foods. In Canavari, M. and Olson, K.D. (eds) *Organic Food: Consumers' Choices and Farmers Opportunities*, Springer, New York, pp. 157–70.

Douglas, M. (1966) *Purity and Danger: An Analysis of Concepts of Pollution and Taboo*, Routledge & Kegan Paul, London.

——. (2004) *Jacob's Tears: The Priestly Work of Reconciliation*, Oxford University Press, Oxford.

Dumont, L. (1980 [1966]) *Homo Hierarchicus: The Caste System and Its Implications*, University of Chicago Press, Chicago.

Durham, C.A. (2007) The Impact of Environmental and Health Motivations on the Organic Share of Purchases, *Agricultural and Resource Economics Review*, 36(2): 304–20.

Durkheim, E., and Mauss, M. (2010 [1903]) *Primitive Classification*, Routledge, Abingdon.

Duschinsky, R. (2016) Introduction. In Duschinsky, R., Schnall, S. and Weiss, D. (eds) *Purity and Danger Now*, Routledge, Abingdon, pp. 1–20.

Duschinsky, R., Schnall, S. and Weiss, D. (eds) (2016) *Purity and Danger Now*, Routledge, Abingdon.

Eurostat.eu. (2022) Organic Farming Statistics. Published at: https://ec.europa.eu/eurostat/statistics-explained/index.php?title=Organic_farming_statistics. Accessed on 02 February 2023.

Evans, B. (2012) Jainism's Intersection with Contemporary Ethical Movements: An Ethnographic Examination of a Diaspora Jain Community, *Journal for Undergraduate Ethnography*, 2(2): 1–12.

Fardon, R. (2013) Citations out of Place, *Anthropology Today*, 29(1): 25–26.

Filimonau, V., Vi, L.H., Beer, S. and Ermolaev, V.A. (2021) The Covid-19 Pandemic and Food Consumption at Home and Away: An Exploratory Study of English households, *Socio-economic Planning Sciences Online*. Published at: https://doi.org/10.1016/j.seps.2021.101125. Accessed on 16 January 2022.

Firth, H. and Theasby, I. (2019) *Bosh! How to Live Vegan, Save the Planet and Feel Amazing*, HarperCollins, London.

Food and Agriculture Organization of the United Nations (2023) Sustainable Development Goals Indicators. Published at https://www.fao.org/sustainable-development-goals/indicators. Accessed on 24 January 2023.

Food Standards Agency (2020) FSA Research Suggests New Higher Estimates for the Role of Food in UK Illness. Published at: https://www.food.gov.uk/news-alerts/news/fsa-research-suggests-new-higher-estimates-for-the-role-of-food-in-uk-illness. Accessed on 16 January 2022.

Freisthler, M.S., Robbins, C.R., Benbrook, C.M., Young, H.A., Haas, D.M., Winchester, D.M. and Perry, M.J. (2022) Association between Increasing Agricultural Use of 2,4-D and Population Biomarkers of Exposure: Findings from the National Health and Nutrition Examination Survey, 2001–2014, *Environmental Health*, 21(23): 1–11.

Fuller, E., Bankiewicz, U., Davies, B. and Mandalia, D. and Stocker, B. (2019) *The Food and You Survey Wave 5. Combined Report for England, Wales and Northern Ireland*, Food Standards Agency, London. Published at: https://www.food.gov.uk/sites/default/files/media/document/food-and-you-wave-5-combined-report.pdf. Accessed on 23 January 2022.

Gogol, P. and Singh, M.S. (2021) Nutritional Status and Parental Socio-economic Conditions among the Adolescent Boys and Girls of Sombaria Village of West Sikkim, Northeast India, *Antrocom Online Journal of Anthropology*, 17(2): 165–72.

Goyal, S. (2021) Blog: 25 Years on, Is McDonald's a Success in India? Published at: https://www.campaignindia.in/article/blog-25-years-on-is-mcdonalds-a-success-in-india/472393. Accessed on 1 January 2022.

Gray, N. (2016) Developing Organic, Fairtrade, and Ethically Produced Products. In Osborn, S. and Morley, W. (eds) *Developing Food Products for Consumers with Specific Dietary Needs*, Woodhead, Sawston, pp. 241–66.

Gregory, J. (2007) *Of Victorians and Vegetarians: The Vegetarian Movement in Nineteenth-Century Britain*, I.B. Tauris, London and New York.

Grunert, K.G., Hieke, S. and Wills, J. (2014) Sustainability Labels on Food Products: Consumer Motivation, Understanding and Use, *Food Policy*, 44: 177–89.

Gunnars, K. (2018) The Paleo Diet – A Beginner's Guide Plus Meal Plan. Published at: https://www.healthline.com/nutrition/paleo-diet-meal-plan-and-menu. Accessed on 27 December 2022.

Harris, M. (1985) *Good to Eat. Riddles of Food and Culture*, Simon & Schuster, New York.

Hashem, S., Migliore, G., Schifani, G., Schimmenti, E. and Padel, S. (2018) Motives for Buying Local, Organic Food through English Box Schemes, *British Food Journal*, 120(7): 1600–14.

Hatch, A.R. (2016) *Blood Sugar: Racial Pharmacology and Food Justice in Black America*, University of Minnesota Press, Minneapolis.

Hetherington, K. (2004) Secondhandedness: Consumption, Disposal, and Absent Presence, *Environment and Planning D: Society and Space*, 22(1): 157–73.

Hjelmar, U. (2011) Consumers' Purchases of Organic Food Products: A Matter of Convenience and Reflexive Practices, *Appetite*, 56(2): 336–44.

Hobsbawm, E. and Ranger, T. (eds) (2012) *The Invention of Tradition*, Cambridge University Press, Cambridge.

Howard, A. (2011 [1945]) *The Soil and Health: A Study of Organic Agriculture*, Oxford City Press, Oxford.

———. (2014 [1940]) *An Agricultural Testament*, Rehák David and Important Books, New York.

Howard, A. and Wad, Y.D. (2011 [1931]) *The Waste Products of Agriculture: Their Utilization as Humus*, Oxford City Press, Oxford.

Inglis, D. (2015) Globalization and Food: The Dialetics of Globality and Locality. In Turner, B.S. and Holton, R.J. (eds) *The Routledge International Handbook of Globalization Studies. Second Edition*, Routledge, Abingdon, pp. 469–91.

Inglis, D. and Gimlin, D. (2009) *The Globalisation of Food*, Berg, London.

Iqbal, J. (2021) Puritanical Vegan Hectoring Should Be Kept off the Menu. Published at: https://www.thetimes.co.uk/article/puritanical-vegan-hectoring-should-be-kept-off-the-menu-8z2jrprxb. Accessed on 26 December 2021.

Jacimovic, D. (2021) 20 Remarkable Vegetarian Statistics for 2022. Published at https://dealsonhealth.net/vegetarian-statistics/. Accessed on 5 February 2022.

Jackson, P. (2010) Food Stories: Consumption in an Age of Anxiety, *Cultural Geographies*, 17(2): 147–65.

Jain, P. (2021) Jain Dharma as a Virtue Ethics for Sustainability. In Kawall, J. (ed.) *The Virtues of Sustainability*, Oxford University Press, Oxford, pp. 115–34.

James, C. and Fitzgerald, J.A. (eds) (2008) *Of the Land and the Spirit: The Essential Lord Northbourne on Ecology and Religion*, World Wisdom, Bloomington.

Janeja, M.K. (2010) *Transactions in Taste: The Collaborative Lives of Everyday Bengali Foods*, Routledge, Abingdon.

Jordan, J.A. (2012) In Search of the Elusive Heirloom Tomato: Farms and Farmers' Markets, Fields and Fieldwork, In Coleman, L. (ed.) *Food. Ethnographic Encounters*, Berg, Oxford and New York.

Kamenidou, I., Rigas, K. and Priporas, C.V. (2017) Household Behavior on Food Security during an Economic Crisis. In Mergos, G. and Papanastassiou, M. (eds) *Food Security and Sustainability*, Palgrave Macmillan, Cham, pp. 243–61.

Kamenidou, I., Stavrianea, A. and Bara, E.-Z. (2020) Generational Differences toward Organic Food Behavior: Insights from Five Generational Cohorts, *Sustainability*, 12: 2299.

Kapuge, K. (2016) Determinants of Organic Food Buying Behavior: Special Reference to Organic Food Purchase Intention of Sri Lankan Customers, *Procedia Food Science*, 6: 303–8.

Katz, D.L. and Meller, S. (2014) Can We Say What Diet Is Best for Health? *Annual Review of Public Health*, 35: 83–103.

Katzen, M. (2014 [1974]) *Moosewood Cookbook*, Random House, New York.

Katzmarzyk, P.T. (2010) Obesity – An Emerging Epidemic: Temporal Trends in North America. In Moffat, T. and Prowse, T. (eds) *Human Diet and Nutrition in Biocultural Perspective. Past Meets Present*, Berghahn Books, Oxford, pp. 223–40.

Kaza, S. (2005) Western Buddhist Motivations for Vegetarianism, *Worldviews: Global Religions, Culture, and Ecology*, 9(3): 385–411.

Kieschnick J. (2005) Buddhist Vegetarianism in China. In Sterckx R. (ed.) *Of Tripod and Palate*, Palgrave Macmillan, New York, pp. 186–212.

Koebnick, C., Strassner, C., Hoffmann, I. and Leitzmann, C. (1999) Consequences of a Long-Term Raw Food Diet on Body Weight and Menstruation: Results of a Questionnaire Survey, *Annals of Nutrition and Metabolism*, 43(2): 69–79.

Kuper, A. (1973) *Anthropology and Anthropologists: The Modern British School*, Allen Lane, London.

Lakhani, N. (2022) One in Three Americans Have Detectable Levels of Toxic Weedkiller, Study Finds, *The Guardian*, 10 February 2022. Published at: https://www.theguardian.com/environment/2022/feb/09/toxic-herbicide-exposure-study-2-4-d. Accessed on 11 February 2022.

The Lancet (2018) Global, Regional, and National Incidence, Prevalence, and Years Lived with Disability for 354 Diseases and Injuries for 195 Countries and Territories, 1990–2017: A Systematic Analysis for the Global Burden of Disease Study 2017, *The Lancet*, 392(10159): 1789–858.

Lappé, F.M. (2021[1971]) *Diet for a Small Planet: From Choice to Necessity*, Random House, New York.

LeBlanc, H. (2020) What Makes Food Super? The Post-eugenic Promises of Fish Flour and Other Super Powders. In McDonell, E. and Wilk, R. (eds) *Critical Approaches to Superfoods*, Bloomsbury, London, pp. 119–34.

Lee, H.J. and Yun, Z.S. (2015) Consumers' Perceptions of Organic Food Attributes and Cognitive and Affective Attitudes as Determinants of their Purchase Intentions toward Organic Food, *Food Quality and Preference*, 39: 259–67.

Lévi-Strauss, C. (1963) *Totemism*, Beacon Press, Boston.

———. (1966) *The Raw and the Cooked: Introduction to the Science of Mythology 1*, Penguin, London.

Loyer, J. (2016) *The Social Lives of Superfoods*. Doctoral dissertation, University of Adelaide. Published at: https://hdl.handle.net/2440/101777. Accessed on 15 September 2022.

Lüthi, D. (2010) Private Cleanliness, Public Mess: Purity, Pollution and Space in Kottar, South India. In Dürr, E. and Jaffe, R. (eds) *Urban Pollution: Cultural Meanings, Social Practices*, Berghahn Books, Oxford, pp. 57–85.

Macfarlane, A. (2006) Interview with Mary Douglas, 26 February 2006. Published at: http://www.alanmacfarlane.com/ancestors/douglas.htm. Accessed on 28 November 2021.

Magnusson, M.K., Arvola, A., Koivisto Hursti, U.K., Åberg, L. and Sjödén, P.O. (2001) Attitudes towards Organic Foods among Swedish Consumers, *British Food Journal*, 103: 209–27.

_____. (2003) Choice of Organic Foods Is Related to Perceived Consequences for Human Health and to Environmentally Friendly Behaviour, *Appetite*, 40: 109–17.

Mattevi, M. and Jones, J.A. (2016) Food Supply Chain: Are UK SMEs Aware of Concept, Drivers, Benefits and Barriers, and Frameworks of Traceability?, *British Food Journal,* 118(5): 1107–28.

Max-Müller, F. (2000) *The Thirteen Principal Upanishads*, Wordsworth Editions, Ware.

Mayo Clinic (2020) Paleo diet: What Is It and Why Is It So Popular? Published at: https://www.mayoclinic.org/healthy-lifestyle/nutrition-and-healthy-eating/in-depth/paleo-diet/art-20111182. Accessed on 27 November 2021.

McDonell, E. and Wilk, R. (2020) Tracking Superfoods: An Introduction. In McDonell, E. and Wilk, R. (eds) *Critical Approaches to Superfoods*, Bloomsbury, London, pp. 1–16.

McKanan, D. (2017) *Eco-alchemy: Anthroposophy and the History and Future of Environmentalism*, University of California Press, Oakland.

Medina, F.X. and Macbeth, H. (2021) Introduction. In Medina, F.X. and Macbeth, H. (eds) *The Mediterranean Diet from Health to Lifestyle and a Sustainable Future*, ICAF Alimenta Populorum Series, UK. Available at https://archive.org/details/the-mediterranean-diet-isbn-978-0-9500513-1-4. Accessed on 17 April 2022.

Mendenhall, E. (2019) *Rethinking Diabetes: Entanglements with Trauma, Poverty, and HIV*, Cornell University Press, Ithaca, NY.

Messer, E. (2007) Cultural Factors in Food Habits: Reflections in Memory of Christine S. Wilson, *Ecology of Food and Nutrition*, 46(3–4): 185–204.

Miller, C.J. and Dickstein, J. (2021) Jain Veganism: Ancient Wisdom, New Opportunities, *Religions*, 12(7): 512.

Moffat, T. (2010) The 'Childhood Obesity Epidemic': Health Crisis or Social Construction?, *Medical Anthropology Quarterly*, 24(1): 1–21.

Moffat, T. and Prowse, T. (2010) Introduction: A Biocultural Approach to Human Diet and Nutrition. In Moffat, T. and Prowse, T. (eds) *Human Diet and Nutrition in Biocultural Perspective. Past Meets Present*, Berghahn Books, Oxford, pp. 1–12.

Monier-Dilhan, S., and Bergès, F. (2016) Consumers' Motivations Driving Organic Demand: Between Self-Interest and Sustainability, *Agricultural and Resource Economics Review*, 45(3): 522–38.

Nagy-Pércsi, K. and Fogarassy, C. (2019) Important Influencing and Decision Factors in Organic Food Purchasing in Hungary, *Sustainability*, 11(21): 6075.

Nandini, A.S. (2014) McDonald's Success Story in India, *Journal of Contemporary Research in Management*, 9(3): 22–31.

National Sample Survey Office (2013) *Note on Sample Design and Estimation Procedure of NSS 68th Round*, Ministry of Statistics and Programme Implementation, New Delhi.

Natrajan, B. and Jacob, S. (2018) 'Provincialising' Vegetarianism. Putting Indian Food Habits in Their Place, *Economic & Political Weekly*, LIII(9): 54–64.

Navaro-Yashin, Y. (2009) Affective Spaces, Melancholic Objects: Ruination and the Production of Anthropological Knowledge, *Journal of the Royal Anthropological Institute*, 15(1): 1–18.

Newman, T. (2017) Nine Most Popular Diets Rated by Experts 2017, *Medical News Today*. Published at: https://www.medicalnewstoday.com/articles/5847#3-ketogenic-diet. Accessed on 14 January 2022.

Ngo Dinh Bao, H. and Mahathanadull, S. (2019) The Concept and Practices of Mahayana Buddhist Vegetarianism in Vietnamese Society, *Journal of International Association of Buddhist Universities*, 12(1): 77–87.

Northbourne, Lord. (2003 [1940]) *Look to the Land*, Sophia Perennis, Hillsdale, NY.

Otterbine, J.R. (2014) *Youth-Led Environmental Awareness: Initiatives towards a Jain Faith Community Empowerment,* University of North Texas. ProQuest Dissertations Publishing, 1601246. Published at: https://digital.library.unt.edu/ark:/67531/metadc700090/. Accessed on 16 July 2021.

Padel, S. and Foster, C. (2005) Exploring the Gap between Attitudes and Behavior: Understanding Why Consumers Buy or Do Not Buy Organic Food, *British Food Journal,* 107: 606–25.

Park, W. (2020). Why Vegan Junk Food May Be Even Worse for Your Health. Published at: https://www.bbc.com/future/article/20200129-why-vegan-junk-food-may-be-even-worse-for-your-health. Accessed on 2 January 2022.

Paxson, H. (2019) Rethinking Food and Its Eaters: Opening the Black Boxes of Safety and Nutrition. In Klein, J.A. and Watson, J.L. (eds) *The Handbook of Food and Anthropology*, Bloomsbury Academic, London and New York, pp. 268–88.

Paull, J. (2006) The Farm as Organism: the Foundational Idea of Organic Agriculture, *Elementals: Journal of Bio-Dynamics Tasmania*, 80: 14–18.

_____.(2014) Lord Northbourne, the Man Who Invented Organic Farming, a Biography, *Journal of Organic Systems*, 9(1): 31–53.

Petrescu, D.C., Vermeir, I. and Petrescu-Mag, R.M. (2020) Consumer Understanding of Food Quality, Healthiness, and Environmental Impact: A Cross-National Perspective, *International Journal of Environmental Research and Public Health*, 17(1): 169.

Pfeiffer, E. (1938) *Bio-Dynamic Farming and Gardening: Soil Fertility Renewal and Preservation* (F. Heckel, trans.), Anthroposophic Press, New York.

Pham, H.C. (2020) Antecedents of Organic Food Products Intention and Behaviors: Evidence from Vietnam, *Journal of Asian Finance, Economics and Business*, 7(11): 429–37.

Plant Based News.org (2022) Number of Vegans in Britain Skyrocketed by 40% in 2020 Claims Survey. Available at https://plantbasednews.org/culture/ethics/vegans-in-britain-skyrocketed/. Accessed on 29 January 2022.

Portalatín, M.J. (2007) Eating Snot: Socially Unacceptable but Common. Why? In MacClancy, J., Henry, J. and Macbeth, H. (eds) *Consuming the Inedible. Neglected Dimensions of Food Choice*, Berghahn Books, Oxford, pp. 177–88.

Poulain, J-P. (2017) *The Sociology of Food: Eating and the Place of Food in Society*, Bloomsbury, London and New York.

Pushpangadan, P., Sharma, J. and Kaur. J. (1987) Environmental Health and Hygiene in Ancient India: An Appraisal, *Ancient Science of Life*, VII(1): 1–5.

Raba, D.-N., Iancu, T., Bordean, D.-M., Adamov, T., Popa, V.-M. and Pîrvulescu, C.L. (2019) Pros and Cons of Raw Vegan Diet, *Advanced Research in Life Sciences*, 3(1): 46–51.

Rahman, S.M., Mele, M.A., Lee, Y.T. and Islam, M.Z. (2021) Consumer Preference, Quality, and Safety of Organic and Conventional Fresh Fruits, Vegetables, and Cereals, *Foods*, 10: 105.

Rankin, A. (2018) Obligation and Interdependency: Towards a Jain Theory of Organic Growth. In Shah, A.K. and Rankin, A. (eds). *Jainism and Ethical Finance: A Timeless Business Model*, Routledge, Abingdon, pp. 74–92.

Reinhart, R.J. (2018) Snapshot: Few Americans Vegetarian or Vegan. Published at: https://news.gallup.com/poll/238328/snapshot-few-americans-vegetarian-vegan. aspx. Accessed on 30 January 2022.

Reisman, E. (2020) From Seasonal Specialty to Superfood: Almonds, Overproduction, and the Semiotics of the Spatial Fix. In McDonell, E. and Wilk, R. (eds) *Critical Approaches to Superfoods*, Bloomsbury, London, pp. 17–36.

Rodale, J. (2017 [1945]) *Pay Dirt: Farming & Gardening with Composts*, Sportsman's Vintage Press, Boston.

Rozin, P., Haidt, J. and McCauley, C.R. (2010). Disgust. In Lewis, M., Haviland-Jones, J.M. and Barrett, L.F. (eds) *Handbook of Emotions (3rd Edition)*, Guilford Publications, New York, pp. 757–76.

Ruby, M.B, Heine, S.J., Kamble, S., Cheng, T.K. and Waddar, M. (2013) Compassion and Contamination: Cultural Differences in Vegetarianism, *Appetite*, 71: 340–8.

Scalvedi, M.L. and Saba, A. (2018) Exploring Local and Organic Food Consumption in a Holistic Sustainability View, *British Food Journal*, 120(4): 749–62.

Schiefenhövel, W. and Blum, P. (2007) Insects: Forgotten and Rediscovered as Food. Entomophagy among the Eipo, Highlands of West-New Guinea, and in Other Traditional Societies. In MacClancy, J., Henry, J. and Macbeth, H. (eds) *Consuming the Inedible. Neglected Dimensions of Food Choice*, Berghahn Books, New York, Oxford, pp. 163–76.

Schmidt, G.H. (2018) Is Vegetarianism a Personal Choice for Buddhists? A Contrast between Doctrine and Popular Opinion, *Buddhist Research Studies*, 4: 15–36.

Schumacher, E.E. (1973) *Small Is Beautiful: A Study of Economics as if People Mattered*, Blond and Briggs, London.

Schweers, B.W. (2021) The Emergence of Vegetarianism alongside the British Suffrage Movement from the Mid Nineteenth to the Early Twentieth Centuries. BA thesis, Saint Mary's University, Halifax, Nova Scotia. Published at: https://library2.smu.ca/handle/01/29507. Accessed on 1 January 2022.

Scofield, A.M. (1986) Organic Farming – the Origin of the Name, *Biological Agriculture and Horticulture*, 4(1): 1–5.

Scuderi, A., Bellia, C., Foti, V.T., Sturiale, L. and Timpanaro, G. (2019) Evaluation of Consumers' Purchasing Process for Organic Food Products, *AIMS Agriculture and Food*, 4(2): 251–65.

Sen, C.T. (2004) *Food Culture in India*, Greenwood, Westport, CT.

Seyfang, G. (2006) Ecological Citizenship and Sustainable Consumption: Examining Local Organic Food Networks, *Journal of Rural Studies*, 22: 383–395.

Shah, A.K. (2018) Ethical Investment. Social and Environmental Transformation and Jain Business. In Shah, A.K. and Rankin, A. (eds) *Jainism and Ethical Finance: A Timeless Business Model*, Routledge, Abingdon, pp. 93–107.

Sherman, G.D., Haidt, J. and Clore, G.L. (2012) The Faintest Speck of Dirt: Disgust Enhances the Detection of Impurity, *Psychological Science*, 23: 1506–14.

Singer, P. (1995 [1975]) *Animal Liberation*, Pimlico, London.

Skrovan, S. (2017) The Origins and Evolution of Nutrition Facts Labelling. Published at: https://www.fooddive.com/news/the-origins-and-evolution-of-nutrition-facts-labeling/507016/. Accessed on 1 January 2022.

Soil Association (2021) Our History. Published at: https://www.soilassociation.org/who-we-are/our-history/. Accessed on 26 December 2021.

Stahler, C. (2021) How Many People Are Vegan? How Many Eat Vegan When Eating out? Asks the Vegetarian Resource Group. Published at: https://www.vrg.org/nutshell/Polls/2019_adults_veg.htm. Accessed on 30 January 2022.

Steiner, R. (2020 [1924]) *Agricultural Course* (J. Paull, trans.). Published at: https://www.researchgate.net/figure/Translations-of-the-Agriculture-Course-presented-by-Rudolf-Steiner-in-German-at_tbl1_345431245. Accessed on 20 February 2022.

Stewart, J.J. (2010) The Question of Vegetarianism and Diet in Pāli Buddhism, *Journal of Buddhist Ethics*, 17: 99–140.

Stewart, J.J. (2015) *Vegetarianism and Animal Ethics in Contemporary Buddhism*, Routledge, Abingdon.

Stuart, T. (2008) *The Bloodless Revolution: A Cultural History of Vegetarianism from 1600 to Modern Times*, W.W. Norton & Company, New York.

Tessitore, S., Iraldo, F., Apicella, A. and Tarabella, A. (2020) The Link between Food Traceability and Food Labels in the Perception of Young Consumers in Italy, *International Journal of Food System Dynamics*, 11(5): 425–40.

Thomas, T. and Gunden, C. (2012) Investigating Consumer Attitudes toward Food Produced via Three Production Systems: Conventional, Sustainable and Organic, *Journal of Food, Agriculture and Environment*, 10: 132–35.

The Times Literary Supplement (1995) The Hundred Most Influential Books since WWII, *Times Literary Supplement*, 6 October.

Tiwari, A. (2016) Mystery Date: Advocating for a Harmonized System of Expiration Date Labeling of Food, *Vanderbilt Journal of Transnational Law*, 49: 1447.

Tobler, C., Visschers, V.H. and Siegrist, M. (2011) Eating Green. Consumers' Willingness to Adopt Ecological Food Consumption Behaviors, *Appetite*, 57: 674–82.

Toma, L., Costa Font, M. and Thompson, B. (2020) Impact of Consumers' Understanding of Date Labelling on Food Waste Behaviour, *Operational Research*, 20(2): 543–60.

Twigg, J. (1979) Food for Thought: Purity and Vegetarianism, *Religion*, 9(1): 13–35.

UN Environment Programme (2021) *Food Waste Index Report 2021*, UN, Nairobi.

_____. Facts about Food Waste. Published at: https://www.unep.org/thinkeatsave/get-informed/worldwide-food-waste. Accessed on 30 August 2022.

US Department of Agriculture (2022). Why Should We Care about Food Waste? Published at: https://www.usda.gov/foodlossandwaste/why. Accessed on 30 August 2022.

US Food and Drug Administration (2022a) How to Cut Food Waste and Maintain Food Safety. Published at: https://www.fda.gov/food/consumers/how-cut-food-waste-and-maintain-food-safety. Accessed on 30 August 2022.

_____. (2022b) Food Loss and Waste. Published at: https://www.fda.gov/food/consumers/food-loss-and-waste. Accessed on 24 January 2023.

Vågsholm, I., Arzoomand, N.S. and Boqvist, S. (2020) Food Security, Safety, and Sustainability – Getting the Trade-offs Right, *Frontiers in Sustainable Food Systems*, 4: 16.

Vainio, A., Kaskela, J., Finell, E., Ollila, S. and Lundén, J. (2020) Consumer Perceptions Raised by the Food Safety Inspection Report: Does the Smiley Communicate a Food Safety Risk?, *Food Control*, 110: 1–8.

Van Boxstael, S., Devlieghere, F., Berkvens, D., Vermeulen, A. and Uyttendaele, M. (2014) Understanding and Attitude Regarding the Shelf Life Labels and Dates on Pre-packed Food Products by Belgian Consumers, *Food Control*, 37: 85–92.

Van Loo, E.J., Diem, M.N., Pieniak, Z. and Verbeke, W. (2013) Consumer Attitudes, Knowledge, and Consumption of Organic Yogurt. *Journal Dairy Science*, 96: 2118–29.

Vegan.com (2022) Level Five Vegan. Published at: https://vegan.com/info/level-5-vegan/. Accessed on 23 January 2022.

Veganuary.com (2023) The Go Vegan 31 Day Challenge. Published at https://veganuary.com. Accessed on 24 January 2023.

Waitrose and Partners (2018) *Waitrose and Partners Food and Drink Report 2018–19*. Published at: https://waitrose.pressarea.com/pressrelease/details/78/NEWS_13/10259. Accessed on 6 February 2022.

Ward, T. (2015) *The Naked Diet*, Quadrille, London.

Wartella, E.A., Lichtenstein, A.H. and Boon, C.S. (eds) (2010) *Institute of Medicine (USA) Committee on Examination of Front-of-Package Nutrition Rating Systems and Symbols*, National Academies Press, Washington DC.

Watson, J.L. (2006) Introduction. Transnationalism, Localization, and Fast Foods in East Asia. In Watson, J.L. (ed.) *Golden Arches East: McDonald's in East Asia. Second Edition*, Stanford University Press, Redwood City, CA, pp. 1–38.

Watson, J.L. and Klein, J.A. (2019) Introduction. Anthropology, Food and Modern Life. In Klein, J.A. and Watson, J.L. (eds) *The Handbook of Food and Anthropology*, Bloomsbury Academic, London and New York, pp. 1–27.

Weaver, L.J. (2018) *Sugar and Tension: Diabetes and Gender in Modern India*, Rutgers University Press, New Brunswick, NJ.

Weinstein, S.B., Buck, J.C. and Young, H.S. (2018) A Landscape of Disgust, *Science*, 359(6381): 1213–14.

Wier, M., O'Doherty, K., Andersen, L., Millock, K. and Rosenkvist, L. (2008) The Character of Demand in Mature Organic Food Markets: Great Britain and Denmark Compared, *Food Policy*, 33(5): 406–21.

Willer, H., Meier, C., Schlatter, B., Dietemann, L., Kemper, L. and Trávníček, J. (2021) The World of Organic Agriculture 2021: Summary. In Willer, H., Trávníček, J., Meier, C. and Schlatter, B. (eds) *The World of Organic Agriculture Statistics and Emerging Trends*. Research Institute of Organic Agriculture FiBL/IFOAM – Organics International, Frick/Bonn, pp. 20–31.

Wojciechowska-Solis, J. and Soroka, A. (2017) Motives and Barriers of Organic Food Demand among Polish Consumers: A Profile of the Purchasers, *British Food Journal*, 119: 2040–8.

WRAP (2020) Redistribution Labelling Guide. Date Labels, Storage Advice and Freezing for Food Safety. Published at: https://wrap.org.uk/sites/default/files/2020-07/WRAP-surplus-food-redistribution-labelling-guide-May-2020.pdf. Accessed on 31 August 2022.

WRAP (2022) Food and Surplus Waste in the UK – Key Facts. Published at: https://wrap.org.uk/sites/default/files/2021-10/food-%20surplus-and-%20waste-in-the-%20uk-key-facts-oct-21.pdf. Accessed on 30 August 2022.

Wright, L. (2021) Framing Vegan Studies: Vegetarianism, Veganism, Animal Studies, Ecofeminism. In Wright, L. (ed.) *The Routledge Handbook of Vegan Studies*, Routledge, Abingdon, pp. 3–14.

Wunsch, N.-G. (2020) Global Organic Food and Beverage Market Value in 2018 & 2027. Published at: https://www.statista.com/statistics/869052/global-organic-food-and-beverage-market-value/. Accessed on 27 November 2021.

Wunsch, N.-G. (2021) Worldwide Sales of Organic Foods 1999–2019. Published at: https://www.statista.com/statistics/273090/worldwide-sales-of-organic-foods-since-1999/. Accessed on 27 November 2021.

Xiu, C. and Klein, K.K. (2010) Melamine in Milk Products in China: Examining the Factors That Led to Deliberate Use of the Contaminant, *Food Policy*, 35(5): 463–70.

Yates-Doerr, E. (2015) *The Weight of Obesity: Hunger and Global Health in Postwar Guatemala*, University of California Press, Berkeley.

Young, J.H. (1989) *Pure Food: Securing the Federal Food and Drugs Act of 1906*, Princeton University Press, Princeton.

Yuan, C., Wang, S. and Yu, X. (2020) The Impact of Food Traceability System on Consumer Perceived Value and Purchase Intention in China, *Industrial Management & Data Systems*, 120(4): 810–24.

Zivkovic, T., Warin, M., Moore, V., Ward, P. and Jones, M. (2018) Fat as Productive: Enactments of Fat in an Australian Suburb, *Medical Anthropology*, 37(5): 373–86.

CHAPTER 1
THE IMPURITIES OF PURITY

Jeremy MacClancy

'P$_{ure}$' is impure, its claims to clarity more misleading than clarificatory. Yet its purveyors and promoters argue the very opposite. My plan is to demonstrate the workings of this apparent conundrum and to offer reasons for its continued existence.

For 'purity', its most common thread of meaning appears to be 'unmixed' or, as the *Oxford English Dictionary* puts it, 'the thing itself, not something else'. Yet that dictionary lists thirty-one further meanings for the term, most of which are concerned with 'lack of admixture' in various specialised contexts. Many of these diverse meanings are approbatory, whether openly or by implication: the pure breed versus the mongrel; the pure or chaste versus the defiled; a pure tone better than a discordant one; and so on.

The pure is to be lauded, the impure denigrated. Importantly, frequently, this moral yardstick is lined up with those of spirituality and cleanliness, as though the pure is to be triangulated against immorality, defilement and dirt. But the weight given to these different dimensions, the terms alongside and against which the 'pure' is defined shift and budge according to space, context and time. A central objective of this chapter is to track some of those shifts and the changing prominence given to purity at different times, and what those changes tell us about those times. I pay special attention to who is deploying what notion of purity, when and for what ends.

My structure: first I broach the founding text in this forum – Mary Douglas on the gastronomic code of the Ancient Hebrews. I then attempt to compare their notion of purity with that that of the Victorians in both the United Kingdom and the United States. I pass from there to today, looking at the conceptual nexus within which 'purity' is now sited, and who are the present actors with a stake in its definition. Next, I follow up with who benefits from deploying a particular notion of purity, for whatever end, including the self-promotional.

Deploying all this for my own ends, I then strive to characterise aspects of 'purity' and cognate terms. In the next section, I query the seemingly universal association of purity and the positive. I close by trying to sum up what kind of concept 'pure' is: a concept that, on its own terms, is forever impure.

If this be so, dare we call this chapter an exercise in purification?

Taboo, or Not Taboo? What Is the Question?

The foundational work in this area is Douglas' *Purity and Danger* (Douglas 1966), her most influential book. As an opener to my discussion, I need to review, however briefly, her style of analysis, her later revisions of it, and others' reactions.

The most famous chapter of this celebrated work is the third, 'The Abominations of Leviticus', a structuralist interpretation of the Old Testament book that collates Ancient Hebrew dietary regulations. According to Douglas, its scribes equated purity with wholeness and holiness. Their particular classification of the animal world created anomalies, and since dirt was matter out of place, the anomalous were dirty. Hence, to follow Ancient Hebrew categorisation of the animals around them, pigs, because they are cloven-hooved but do not 'chew the cud', were polluting. Further, as impure creatures, they were dangerous to Jews who, to be holy, had to avoid them (Douglas 1966).

At its time, this structuralist approach was striking and became extremely influential both within anthropology and, to a notable extent, beyond. *Purity and Danger* has never been out of print, though it was first published over five decades ago (Leathem 2020; Zaloom 2020). In subsequent years Douglas, who rarely let her texts lie, both criticised and revised her argument. She criticised it for not relating a cultural classification to the social forms of the classifiers, here the Ancient Hebrews. To a good neo-Durkheimian like herself, cultural categorisation was congruent with, if not derived in structure from, social classification. Decades later, she revised her argument by (1) reconceiving the structure of its argument as less grid-like and more annular; (2) coming to view the Book of Leviticus as a rabbinical attempt to coax the general populace according to their learned guidelines. On this rereading, the Levitical rules of purity were not for separating out groups of people, but to proclaim an egalitarian doctrine that, though universal in scope, lent power of authority to the priestly office-holders. Some animals were not abominable, and therefore dangerous, but simply to be avoided. These rules against their polluting consumption thus served indirectly to protect certain animals that represented fertility. As much as humans, they were part of God's creation (Douglas 1999; Fardon 1999: Ch.9).

Both anthropologists and biblical scholars may question details of Douglas' argument but all laud its imaginative, stimulating power (e.g. Klawans 2003; Grabbe 2004; Heald 2004; Hendel 2004; Datta 2005). None would now think of attempting to explain Levitical regulations individually. They recognise that Douglas might have developed and rethought the functionalist dimension of her interpretations over the years, but their grounding on the central integrity of classifications remained central to her mode of understanding until her end; as exemplified by her last book published during her lifetime, *Jacob's Tears: The Priestly Work of Reconciliation* (Douglas 2004). Purity was never to be viewed piecemeal, but as an integral, integrating consequence of a categorical system.

Impurity as Unwanted Admixture in the Nineteenth Century

I wish to follow Douglas' example, placing the study of purity within its classificatory schema at different times and places. But there are at least two key differences between us.

First, the nature of classification: Douglas understood the categorical system of the Ancient Hebrews in monothetic terms, i.e. as a stable, elaborated structure of clearly defined taxa organised hierarchically (Handelman 2004: 165). Since I look at the fractious, evolving food systems in Western Europe and the United States of the last 150 years, I cannot assume such stability, rigid conceptual organisation or monothesis. Instead, I turn to the evidence we have and see what it allows us to say.

Second, the nature of food systems: like the Ancient Hebrews, most villagers in pre-industrial Europe and North America were to a great extent self-sufficient. They produced much of their own food themselves. But from the late eighteenth century onwards, areas in both continents began to experience an interlocking series of profound changes: the mechanisation of agriculture, mass immigration into mushrooming cities, salaried labour in factories and the development of a food industry.

In pre-industrial times, most people could usually trust in the food they were eating: either they cultivated it themselves or bought it from a merchant they knew personally. There were, of course, some infamous exceptions: for instance, miscreants' padding out expensive spices to increase their profits, and bakers' adulteration of bread with chalk, sawdust, clay and other materials. Despite the patchy persistence of these swindling practices, the general point stands: until the late eighteenth century, general trust in food was not an overly endangered value, for there was no or very little distance between most consumers and what they consumed. That comforting proximity disappeared with industrialisation and its concomitants (Fischler 1995: 209). These revolutionary changes together created a chain of distancing links between consumers and the source of what they consumed. The proletariat had now to rely on farmers, who sold to middlemen, who transported and distributed the foods, which were put on sale by grocers. Also, that is just the very simplest rendering of what was becoming an increasingly complex, extended food chain.

To modern readers, governments of this time can appear generally neglectful of their citizens, as though they were more concerned with raising taxes than securing the long-term health of the population. To employ contemporary terms, the state was, by and large, socially non-interventionist. This orientation elsewhere of the administration plus the introduction of so many participants into a commercially driven ever more fractured market enabled the adulteration of foods to prosper or to fester, according to one's view. When the level of abuse became too medically dangerous or morally outrageous, energetic activists launched campaigns that, eventually, led to legislative implementation.

From the late eighteenth century onwards, townspeople in Britain became increasingly suspicious of the ingredients within food on sale. The pioneering campaigner against these unspoken additives to urban diets was Friedrich Accum, an innovative chemist and gifted publicist. Accum devised simple scientific tests to analyse the contents of foodstuffs that he described in accessible prose in his best-selling *Treatise on Adulteration of Food and Culinary Poisons* (Accum 1820). On its cover a skull surmounts a spider's web, and beneath, the line from the Book of Kings, 'There is poison in the pot'. Mercantile reaction was widespread and negative. And when the Royal Institution accused him of severing pages from its books, he fled to his native Germany. He never returned (Cole 1951).

By the mid-nineteenth century, adulteration was so widespread that it had become very difficult in cities to buy several basic foods free of modification (Burnett 1979: 240; Freeman 1989: 26–29, 87–93). In 1850 the leading medical journal *The Lancet*, then edited by a campaigning coroner, commissioned Arthur Hassall, a clinical academic, to conduct a systematic investigation into the methods and range of adulteration. In a weekly series over the next four years, the industrious Hassall exposed the tricks of food fraudsters and the astonishing range of their practice. The re-publication of his findings in the daily press galvanised sectors of the public, in turn stimulating a notable number of food producers and traders into voluntary reform of their own practices. Parliament responded by establishing an official inquiry, and in 1860 passing the first Adulteration of Foods Act. The Act, an unsatisfactory compromise between commercial interests and consumer concerns, changed little; it did, however, establish the important precedent that the state should protect consumers from fraud and risks to health. Interventionism was no longer taboo. Throughout the 1860s, sustained campaigning by a broad coalition of learned bodies and socially minded medics kept up the pressure on Parliament. The progressively more powerful Acts it passed, in 1872 and 1875, plus chemists' development of new analytical tests, led within a decade to major improvement in the quality of basic foods (Drummond and Wilbraham 1939: 340–70; Burnett 1979: 99–120, 240–67; Rioux 2019).

The development of the food system in the United States was roughly comparable. Pervasive adulteration followed in the wake of the industrial and rural revolutions. Tampering with produce, profit-driven but ill-considered, led to spasmodic food scares and some deaths. Inspired activists exploited these attacks on public wellbeing by launching their own campaigns. The 'Pure Foods Movement' was a broad coalition active from the 1870s, spearheaded by women's clubs. Its speakers, many of whom had already been militant in the temperance movement, regarded adulterated food as on a moral par with alcohol abuse. Both forms of abuse, especially among the poor, led to malnourishment, violence and other corruptions of the social order. The 1906 publication of Upton Sinclair's *The Jungle* (Sinclair 1906), a still chilling exposé of conditions in the Chicago meatpacking industry, caused a public outcry. This increased the Movement's pressure on politicians for protective legislation. A few months later, the first national regulations for food safety were passed: the 1906 Pure Food Act (Cohen 2020: Chapter 7).

What most marks out the US progress towards greater regulation of food safety was the evangelical zeal of many of those who propounded it, which tended at times towards the messianic. In their campaigns, they advocated a righteous form of food purity, one as spiritual as it was alimentary. Eating the wrong items was sinful. Coffee and mustard, no matter how unadulterated, were classed as evil stimulants and therefore 'impure' (Wilson 2020: 164–66). Sylvester Graham, a pro-temperance minister and inspirer of the eponymous cracker, went even further, preaching against condiments, spices and a surprising range of other foods (Spencer 1993: 273–74). In these radical Christian contexts, the campaign against margarine was exemplary. The spread, it was said, attacked both body and soul, stimulated promiscuity and lowered the level of life (Wilson 2020: 171).

I have underlined the differences between the Ancient Hebrews and modern Westerners, of taxonomic stability and food chain complexity. But there is a primary commonality, which should be starkly evident by now: the centrality of notions of purity for both populations. In her biblical works, Douglas underlines the social significance of the Levitical food taboos: whether, as she first claimed, to draw the Jews together through the embodied solidarity of common routines and so differentiate them from other nonpracticants or, as she later argued, to set a universalising standard, in Hebraic terms, for all humanity.

Similar statements can be made about Britons and Americans in the second half of the nineteenth century. For many urban consumers, it was key for their conception of life itself that their food was pure, i.e. unadulterated, especially by potentially poisonous additives. Their campaigns became so powerful because this concern was so extensive and profound. In the United States, the campaigns gained patently spiritual dimensions, with some of its protagonists making their proposed reforms not just a central strut of their lives, but a comprehensive code to restructure their quotidian food routines within the frame of a sternly delineated morality.

Ancient rabbis, upright Victorians: these people were whom they were because they strove to be pure. Ideas of purity and its opposite gave meaning and structure to their lives, throughout their lives.

Trusting in Purity, Today

In this section I comment on contemporary roles of purity, primarily in the United Kingdom and the United States. First, I look at official approaches to this general area. Then I chase up the modern evolution of popular versions of 'purity' and associated terms: who said and did what, and to what effect. Finally, I discuss some more developed, potentially pathological interpretations of the concept.

Officialdom

Today, the webpages of global health agencies, international bodies and national ministries tell a comparably interlinked tale to that sketched above for the nineteenth century. Many of these digital digests underline the mutual reinforcing of safe food, health concerns, buoyant trade and public trust. As the World Health Organization (WHO), a UN agency, states:

> Food safety, nutrition and food security are closely linked. Unsafe food creates a vicious cycle of disease and malnutrition, particularly affecting infants, young children, elderly and the sick. In addition to contributing to food and nutrition security, a safe food supply also supports national economies, trade and tourism, stimulating sustainable development.[1]

The WHO is medically oriented. In qualified contrast, the Food and Agriculture Organization (FAO), also a UN agency, emphasises the active roles industry and consumers can and should play in maintaining trust in the foods they are offered for sale:

> Food control – a mandatory activity – can improve the national food system, protect the consumer and promote trade only if it enjoys the active cooperation and participation of the industry, which is subject to regulation, and consumers, who they benefit from better protection.

> … For consumer groups … the most important aspect is the presence of chemical substances in food. To be able to cover all aspects, an effective control system is needed, based on sound food laws and regulations and the necessary technical knowledge. The system must be trustworthy and transparent, in which consumers and industry can place their trust.[2]

The FAO furthers the point by quoting a representative of a US grocers' association:

> Private enterprise recognizes that its success – measured in terms of profitability – is completely dependent on consumer satisfaction. A reflection of consumers' satisfaction is their continuing purchase of the same products. Food manufacturers and marketers thus have an investment in their product identities (brand names) that they naturally wish to protect. It is in their interest, therefore, to establish and administer the controls that ensure that their products do indeed meet consumer expectations of safety and quality.[3]

In the United Kingdom, the Food Standards Agency of the British government upholds the Food Safety Act 1990. According to its website, this legislation is meant to assure openness, purity and trust in the food network:

> The main responsibilities for all food businesses under the Act are to ensure that:
>
> ... businesses do not include anything in food, remove anything from food or treat food in any way which means it would be damaging to the health of people eating it
>
> ... the food businesses serve or sell is of the nature, substance or quality which consumers would expect
>
> ... the food is labelled, advertised and presented in a way that is not false or misleading.[4]

In a similar vein, the European Commission (EC) states that the principles of its food safety regulations are to:

> ... guarantee the protection of human health and life ... consumers' interests, ... fair practices in food trade ... and to facilitate the global trade in safe, wholesome food.[5]

These various official bodies, operating on a range of geographical scales, all highlight the same intertwining of consumer, commercial and public concerns. The idea of 'food safety' only gains meaning within this nexus. What these websites do not mention are the nationalist and regionalist dimensions to this global network. Governments of individual countries and of blocs such as the European Union (EU) have to juggle electoral support and business interests. The constant concern is that governments, for the sake of strengthening the economy, quietly allow the sale of new foods or additives whose long-term safety has yet to be exhaustively tested. A notorious example is the outbreak in the 1990s of bovine spongiform encephalopathy (BSE), 'mad cow disease', caused by including animal carcasses in feed for livestock, which led to several countries banning the import of British beef (Parasecoli 2017: 194–97; see also Messer 2007; Thomas 2014). Further, these official statements hide as much as they clarify: for example, the EC statement gives no clear idea what 'fair', 'safe' or 'wholesome' should mean; all of these terms are up for angry debate. In a similar mode, the FAO statement comes across as disingenuous: that 'private enterprise recognizes … success … is completely dependent on consumer satisfaction' ignores the well-grounded, much-practised commercial strategy of food companies indirectly conditioning popular tastes, via aspirational advertising and other marketing means. It also ignores the economic reality of testing (Loria 2017; Subramanian 2021): innovative private companies may offer the latest technology for testing – element analysis, plasma spectrometers, etc. – but who is prepared to foot their bill?

This regulatory system, however loose, is meant to be held together by a contested, unsteady notion of trust (Gambetta 2000). As we have seen, the adulteration of food is a question of public health, economic interests, political disposition and public order. The food historian Bee Wilson goes further: she argues that general worries about what is in our food can constitute a threat to civilised politics, for a government that allows food fraud to proliferate is indirectly enabling anarchy. In her terms, a society whose members accept that swindling is rife is 'one where the fundamental trust between citizens has broken down' (Wilson 2020: xiii). In 2017 a promoter of a mobile compliance app put across much the same message, albeit in a more dramatic manner, perhaps with one eye on prospective sales:

> One slip in food safety compliance could cost someone their health or life, and this information spreads mistrust in the general public toward the company who sold the product, and also the entire product across companies throughout an entire country and beyond.[6]

Whether we accept Wilson's argument or not, the main point remains: a generalised sense of trust, however fragile or fractured, is necessary for the maintenance of Western food systems. I now look at modern-day examples where that sense of trust has begun to crack, and debates about 'purity' return to the fore.

Food Activists, Discourse Developments

This distributed sense of trust, though officially endorsed, is insufficient for some individuals. They have questioned the interests of parties involved in the tripartite equation of the public good, big business and government. Like the campaigners and concerned members of the populace of the late nineteenth century, these modern-day food activists have fought to achieve in their own lives greater control of what goes into their bodies, and to persuade others to follow suit. Investigative journalists have long played their part here (e.g. Cannon 1987; Blythman 1996; Schlosser 2001; Lawrence 2004; Spurlock 2006), but in this subsection I wish to concentrate on the work of self-proclaimed alternatives.

Let us start with the hippies and other protagonists within the emergent counterculture who, in the early 1960s, urged a 'return to nature'. Many were emboldened by Rachel Carson's seminal *Silent Spring* (Carson 1962), a groundbreaking critique of the overuse of insecticides and pesticides. The heavy-handed attempt by the chemical industry to forestall its publication and then to condemn it only helped its massive sales. Aspirant farmers were also inspired by the example of pioneers such as Lady Eve Balfour, founder of the UK Soil Association, who had practised and developed non-intensive modes of agriculture since the 1930s. Thousands entered newly established communes to 'live off the land' without relying on industrial intermediaries: some of these groups survived (Guthman 2014: 24–44). Many, whether in rural or urban settings, claimed free-thinking opposition to 'mass production, efficiency, rationalization, limits' (Belasco 1989: 40). Using culinary bibles such as *Diet for a Small Planet, The Whole Earth Catalogue* and *Organic Gardening and Farming,* they strove to eschew additives from their diet and, if they had the disposable income, to patronise independent greengrocers. In sum, they wished to make themselves anew, to live as 'naturally' as possible, eating above all 'honest', 'natural' foods.

New styles of restaurant also began to open, disseminating much the same message. The exemplar I choose to single out here is Alice Waters, whose foundational work since the 1970s in both the San Francisco area and later nationally embodies many of our themes. In the name of taste, she developed and propounded a very influential style of farm-to-fork feeding for her restaurants, grounded on local, market-fresh, organic food. In recent decades, she has campaigned for 'edible education' in secondary schools, while chefs who trained in her kitchens and other converts to her food philosophy disseminate her approach yet further. She both created a commercially viable new style of cuisine and enabled its directed diffusion across both coasts (Waters et al. 1984; McNamee 2006; Waters 2007, 2015, 2017).

'Natural' became such a shibboleth for back-to-the-land hippies and other would-be changemongers because it is usefully complex. It can refer to a people-free environment, untrammelled by the evils of agribusiness; health-enhancing foodstuffs, considered 'pure' because they are unpolluted by preservatives and other chemical additives; the normal or expected, with the unvoiced implication that what is should be, as though one could pretend to derive a moral position from a factual statement. What was quietly shunted aside was the established idea of nature as 'red in tooth and claw' (Coward

1989: 141). For those hippies more enamoured of Eden before the Fall, the 'natural' could also connote 'simplicity, humility, lack of pretension, a healthy lack of self-consciousness or sophistication', though their mainstream opponents might signal how ill-defined, even contradictory, use of the term was within the countercuisine (Belasco 1989: 41).

By turn of the millennium, 'organic' had to a significant extent replaced 'natural' as the favoured adjective for food-focused hippies and those equally inclined albeit less extreme in their opposition to the mainstream. Though the two terms are similar, their differences when applied to food are important. Within the self-styled 'alternative movement', 'natural' tended to mean additive- or preservative-free, unprocessed, whereas 'organic' signalled a mode of cultivation where pesticides and other chemical killers were taboo. The first referenced factories; the second, farms. Then again, 'organic', like 'natural', can bear multiple meanings. According to the *Oxford English Dictionary*, besides its specific technical usages in medicine, music, mechanics, mathematics, the law, linguistics, architecture, economics, chemistry and commerce, 'organic' can denote 'of, relating to or derived from a living organism or organisms; having the characteristics of a living organism'; 'belonging to the constitution of an organised whole; structural'; 'of or relating to an organized structure compared to a living being; of, relating to, or derived from living matter'. Counterculturalists extended this semantic range yet further by giving the term connotations of:

> integration, wholeness, health. Living organically meant experiencing basic processes of growth, change, renewal. Embracing enduring life processes such as natural child birth, breastfeeding, bread baking, and gardening, the organically inclined saw nature as an ally rather than a nuisance or conquest. (Belasco 1989: 69)

Today, 'organic' has long been co-opted into the mainstream. A diversity of official modes of certification are now available, with all the attendant bureaucracy that comes in their train. The set of associations Belasco identified in the 1980s have also lost their alternative edge: today, not just foodies have bread machines, and in the United Kingdom at least, kitchen gardening, often with exotic variants, continues its steady rise, and competition for municipal allotments has returned in recent decades.

Just as the use of the term 'organic' tended to push that of 'natural' off centre-stage, the use of 'local' appears to have recently done much the same for 'organic'. It seems the idea of giving priority to proximity of production was stimulated by the idea of 'food miles', first formulated by Tim Lang, a British professor of food policy (see e.g. Lang 2006). Though it has proved overly simplistic and needs to be assessed in conjunction with other factors in order to gauge environmental impact, the phrase has been incorporated into common foodie parlance in the United Kingdom, along with 'local', as positive terms employed by those who see themselves as ecologically minded. One difference, at least in Britain, is that 'organic' is still widely regarded as an identity-making marker for the comfortably off, while 'local' appears unhindered by perceived social class bias.

Despite these shifts in terminology and their particular foci, one common thread to these modern trends is that today concerns about food do not overly stress hygiene and sterility. It would seem the populace trust food regulators to ensure that what they consume will not make them immediately ill. However, as recent work in Denmark demonstrates, some people have reassessed the importance of these concerns for them and their families. Researchers there found that interviewees had continuing worries about environmental mismanagement and mercantile self-interest. These made them anxious about corporeal contamination. As consumers, their choices were primarily guided by a striving for purity, in the sense of 'free from additives or preservatives' or 'untampered-with nature' (Ditlevsen et al. 2019). Buyers focused on perceived naturalness, 'even though "natural" products are known to incorporate objectively dirty and non-sterile elements' (Ditlevsen and Andersen 2021). In other words, it's OK if a purchased parsnip has bits of earth clinging to it, as the soil won't have been soaked in pesticides. Toxins commonly encountered in the countryside are acceptable or ignored; agrichemical additives are not.

The Dark Side of Cooking the Books

These various shifts in terminology and consumer practice are also refracted and boosted through an array of culinary and restaurant developments, plus an accumulating plethora of cookbooks, dietary guides and exposés of the food industry.

An overview of recent cookbooks gives some idea of the variety of positions, within the remit of this chapter, taken today. Many encapsulate their message for a healthy, additive-free, 'natural' diet as 'pure food'. In the United States, the prize-winning *Pure Food* by chef and food educator Kurt Dammeier proclaims: 'You are what you eat. And what you're eating isn't good.' To break the deadly cycle of poor nutrition and epidemic levels of obesity and diabetes, he promises to show readers how to 'take control of your diet ... how easy – and how much healthier it is to cook clean, delicious foods' (Dammeier 2016; see also Amilian 2018). Veronica Bosgraaf, who presents herself as a biology teacher-turned-food advocate because of her children, runs The Pure Bar Co., selling snack bars that compete with mainstream competitors on taste but are made only with 'simple, organic ingredients': 'We make clean, exceptionally delicious food for all ages. This is what makes Pure special.'[7] Her book, its blurb states, will 'clean' your kitchen and your lifestyle (Bosgraaf 2017). The best-selling food writer David Joachim cut a new niche in his *Fresh Choices: More Than 100 Easy Recipes for Pure*

Food When You Can't Buy 100% Organic, in which he uses official data 'to identify conventionally supplied foods that are among the safest to consume when organic alternatives are unavailable' to include in his 'healthy' recipes (Joachim 2004). The term 'purity' may also be used by raw foodies. They tend to eat only raw or mildly heated foods, which, if processed, are only simply so, e.g. sprouted seeds and fermented items. They eschew any pasteurised, homogenised, non-organic foods and all additives. According to its devotees, following this dietary practice is the path towards 'purity without limits' (Wollin 2014; see also Cushing 2007).

In the United Kingdom, already in 1985, cookery writer Pauline Hemmings was advocating 'healthy eating without additives' in her *Pocket Book on Pure Food* (Hemmings 1985). Twenty years later, Max Tomlinson, the country's 'top naturopath', broadened much the same programme and developed the language. In his *Clean up Your Diet: The Pure Food Programme to Cleanse, Energize and Revitalise*, he promises to restore one's health and energy by capitalising on 'the inherent power of food' that is not processed or 'chemical-laden': the judicious choice of 'delicious recipes' will 'kick-start your energy levels' and relieve common ailments (Tomlinson 2006). In Australia, the leading chef Peter Gilmore says in his *Organum: Nature Texture Intensity Purity* that he seeks through his cuisine for the idea of organum: 'a sense of purity, which is the essence of something which is complete, where all the elements work together to create something new' (Gilmore 2014; see also Church 2016).

These productions seem unremarkable: chefs and cookery writers advancing their careers, raising their profile and maybe making a bit of money in the process. They are selling a way to rejig your diet and ground your health in the right culinary habits. But in recent years in both the United Kingdom and the United States, this concern with achieving a notion or sense of purity through 'clean eating' has taken on extreme, worrying forms. Boosted by social media, some of its promoters have moved towards the absolutist and have gained an increasing number of followers along the way. The exact forms taken by its adherents, which range from veganism to the praising of wild meats, are less important than some of its practitioners' life-consuming, rigid approaches (Wilson 2017). They are said to suffer orthorexia, a condition still awaiting consensual medical definition, but characterised as an obsession with eating only foods considered pure and perfect (Beat Eating Disorders 2017). Dieticians view it as potentially dangerous because it lacks a scientifically grounded nutritional rationale, and some versions prohibit the intake of whole food groups usually considered essential (Yuen 2015; McGregor 2017).

To prominent food critics, 'clean eating' has taken on an overly righteous tone, upheld by zealots and edging perilously close to a foodie fundamentalism. To them, clean-eating crusaders confine mealtimes to a moralising frame and put tenets before taste. Here clean eating is more about lifestyle than diet, and comes with a strong evaluatory charge. As the very successful cookbook writer Nigella Lawson complained in 2015 on BBC Radio:

What I think is behind the notion of clean eating is an implication that any other form of eating is dirty or shameful. I think there is, err, a slight puritanism which is as much about the horror of the flesh, one's own flesh and the flesh one might be eating ... I think food should not be used as a way of persecuting oneself, and I think one should look to get pleasure and revel in what's good, rather than think, 'Oh no. That's dirty, that's bad, and that's sinful,' and the other sort of eating is virtuous. And also I don't like people thinking they're better people themselves for the way we eat. We make choices for ourselves, either for our health, our life, according to our income and according to our taste buds. (Lawson 2015)

The following year, Ruby Tandoh, another successful food writer, in a much-quoted article, railed against evangelical clean-eating advocates who have surrendered to the pseudo-science of a narrowly prescriptive diet. She complained of gluten being branded 'evil', 'poison' and 'contaminating':

There's even a leading Australian gluten-free site called glutenisthedevil. com ...

This isn't just about nutrition, it's about morality, and when food becomes imbued with this kind of scandalizing language, the dinner table becomes a minefield. (Tandoh 2016)

Eating as ethics? Chasing a dream, however toxic or divisive, of purity? Douglas was here, decades ago. The Ancient Hebrews who wrote Leviticus would recognise the logic of the modern-day style.

Wielding Purity

It should be patently obvious by now that there is no pure 'purity'. It is an always-contested concept and thus is best understood in strategic terms. It is much more an instrumental category than a neutral one. The immediate, important question therefore becomes: who is upholding or promoting which version, when, to what end and to what effect?

If we follow Douglas, the 'purity' of Levitical times is to be understood in terms of conceptual structure, as a reinforcing mechanism of classificatory integrity. Douglas changed her mind about the broader aims of the Levitical regulations – what she terms their 'cultural bias'. In *Purity and Danger*, she speculated that the Levitical regulations were deployed by farsighted rabbis to rally the faithful; in her later book on Leviticus, she viewed them as universalising rules whose purpose was not to erect barriers between believers and infidels, but to draw others into the fold (Douglas 1966, 1999). If we follow Douglas' style of functionalist free-thinking, it is also possible to regard the rabbinical authors of the Book of Leviticus as dissimulating self-promoters: if their words held sway, they would accrue further authority and accumulate prestige. This might be speculation. But whatever their self-confessed motives, to regard these ancient scribes as holy innocents would be wilfully naïve.

The pure food protagonists of the late nineteenth century can be viewed in a comparable manner. In the United Kingdom, their worries about purity were guided by concerns about health and fraud. By definition, the 'pure' is unadulterated. For UK campaigners, it was also honest: a consumer was buying what they were told they were buying and nothing more; they had not entered a food shop to be pawned off with additives, whether noxious or not. Self-styled champions of the people, such as Accum, were viewed as men and women of probity. At the same time, for a publicity-seeking immigrant like Accum, a moral campaign against demon grocers only served to boost his profile. This is but a common, though usually unvoiced, part of the agenda of any groundbreaking militant (MacClancy and Fuentes 2013: 19).

In the United States, campaigners gave the 'pure' stridently religious charge. 'Impure' food was a sin against a divinely ordained order, a corrupting transgression of the Lord's design for us all. The scientific dimension of this Pure Foods Movement was led by Harvey Washington Wiley, Chief Chemist at the Department of Agriculture. His work was particularly persuasive because he devised simple but effective experiments into the deleterious effects of additives, such as salicylic acid and formaldehyde, and had the results broadcast by a journalist friend. He was so successful that he continued to gain increased funding for his unit and was able to persuade Theodore Roosevelt to promote protective legislation. The President was keen to gain kudos for the passing of the 1906 Act, but it still became known as 'Wiley's Law'. Though Wiley resigned in 1912 saying he 'had been antagonized in the implementation of the pure food law', he assumed control of the laboratories of a popular magazine, where for the next twenty years he continued his investigative chemistry and publicised his team's results.[8] His industrious championing of this movement made him a national figure, garlanded with many honours both during and after his life (Figure 1.1) (Root and de Rochemont 1976: 245; Levenstein 1988: 39–40, 2012: 61–78; Blum 2019).

Most campaigners for purity appear to benefit from a popular logic that purity of motive underlies calls for purity in food. If so, Wiley appears to have benefited from his own style of food fraud. Though many looked up to him as a champion of the people, some commentators of the time did question the conclusions he drew from his most significant experiments. His latest biographer's re-examination of his scientific work suggests their concerns were well-grounded (Rees 2021). The popular impact of his proselytising relied more on the fear he instilled than the quality of his research.

Energetic activists in the women's clubs movement did not aspire as high as Wiley, but their campaigning still benefited their own position and others of their gender. Food reform was one of a raft of initiatives they put out over this period. Participation in these activities gave women a platform from which to argue for the transformation of public policy, a sense of political standing and greater influence within their own communities. In those gender-divisive times, fighting for food gave women a rare opportunity to be taken seriously beyond domestic confines.

I have already mentioned clean-eating cookbooks as self-promoting vehicles for careerist chefs and writers. The most egregious example I found of a foodie entrepreneur exploiting this movement for the sake of their own advancement is that of Sarma Melngailis. In the early 2000s she cofounded Pure Food and Wine, the first upmarket 'raw food' restaurant in New York, then opened three juice bars and launched a brand of snacks. The restaurant gained a name and, with customers like Anne Hathaway, Stevie Wonder, Chelsea Clinton and Alec Baldwin (who met his second wife there), Melngailis was classed a 'food-world star', the 'Queen of Vegan Cuisine' (Salkin 2016). She also produced two 'raw food' cookbooks, the first cowritten with her chef: *Raw Food/Real World: 100 Recipes to Get the Glow* (Kenney and Melngailis 2006; see also Melngailis 2009). But after staff walked out, claiming unpaid wages, both restaurant and juice bars closed down. Melngailis, now dubbed 'the Vegan Fraudster' by the press, went on the run. She was later jailed for theft and other charges (Tempey 2017). Comments left on her postprison blog (sarmaraw.com) suggest she still has committed, forgiving former clients, buoyed by remembrance of 'raw' repasts.[9]

A Time to Purify the Dialect of the Tribe

Let me try to plait my points into some kind of pleasing order.

To the authors and readers of Leviticus, purity was a classifying term of spiritual consequence. It was a taxonomic mode that created products: the edible and the inedible. In the nineteenth century law-abiding food manufacturers turned purity into a processual term: their regulated processes of production ensured their foods could be legally branded as 'pure'. Modern modes of chemical analyses grounded these regulations. They were also innovative in another way: they turned purity into a measurable quality, which could be expressed in percentile terms: e.g. 'Flour from 100% wheat' (Booker 2019: 158).

This quantitative shift may sound like a positive move. But new, more exact modes of measurement do not just allay old anxieties; they create new ones as well. For novel scientific analyses may well demonstrate the absence of deliberately introduced additives, but they can also reveal the presence of other material. In traditional modes of production, food is a biological product and therefore the composition of all its constituents cannot be completely controlled. Even in industrial times, food factories, despite their attempts, fail to remove all unwanted items; trace elements remain, as packet warnings to the potentially allergic attest. Lowering percentages of undesired ingredients to a physically undetectable level comes with a financial cost. Official agencies have to balance risks to public health against commercial viability. Therefore, they establish the maximal criteria of tolerable levels of these unwanted components. This bureaucratic code is popularly known as the 'filth regulations', specifying officially accepted percentages of items such as 'maggots, mould, rodent pellets, rat hairs, and insects'. In 1972 the US Food and Drug Administration (FDA) tried to practise the laudable democratic aim of transparency: it began to reveal some of its hitherto secret 'filth guidelines':

> Weems Clevenger, an FDA spokesperson, announced it was impossible to make food 100 percent pure, 'There are insect fragments in every loaf of bread', he stated, and 'An allowance of one rodent pellet per pint of white flour'. (Wilson 2020: 306)

The public reaction was so great and so negative that the experiment was quickly ended and was not repeated.

The meanings of 'purity' evolve in a jerky fashion over time, but so do those of neighbouring concepts, for instance, 'adulterant' and 'stimulant'. This is especially so if there are interests in play – commercial, religious, political – as evidenced earlier. 'Natural' is a similarly slippery notion in the contemporary food world. According to the FDA, 'natural flavours' have to be derived entirely from natural sources, i.e. the biological world (for example, herbs, roots, fruits, yeast and bark). Yet natural and artificial flavours may be composed of identical chemicals, albeit thanks to different methods. The popular assumption is that natural flavours are somehow healthier than artificial ones. This is not always the case:

> When almond flavour (benzaldehyde) is derived from natural sources, such as peach and apricot pits, it contains traces of hydrogen cyanide, a deadly poison. Benzaldehyde produced through a different process – by mixing oil of cloves and the banana flavour, amyl acetate – does not contain any cyanide. Nevertheless, it is legally considered an artificial flavour and sells at a much lower price. Natural and artificial flavours are now manufactured at the same chemical plants ... Calling any of these flavours 'natural' requires a flexible attitude to the English language and a fair amount of irony. (Schlosser 2001: 127)

The definition, and redefinition, of terms is centrally relevant to our central theme. So is their divisive potential as social markers. For there is both historical and contemporary evidence suggesting that a concern with purity is the preserve of the well-to-do. In the late nineteenth century in the United States, producers of quality baking powder used cream of tartar, a byproduct of winemaking, as a central ingredient. They inveighed against their rivals who instead used the much cheaper alum (aluminium potassium sulphate). To the Royal Baking Company, alum was a 'toxic' adulterant, while its powder was pure, and 'from the grape'. In the early twentieth century in the United Kingdom, Cadburys argued that the purity of its chocolate was the guarantee of its quality, and so refused to follow the 'Dutch process', which utilised potassium carbonate. The result was the same in both cases: the majority of consumers chose to bypass the battle and to buy the cheaper product (Civitello 2018: 52, 73–76).

More modern studies demonstrate much the same point: those with the means can decide to exercise choice. Those with lesser means have fewer choices, no matter what their desires (Padel and Foster 2005: 608; Fanzo 2021: 84). Recent work in Denmark revealed that consumers of organic food were much more likely to give weight to environmental issues when deciding what foods to buy, and were both more likely to be urban-based and to have had a longer period of education than consumers of local foods. Committed consumers of local foods, those for whom place of production was an important factor in their food choice, were more likely to have had a vocational education (Ditlevsen et al. 2020). Work in the Netherlands also showed that a greater percentage of adolescents preparing for university valued organic food compared to the percentage of pupils on vocational courses (Stobelaar et al. 2007). In other words, manifesting and acting on a preference for organic or pure food threatens to become an indicator of social class. Moreover, it is a gender-biased one as well: more women purchase 'sustainably produced' food than men (e.g. Piester et al. 2020). Purity, it would seem, is not for all. On this reading, it appears more and more an elitist notion, and one more practised by well-to-do women than by their male counterparts.

This common instrumental exploitation of purity leads to my next point. I have yet to read an essay on purity, in anthropology, theology or philosophy, whose author attempts to ponder why a concept denoting 'without admixture' or 'unadulterated' is also always positive. This tying together of the classificatory and the moral goes unquestioned. Indeed, it holds good not just in English, but in Spanish, French, Basque, German and Latin as well – and maybe more, but those are the European languages I am most familiar with. This seemingly indissoluble conjunction of the categorical and the evaluatory comes across as though it were a fundamental dimension of 'purity', which could not be questioned, without deconstructing the concept in the process. Yet, I wish to query, why should a category that denotes classificatory order be automatically, necessarily positive? It is as though we practise and so reproduce an adjudicatory discourse that places value on categorical order. And no one asks why.

The only academics I know of who have approached this question, albeit in their own manner, are those associated with evolutionary psychology. In the late 1990s and early 2000s, Paul Rozin, the eminent psychologist of food choice, and colleagues argued that, across cultures, disgust was typically elicited by violation of a moral code of purity. They took purity to be integrally associated with sanctity. Since they accepted that disgust was not necessarily linked to sanctity, they constructed an evolutionary logic to explain it:

> Disgust originated in animals as a response to distasteful food; the gape response and nausea protected omnivorous mammals from ingesting potentially dangerous foods. In cultural evolution, the output side of disgust (expression, physiology, behavior) remained relatively rather constant, but the range of elicitors expanded dramatically, coming under cultural control. We believe that in this expansion the original elicitor of the disgust program, distaste, ceased to function as an elicitor of disgust, or at least failed to share some of the offensiveness and contamination features of the newer elicitors of disgust. By the process of preadaptation in cultural evolution (use of a mechanism evolved in one system for a novel use in another system), the elicitor category gradually expanded, as the offense/disgust system was harnessed to a wider and wider range of entities that a given culture considered negative and to be avoided. The guardian of the mouth became a guardian of the soul. (Rozin et al. 2000: 190; see also Rozin et al. 1999)

The work of Rozin and his fellows was incorporated into the development of moral foundations theory, whose proponents argued for the existence of three basic moral domains: autonomy, community and divinity. Divinity they coupled with purity, as a domain of values and principles for protecting the sanctity of body and soul. They strove to explain the emergence of this domain in evolutionary terms:

> These values originally related to the evolutionary challenges of avoiding the consumption of toxins, parasites, or bacteria. What began as concerns over purity and contamination of the physical form, however, subsequently extended to include concerns over the purity of the individual's character and social conduct, thus promoting beliefs in the moral value of a physically and mentally pure lifestyle. (Horberg et al. 2009: 964)

Critiques of this intellectual style are manifold. It can be attacked as biologically implausible, confused, inadequate, disingenuous and ideologically suspect (Suhler and Churchland 2011; Grossi et al. 2014). Moreover, its claimed developmental sequences are unevidenced. In 1965 Evans-Pritchard had famously contended that evolutionist explanations were too often 'just so stories', imaginative but pseudo-historical accounts (Evans-Pritchard 1965: 86). His criticisms retain their power and are specifically deployed today in assessments of evolutionary psychologists (e.g. Talmont-Kaminski 2020).

Moral foundation theorists can also rely explicitly on anthropological work. The most pertinent for our purposes was their lauding of *Purity and Danger* as providing an ancient ethnographic match of purity practices regulating food and sex with the evolutionary literature on disgust (Graham et al. 2011). Yet, research indicates that disgust does not arise just in response to impurity, as evolutionary psychologists argue, but also in reaction to evidence of bad moral character (Giner-Sorolla and Chapman 2017; Kupfer et al. 2020). Further, scholars of the ancient Hebraic world underline that disgust at a biological phenomenon may be linked to moral thought, but the connection is not a necessary one:

> Failing to protect the sancta from pollution or to purify oneself in a timely fashion (Numbers 19:13, 20) constitute transgressions, but pollution itself, though inherently undesirable, is often unavoidable and can even be necessary in the service of a moral good, such as caring for deceased relatives. Rather than imparting moral values, the ritual purity laws guard the sacred from that which offends. In so doing, they demarcate various sancta and maintain reverence for the Deity who is the source of their holiness. (Feinstein n.d.)

On top of that, as discussed earlier, Douglas herself came to question the equation of purity and disgust.

Some evolutionary psychologists, especially those propounding moral foundations theory, are aware that the association of purity and positive moral evaluation seems near-universal and in need of explanation. But the developmental answer they provide is too logically questionable for many commentators, and so speculative as to make mainstream anthropologists blanch. These theorists' appreciation of Douglas' work is out of date, being reliant on an association she did make but later repudiated. At the same time, biblical scholars have taken a more radical step by separating ancient Hebraic notions of purity from ethical values. The case of moral foundations theorists is illuminating, but, for our purposes, only its relative failure is relevant. The link between purity and positive moral evaluation remains unexplained, to my satisfaction at least.

In sum, 'purity' and associated concepts are all highly contested terms, employed by different sectors for their own ends: by companies to sell their products, by governments to stay in office, by hierophants to win or retain control of the faithful, and by sectors of the public to reinforce their already privileged positions. Of course, these strategic uses do not necessarily imply that relevant actors do not at the same time believe in their ideals of purity. Nevertheless, the continued rationale for these tactics does mean that we cannot regard use of the category in innocent terms. On these grounds, deployment of 'purity' must also be regarded as a conceptual gambit, as an interested claim rather than a mere, disinterested exercise in classifying.

Handelman classed the classificatory style of the Levitical authors as monothetic: a stable hierarchy of clearly defined taxa. The same cannot be said of 'purity' and associated concepts in modern times, as we have seen. At the same time, these contemporary terms cannot be classed as polythetic: terms with multiple defining characteristics, none of which is necessary, but groups of which may be sufficient, akin to Wittgenstein's family-resemblant concepts (Needham 1975). 'Purity' does have a common single definition, 'without admixture', 'that is the thing itself', alongside a varying range of metaphorical extensions from that. Much the same can be said for the terms against which it jostles: 'additive', 'adulterant', 'local', 'natural' and so on. These modern-day classifications are neither monothetic nor polythetic; rather, they exhibit somewhat loose structures, subject to historical agency. And, like many much-used terms with multiple meanings, each particular employment of the term often resonates with its other connotations. For instance, in many contexts, it is difficult to speak of 'purity' without sounding its spiritual overtones. This is not to regard purity as akin to alphabet soup, but as a labile category nested within a tense nexus of equally mobile terms. In other words, 'purity' is more a shapeshifter than a statue.

One possible alternative is to speak of 'purities' rather than 'purity'. This could be judged insufficient as, either way, whether singular or plural, we remain with an abstract noun. Perhaps it would be more informative to see 'purity' in processual terms and to speak of 'modes of purification'. This would provide a needed sense of agency acting in specific times and places. The benefit is clear, but other, parallel examples of this proposed shift have not been followed up. Svasek, in her work on the anthropology of art, propounds persuasively that we should put 'aesthetics' aside for the sake of studying modes of 'aestheticisation'; similarly, scholars of identity have contended we should instead talk of 'modes of identification' (Jenkins 2002; Svasek 2007). I agree with both positions, but have still to see either put into sustained practice except by their proposers.

'Purity' is an oddball, as it is not just a term within a classificatory system but a classifying term, putting others in their place. It's a second-order classifier, if you will. However, the oddities here are multiple, for the purity of purity is another unquestioned dimension of this concept when used in the vernacular. Academic commentators in food studies may isolate the differing ways in which it is understood and deployed. Yet, as far as I have ascertained, within the particular contexts examined by the academics I have referenced in this chapter, the concept itself is never subject to critical scrutiny. It is as though a concept denoting integrity is also meant to display it. Yet if, as I have striven to demonstrate in this chapter, 'purity' is merely yet another term victim to the vagaries of time, then 'purity' on its own terms is forever impure.

Acknowledgements

Big thanks to Jeremy Cherfas, producer and host of the praiseworthy 'Eat This Podcast', and to my son Jack MacClancy, for assistance with the references.

Jeremy MacClancy is Professor of Social Anthropology in the School of Social Sciences at Oxford Brookes University, United Kingdom.

Notes

1. 'Food Safety', World Health Organization, n.d., https://www.who.int/health-topics/food-safety (last accessed 11 March 2021).
2. 'Integration of Consumers and Industry in Food Control', FAO, n.d., http://www.fao.org/3/v2890t/v2890t04.htm#TopOfPage (last accessed 11 March 2021).
3. 'Consumers and Food Safety: A Food Industry Perspective', FAO, n.d., http://www.fao.org/3/v2890t/v2890t05.htm#TopOfPage (last accessed 11 March 2021).
4. 'Key Regulations', Food Standards Agency, n.d., https://www.food.gov.uk/about-us/key-regulations (last accessed 11 March 2021).
5. 'Food Law General Principles', European Commission, n.d., https://ec.europa.eu/food/safety/general_food_law/principles_en (last accessed 11 March 2021).
6. 'Why Is Food Safety Important to the Food Industry?', *Quora Digest*, 3 July 2017, https://www.quora.com/Why-is-food-safety-important-to-the-food-industry (last accessed 11 March 2021).
7. 'Our Values', *Pure Organic*, https://www.pureorganic.com/en_US/about-pure/our-values.html (last accessed 17 March 2021).
8. 'Dr Harvey Wiley Explains His Resignation', *The Daily Princetonian*, 16 March 1912, https://theprince.princeton.edu/princetonperiodicals/cgi-bin/princetonperiodicals?a=d&d=Princetonian19120316-01.2.2# (last accessed 15 March 2021)
9. Sarmaraw.com (last accessed 24 March 2021).

References

Accum, F. (1820) *A Treatise on the Adulteration of Food and Culinary Poisons. Exhibiting the Fraudulent Sophistications of Bread, Beer, Wine, Spirituous Liquors, Tea, Coffee, Cream, Confectionery, Vinegar, Mustard, Pepper, Cheese, Olive Oil, Pickles, and Other Articles Employed in Domestic Economy, and Methods of Detecting Them*, Longman, Hurst, Rees, Orme and Brown, London.

Amilian, L. (2018) *Pure Food Project for Kids! Whole Food, Real Food, Power Food for Kids: A Wellness Guide for Parents*, Pure Sweat Project, LLC, Edmond, OK.

Beat Eating Disorders (2017) Orthorexia. Published at: https://www.beateatingdisorders.org.uk/types/orthorexia. Accessed on 19 March 2021.

Belasco, W.J. (1989) *Appetite for Change: How the Counterculture Took on the Food Industry 1966–1988,* Pantheon, New York.

Blum, D. (2019) *The Poison Squad: One Chemist's Single-Minded Crusade for Food Safety at the Turn of the Twentieth Century*, Penguin/Random House, New York.

Blythman, J. (1996) *The Food We Eat: The Book You Cannot Ignore,* Penguin, London.

Booker, M.M. (2019) Who Should Be Responsible for Food Safety? Oysters as a Case Study. In Ludington, C.C. and Booker, M.M. (eds) *Food Fights: How History Matters in Contemporary Food Debates*, University of North Carolina Press, Chapel Hill, pp. 146–60.

Bosgraaf, V. (2017) *Pure Food: Eat Clean with Seasonal, Plant-Based Recipes*, Clarkson Potter, New York.

Burnett, J. (1979) *Plenty and Want: A Social History of Diet in England from 1815 to the Present Day*, Methuen, London.

Cannon, G. (1987) *The Politics of Food*, Century Hutchinson, London.

Carson, R. (1962) *Silent Spring,* Houghton Mifflin, New York.

Church, A.B. (2016) *Pure Food: As Nature Intended*, Best Seller Success, Sydney.

Civitello, L. (2018) *Baking Powder Wars: The Cutthroat Food Fight That Revolutionised Cooking*, University of Illinois Press, Urbana.

Cohen, B. (2020) *Pure Adulteration: Cheating on Nature in the Age of Manufactured Food*, University of Chicago Press, Chicago.

Cole, R.J. (1951) Friedrich Accum (1769–1838): A Biographical Study, *Annals of Science*, 7: 128–43.

Coward, R. (1989) *The Whole Truth: The Myth of Alternative Health*, Faber, London.

Cushing, C. (2007) *Pure Food. How to Shop, Cook and Have Fun in Your Kitchen Every Day,* Whitecap Books, Vancouver.

Dammeier, K.B. (2016) *Pure Food. A Chef's Handbook for Eating Clean, with Healthy, Delicious Recipes*, BenBella Books, Dallas.

Datta, R.P. (2005) Book Review: Purity and Danger, *Anthropological Theory*, 5(3): 301–2.

Ditlevsen, K., Denver, S., Christensen, T. and Lassen, J. (2020) A Taste for Locally Produced Food – Values, Opinions and Sociodemographic Differences among 'Organic' and 'Conventional' Consumers, *Appetite* 147: 104544.

Ditlevsen, K., and Andersen, S. S. (2021) The Purity of Dirt: Revisiting Mary Douglas in the Light of Contemporary Consumer Interpretations of Naturalness, Purity and Dirt, *Sociology*, 55(1): 179–96.

Ditlevsen, K., Jandoe, P. and Lassen, J. (2019) Healthy Food Is Nutritious, But Organic Food Is Healthy Because It Is Pure: The Negotiation of Healthy Food Choices, by Danish Consumers of Organic Food, *Food Quality and Preference*, 71: 46–53.

Douglas, M. (1966) *Purity and Danger: An Analysis of Concepts of Pollution and Taboo*, Routledge & Kegan Paul, London.

———. (1999) *Leviticus as Literature*, Oxford University Press, Oxford.

———. (2004) *Jacob's Tears: The Priestly Work of Reconciliation*, Oxford University Press, Oxford.

Drummond, J.C., and Wilbraham, A. (1939) *The Englishman's Food: A History of Five Centuries of British Diet*, Jonathan Cape, London.

Evans-Pritchard, E. (1965) *Theories of Primitive Religion*, Oxford University Press, Oxford.

Fanzo, J. (2021) *Can Fixing Dinner Fix the Planet?* Johns Hopkins University Press, Baltimore.

Fardon, R. (1999) *Mary Douglas: An Intellectual Biography*, Taylor & Francis, London.

Feinstein, E.L. (n.d.) Purity Laws, *Oxford Biblical Studies Online*. Published at: http://ezproxy-prd.bodleian.ox.ac.uk:3973/article/opr/t430/e281?_hi=0&_pos=1#match. Accessed on 17 April 2021.

Fischler, C. (1995) *El (H)Omnivoro. El Gusto, la Cocina y el Cuerpo* (original published in French 1990), Anagrama, Barcelona.

Freeman, S. (1989) *Mutton and Oysters: The Victorians and Their Food*, Victor Gollancz, London.

Gambetta, D. (2000) Can We Trust Trust? In Gambetta, D. (ed.) *Trust. Making and Breaking Cooperative Relations*, Basil Blackwell, Oxford, pp. 213–37.

Gilmore, P. (2014) *Organum: Nature Texture Intensity Purity*, Murdoch Books, Sydney.

Giner-Sorolla, R. and Chapman, H.A. (2017) Beyond Purity: Moral Disgust toward Bad Character, *Psychological Science*, 28(1): 80–91.

Grabbe, L.L. (2004) Review of 'Leviticus as Literature', *Journal of Ritual Studies*, 18(2): 157–61.

Graham, J., Nosek, B.A., Haidt, J., Iyer, R., Koleva, S. and Ditto, P.H. (2011) Mapping the Moral Domain, *Journal of Personality and Social Psychology*, 101(2): 366–85.

Grossi, G., Kelly, S., Nash, A. and Parameswaran, G. (2014) Challenging Dangerous Ideas: A Multi-disciplinary Critique of Evolutionary Psychology, *Dialectical Anthropology*, 38: 281–85.

Guthman, J. (2014) *Agrarian Dreams: The Paradox of Organic Farming in California*, University of California Press, Berkeley.

Handelman, D. (2004) Review of 'Leviticus as Literature', *Journal of Ritual Studies*, 18(2): 162–68.

Heald, S. (2004) Review of 'Leviticus as Literature', *Journal of Ritual Studies*, 18(2): 153–56.

Hemmings, P. (1985) *Pocket Book on Pure Food*, Octopus, London.

Hendel, R.S. (2004) Review of 'Leviticus as Literature', *Journal of Ritual Studies*, 18(2): 172–85.

Horberg, E.J., Oveis, C., Keltner, D. and Cohen, A.B. (2009) Disgust and the Moralization of Purity, *Journal of Personality and Social Psychology*, 97(6): 963–76.

Jenkins, R. (2002) Imagined But Not Imaginary: Ethnicity and Nationalism in the Early Twenty-First Century. In Macclancy, J. (ed.) *Exotic No More: Anthropology on the Front Lines*, University of Chicago Press, Chicago, pp. 114–28.

Joachim, D. (2004) *Fresh Choices: More Than 100 Easy Recipes for Pure Food When You Can't Buy 100% Organic*, Rodale Books, Emmaus, PA.

Kenney, M., and Melngailis, S. (2006) *Raw Food/Real World: 100 Recipes to Get the Glow*, William Morrow Cookbooks, New York

Klawans, J. (2003) Rethinking Leviticus and Re-reading 'Purity and Danger', *Association of Jewish Studies*, 27(1): 89–102.

Kupfer, T.R., Inbar, Y. and Tybur, J.M. (2020) Reexamining the Role of Intent in Moral Judgements of Purity Violations, *Journal of Experimental Social Psychology*, November: 91.

Lang, T. (2006) Locale/Global (Food Miles), *Slow Food*, 19: 94–97.

Lawrence, F. (2004) *Not on the Label: What Really Goes into the Food on Your Plate*, Penguin, London.

Lawson, N. (2015) Nigella: Disgusted by the Mantra of Clean Eating, *Women's Hour*, BBC Radio Four. Published at: https://www.bbc.co.uk/programmes/p034s2dx. Accessed on 4 February 2023.

Leathem, H. (2020) Our (Dis)Orderly World: Thinking with 'Purity and Danger' in the 21st Century, *History of Anthropology Review*, 12 June. Published at: https://histanthro.org/bibliography/generative/our-disorderly-world-thinking-with-purity-and-danger-in-the-21st-century/. Accessed on 10 March 2021.

Levenstein, H. (1988) *Revolution at the Table: The Transformation of the American Diet*, Oxford University Press, New York.

———. (2012) *Fear of Food: A History of Why We Worry about What We Eat*, University of Chicago Press, Chicago.

Loria, K. (2017) Experts Say Fakes Cost the Industry up to $40 Billion a Year and the Problem Is Difficult to Solve, *Fooddive*. Published at: https://www.fooddive.com/news/food-fraud-economic-safety-costs/434237. Accessed on 20 December 2021.

MacClancy, J., and Fuentes, A. (2013) The Ethical Fieldworker, and Other Problems, In MacClancy, J. and Fuentes, A. (eds) *Ethics in the Field. Contemporary Challenges*, Berghahn Books, Oxford, pp. 1–23.

McGregor R. (2017) *Orthorexia: When Healthy Goes Bad*, Nourish, London.

McNamee, T. (2006) *Alice Waters and Chez Panisse: The Romantic, Impractical, Often Eccentric, Ultimately Brilliant Making of a Food Revolution*, Penguin, New York.

Melngailis, S. (2009) *Living Raw Food: Get the Glow with More Recipes from Pure Food and Wine*, William Morrow Cookbooks, New York.

Messer, E. (2007) Food Definitions and Boundaries: Eating Constraints and Human Identities. In Macclancy, J., Henry, J. and Macbeth, H. (eds) *Consuming the Inedible. Neglected Dimensions of Food Choice*, Berghahn Books, Oxford, pp. 53–66.

Needham, R. (1975) Polythetic Classification: Convergence and Consequences, *Man (N.S.)*, 10(3): 349–69.

Padel, S. and Foster, C. (2005) Exploring the Gap between Attitudes and Behaviour. Understanding Why Consumers Buy or Do Not Buy Organic Food, *British Food Journal*, 107(8): 608-25.

Parasecoli, F. (2017) Global Trade, Food Safety and the Fear of Invisible Invaders, *Social Research: An International Journal*, 84(1): 183–202.

Piester, H.E., DeRieux, C.M., Tucker, J., Buttrick, N.R., Galloway, J.N. and Wilson, T.D. (2020) 'I'll Try the Veggie Burger': Increasing Purchases of Sustainable Foods with Information about Sustainability and Taste, *Appetite*, 155: 104842.

Rees, J. (2021) *The Chemistry of Fear: Harvey Wiley's Fight for Pure Food*, Johns Hopkins University Press, Baltimore.

Rioux, S. (2019) Capitalist Food Production and the Rise of Legal Adulteration: Regulating Food Standards in 19th-Century Britain, *Journal of Agrarian Change*, 19(1): 64–81.

Root, W., and de Rochemont, R. (1976) *Eating in America: A History*, Ecco Press, New York.

Rozin, P., Lowery, L., Imada, S., and Haidt, J. (1999) The CAD Triad Hypothesis: A Mapping Between Three Moral Emotions (Contempt, Anger, Disgust) and Three Moral Codes (Community, Autonomy, Divinity), *Personality*, 76(4): 574–86.

Rozin, P., Haidt, J., and McCauley, C. (2000) Disgust. In D. Levinson, J. Ponzetti, and P. Jorgenson (eds) *Encyclopaedia of Human Emotions, 1* (2nd ed.), Macmillan, New York, pp. 188–93.

Salkin, A. (2016) How Sarma Melngailia, Queen of Vegan Cuisine, Became a Runaway Fugitive, *Vanity Fair*, 3 November. Published at: https://www.vanityfair.com/style/2016/11/how-sarma-melngailis-became-a-runaway-fugitive. Accessed on 24 December 2021.

Schlosser, E. (2001) *Fast Food Nation. What the All-American Meal Is Doing to the World*, Houghton Mifflin, New York.

Sinclair, U. (1906) *The Jungle*, Doubleday, New York.

Spencer, C. (1993) *The Heretic's Feast: A History of Vegetarianism*, Fourth Estate, London.

Spurlock, M. (2006) *Don't Eat This Book: Fast Food and the Supersizing of America*, Penguin, London:

Stobelaar, D.J., Casimir, G., Borghuis, J., Marks, I., Meijer, L. and Zebeda, S. (2007) Adolescents' Attitudes towards Organic Food: A Survey of 15- to 16-Year-Old School Children, *International Journal of Consumer Studies*, 31(4): 349–56.

Subramanian, S. (2021) Food Fraud and Counterfeit Cotton: The Detective Untangling the Global Supply Chain, *The Guardian*, 16 September. Published at: https://www.theguardian.com/news/2021/sep/16/food-fraud-counterfeit-cotton-detectives-untangling-global-supply-chains. Accessed on 17 September 2021.

Suhler, C.L. and Churchland, P. (2011) Can Innate, Modular 'Foundations' Explain Morality? Challenges for Haidt's Moral Foundations Theory, *Journal of Cognitive Neuroscience*, 23(9): 2103–16.

Svasek, M. (2007) *Anthropology, Art and Cultural Production*, Pluto, London.

Talmont-Kaminski, K. (2020) Primitive Theories of Religion: Evolutionism after Evans-Pritchard, *E-Rhizome*, 2(1): 1–18. Published at: https://rhizome.upol.cz/artkey/erh-202001-0001_primitive-theories-of-religion-evolutionism-after-evans-pritchard.php. Accessed on 13 March 2021.

Tandoh, R. (2016) The Unhealthy Truth behind 'Wellness' and 'Clean Eating', *Vice*, 13 May. Published at: https://www.vice.com/en/article/jm5nvp/ruby-tandoh-eat-clean-wellness. Accessed on 24 December 2022.

Tempey, N. (2017) Raw Vegan Restaurateur-Turned-Fugitive Pleads Guilty to Fleecing Staffers, Investors, *Gothamist*, 10 May. Published at: https://gothamist.com/food/raw-vegan-restaurateur-turned-fugitive-pleads-guilty-to-fleecing-staffers-investors. Accessed on 19 March 2021.

Thomas, C.I.P. (2014) *In Food We Trust: The Politics of Purity in American Food Regulation*, University of Nebraska Press, Lincoln, NE.

Tomlinson, M. (2006) *Clean up Your Diet: The Pure Food Programme to Cleanse, Energize and Revitalize*, Duncan Baird, London.

Waters, A. (2007) *The Art of Simple Food: Notes, Lessons, and Recipes from a Delicious Revolution*, Clarkson Potter, New York.

———. (2015) *My Pantry: Homemade Ingredients That Make Simple Meals Your Own: A Cookbook*, Random House, New York.

———. (2017) *Coming to My Senses: The Making of a Counterculture Cook*, Hardie Grant Books, London.

Waters, A., Guenzel, L.P. and Dille, C. (1984) *The Chez Panisse Menu Cookbook*, Chatto & Windus, London.

Wilson, B. (2017) Why We Fell for Clean Eating, *The Guardian*, 11 August. Published at: https://www.theguardian.com/lifeandstyle/2017/aug/11/why-we-fell-for-clean-eating. Accessed on 19 March 2021.

_____. (2020) *Swindled: The Dark History of Food Fraud, from Poisoned Candy to Counterfeit Coffee*, Princeton University Press, Princeton.

Wollin, J. (2014) *Comfort Food: Raw: Purity without Limits*, CreativeSpace, Scotts Valley, CA.

Yuen, E. (2015) *Beating Orthorexia and the Memoirs of a Health Freak: Take Back the Control of Your Life Which Your Obsession with Health Took Away*, CreateSpace Independent Publishing Platform.

Zaloom, C. (2020) Mary Douglas, Purity and Danger, *Public Culture*, 32(2): 415–22.

CHAPTER 2
'PURE' FOOD AND FOOD TABOOS IN CROSS-CULTURAL AND HUMAN ETHOLOGICAL PERSPECTIVE
....

Wulf Schiefenhövel

Introduction

This chapter will examine the ubiquitous, universal preoccupation with 'pure' and 'impure' foods by examining, in a small number of cultures, sociocultural and biopsychological categories of acceptance and rejection, to which specific foods are subjected. Every person on the planet, it seems, has likes and dislikes of foods. So have societies, whose members are often quite stuck in the culturally transmitted and then internalised notions of what is proper to eat and what is not. Frederick and Elizabeth Simoons (Simoons 1961, 1991; Simoons and Simoons 1967) were the first to focus on food prohibitions and discussed, among other topics, the extreme rejection of pork in Halakhic food laws. The aspect of pollution, namely that purity is a way to keep the body and the group out of danger, was described in the classic account by Mary Douglas (1966). The approach of Marvin Harris (1974, 1979, 1985) was fundamentally different, as he attempted to link dietary and other religious rules to functionally meaningful behaviour. Meyer-Rochow (2009) published a cross-cultural account on food taboos, which sets out to reconcile the religious-symbolic and the materialistic-functional explanatory strategies of previous authors.

During the four years he was kept as a prisoner of war in a Russian army camp, the zoologist and medical doctor Konrad Lorenz greatly surprised his fellow prisoners because he ate flies, other insects and all kinds of small creatures that he could find (Bateson 1990). First, they were repelled by this strange diet. However, because Lorenz was a charismatic figure who maintained his good health during his imprisonment, they soon followed his example. Even small quantities of animal protein can make a big difference in time of famine. Until recently, our Western societies did not regard insects as proper, let alone good and ecologically sensible, food, whereas they represent an important source of protein in many ethnic groups of the world (Schiefenhövel and Blum 2007), as they do for many other primates (cf. McGrew 2001). Certain chic restaurants that have started serving insects in recent years often specifically select them to engender feelings of aversion and disgust, thus playing with the ambivalence of their customers. It is a sign of courage not to turn down an invitation to such a meal by one's friend or business partner, just as to be invited to participate in the eating of a dish of *fugu* (a potentially deadly pufferfish that has to be prepared very carefully to remove the poisonous tissue) in Japan is at the same time a big honour and for most people a big challenge. In such cases, the mind of the guest is tickled by a mixture of disgust, rejection, fear and bravery. So, what was considered 'impure' yesterday might, in our fast-evolving cultural world, be completely acceptable, even high class, tomorrow.

The spectrum of edible food is much bigger than what is actually consumed by members of the different cultures of the planet. As will be argued here, and in contrast to Marvin Harris (1974, 1979, 1985), this has little to do with the real material (physical, biological, chemical, etc.) property of the rejected foods, but is one of the fascinating aspects of our – in this case often irrational – human mind that sets out, by arbitrary definition and classification into 'pure' versus 'impure' foods, to create order in the bewildering chaos of the world and to set rules for 'proper' nutrition and 'proper' life.

Cultural Examples

The Jewish Kashrut

The oldest known and one of the most amazingly detailed systems of food taboos is that canonised in the dietary laws of Leviticus, Deuteronomy and Exodus.[1] These are also known as *Halakhic* rules (*Halakha*: the system of Jewish religious law, literally meaning 'behaviour', stemming from *halakh*, 'to walk', 'to go').[2] These rules are part of the Torah (and so the Christian Old Testament) completed about 400 BCE in the Persian era of Jewish history, but apparently having its roots in much earlier traditions.[3] These Mosaic food prescriptions are probably the most elaborated ones in any of the world's religions. Very specific characteristics of animals are to be taken into account in deciding if their meat is allowed for consumption: mammals must have cloven hoofs and chew their cud, i.e. ruminate, to be *kasher* (in ancient Hebrew: proper, fitting, advantageous; hence the Hebrew term *kashrut* for the sets of religious laws governing food consumption)[4] or, as it is pronounced among the Ashkenazim, *kosher*. This latter linguistic variant is now mostly used to describe the Jewish view of 'pure', proper food and 'pure', proper ways of preparing and eating it. Mammals that do not exhibit the above criteria, such as the camel, the hare and the pig, are forbidden as food. This last animal is also strictly tabooed by the Islamic religion (see below).

Deuteronomy also lists the many non-*kosher* birds. Again, it is a very complicated recourse to their anatomy, sometimes including very specific features, which forms the leading principle of dividing this group into *kosher* versus *terefah*; this latter term stems from ancient Hebrew *taraf*, to tear,[5] and also appears in similar spelling like *terefa*, *trefa*, *trefot* and others. The semantic concept linking this term with defining impure food is described in Exodus 22:31, where a taboo is expressed involving eating meat that has been 'torn', killed by a predator, and that might have been lying around for some time. This is a reasonable approach: avoid food that could be infected and thus dangerous (even though thorough heating takes care of all viruses, bacteria and parasites). However, most other Halakhic rules (see below) cannot be explained through this kind of biological, materialistic approach, but have their origin in a very complex set of definitions and symbolisms, the main function of which is, in my view, to keep identity and coherence among members of this religion intact and strong. This is true for other religious nutritional laws as well.

Of the many creatures in the sea, only fish with fins and scales are allowed for Jews, while most other marine animals are not.[6] Of insects, only a few types of locust are declared *kosher*. Perhaps the clearest example of arbitrary classification as 'pure' versus 'impure' is the ban on amphibian animals: they are ambivalent creatures, which have not made up their minds, as it were, whether they want to live in the sea or on land. It is understandable that they are the focus of rule-makers who only allow animal food derived from 'real' animals and thus from a proper, 'pure' source. The thrust of this process of classification is based on certain symbolistic, usually dichotomic views and therefore clearly does not lend itself to be interpreted in a functional way.

Again, very detailed and strict Jewish rules specify how a kitchen should be organised and managed, and which tool must be used for which purpose. *Milchig* versus *fleishig* (in Yiddish terminology – other spellings are also in use)[7] foods must be carefully kept apart and always cooked in separate pots. Some Jews separate the intake of meat and milk or dairy products through the timing of their consumption. This goes back to the rule expressed in Exodus 23:19 and other quotations that a 'kid (of a goat) must not be boiled in its mother's milk'.[8] Many avoid using the dishwasher because small traces of milk and meat may come into contact with each other and thus contaminate the dishes. Until ritually cleansed, a pot will stay 'impure' when non-*kosher* or even the wrong *kosher* food is prepared in it. Even plant food can present a problem because, for example, small quantities of forbidden insects may be mixed with it. All this reflects the amazing attention to symbolic detail in the Jewish religion, whose followers need to respect all of these intricate rules if they want to belong to the real believers. A high mental and social awareness of rules represents a high investment – in both time and in other ways, such as financially. This is typical, as an 'honest signal', of true membership in religions and religious groups, which demand that their norms are strictly followed, no matter how demanding this may be (cf. Blume 2009; Schiefenhövel and Voland 2009). In cases of doubt and to decontaminate foods and tools, a specialist is needed. As in other cases, complex religious rules lead to diversification, special roles, hierarchy and strengthened group identity.

Islamic Food Taboos

One day I walked through the streets of Samarinda in East Kalimantan, chewing some sunflower seeds that I had bought at a stand at the roadside. A young man approaching in my direction spat out, with the signs of deepest disgust, in front of me, hissing *'Ramadan, makan dilarang*!': 'It is Ramadan, eating is forbidden!' It was very stupid of me not to think about the rule to refrain from eating even the tiniest bits of food during the days of holy fasting, thereby insulting this Muslim citizen. The incident made me deeply aware of how volcanic the religiously driven emotion of disgust can be. The role of this psychobiological mechanism, the facial expression of which involves a ritualised vomiting act, has been addressed elsewhere (Schiefenhövel 1997). As will be further elaborated in the discussion below, disgust for the food categories that other ethnic groups eat is involved in creating the sense of one's own moral superiority and is part of the process of pseudospeciation (Erikson 1966).

The Quran or Qur'an echoes the dietary laws of the Torah to an astounding degree, but is less detailed and strict than the latter. Only a few *surahs* specify which kind of food must be avoided and at the same time give some generous, friendly leeway if followers meet certain conditions where this may not be possible. The main quotation is from *surah* 2,[9] where it is written: 'O you who have good faith! Eat of the good things We have provided you, and thank Allah, if it is Him that you worship' (verse 172); and 'He has forbidden you only carrion, blood, the flesh of the swine, and that which has been offered to other than Allah. But should someone be compelled, without being rebellious or aggressive, there shall be no sin upon him. Indeed, Allah is all-forgiving, all-merciful' (verse 173). Other quotations repeat in similar wording this cornerstone of Islamic food laws, e.g. *surah* 6: 'Say I don't find what has been revealed to me that anyone be forbidden to eat anything except carrion or spilt blood or the flesh of the swine – for that is indeed unclean – or an impiety offered to other than Allah. But should someone...' (verse 145) or in *surah* 16: 'He has forbidden you only carrion, blood, the flesh of the swine, and that which has been offered to other than Allah. But...' (verse 115).

Over time, other animals have been added to the ones forbidden by Islamic law or Sharia, which stipulates that 'pure' animals that are allowed to be eaten are the ones that survive on grass and leaves. Therefore, camel meat is allowed in the Islamic but not in the Jewish tradition; the same is true for many other animals. Predator animals and some others as well are *haram*. This Arabic term primarily means forbidden (cf. *harem*), but is globally and commonly understood to signify impure, forbidden food; the opposite – allowed, prescribed food – is called *halal*.[10] Whereas almost all Islamic views of food being 'pure' versus 'impure' are derived from the Mosaic views (quite a surprising fact given the long history of animosity between the two religions, but of course a reflection of their common origins), they are usually much less strict and less detailed.

Muslims may eat the meat of hunted animals, provided they are *halal*, but only in cases where the animal has the ability to run or fly away;[11] young animals that cannot do so are forbidden. Here, again, a straightforward functionalistic as well as quasi-humanistic aspect governs these rules. In the animistic (i.e. non-Muslim) religions of Melanesia, which also hold that animals have human-like souls, these kinds of protective rules are not found.

Other aspects of nutrition-related issues specified in the Sharia are as similarly complex as the Jewish ones. For example, in order to slaughter an animal, Islamic law requires specific rules to ensure that this act is conducted in a proper way; these rules are contained in the Dhabiba (other spellings are also common).[12] In both religions, the specialist (and only he is allowed to perform the act) must say a particular prayer. It seems likely that respect for the life of animals is the motivation behind these rules.

Food Taboos among the Batak of Sumatra

For a study (Strungaru and Schiefenhövel 2001) of food taboos and food preferences (especially with regard to meat), the city of Pematang Siantar was chosen, the second largest urban area in the Province of Northern Sumatra after the capital Medan. This is traditional Batak country. Many megalithic and other monuments give testimony to the prehistoric and historic importance of this region. As is typical for large Indonesian cities, there is a modern mix of various ethnic groups.

Female (45 percent) and male (55 percent) students, ranging in age from fifteen to eighteen, from two large public 'middle schools' (Sekolah Menengah Umum in Indonesian, comparable to the German Gymnasium) participated in the study and returned 1,051 fully filled-out questionnaires. All the Christian students (Protestant and Catholic) were ethnic Batak. Of the Muslim students 47 percent also belonged to the Batak and 43 percent traced their origin to Java, 5 percent to Melayu and Minangkabau, and 5 percent were from other ethnic backgrounds.

The questions concerned the following items:

(1) name and rank the three kinds of food you prefer most;
(2) name and rank the three kinds of meat dishes you prefer most;
(3) how many times per week do you eat meat?;
(4) name and rank three kinds of meat you prefer most;
(5) name and rank three kinds of dishes you are disgusted by;
(6) name kinds of food which are taboo for you.

Discussion of Results Regarding Disgust

Despite the fact that a sizeable number of students mentioned carp as their favourite dish, fish (*ikan*) in general is still the most disgusting food[13] for the majority of the respondents. This is surprising and most likely not connected to Muslim food taboos in Indonesia, where fish in general is *halal*, i.e. allowed. Obviously, as in Europe, the smell and taste of fish is something that children and juveniles have to get used to if they do not grow up in an area where fish is routinely part of the cuisine. In second place is snake (*ular*), which is taboo for Indonesian Muslims. Again, this could well reflect a rather universal attitude: snakes are subject to avoidance and disgust in many parts of the world independent of them being a possible food or not. Then comes dog and cat. Dogs, as carnivores, are *haram* for Muslims, yet are part of normal cuisine in some parts of Indonesia, e.g. among Christians from Sulawesi, far away from Sumatra. Cat as food was named disgusting only by Christian students, even though it would be, as a carnivore, *haram* for Muslims and could have provoked disgust as well. However, the cat is considered a ritually clean animal (in stark contrast to the 'unclean' dog)[14] and is particularly favoured in Islamic tradition. Thus, because of emotional reasons, it would probably not be considered edible anyway. Only in fifth place is pork, which is felt to be disgusting by Muslims, but surprisingly also by a few Christian students. Those who find pork aversive are outnumbered by those (coming from all religious backgrounds) who abhor the idea of eating snakes, dogs and cats. Yet, the rejection and avoidance of pork is, in everyday life and in the perception of the Indonesians, the classic divider between Muslims and non-Muslims, even more so than alcohol versus non-alcohol. Yet, in everyday Indonesian life there are usually no aggressive attitudes connected to this separation of religions.

The Batak people of Sumatra are a good example of the power of religiously stipulated behaviour. While those belonging to communities that became Muslim from the thirteenth century onwards very strictly adhere to the food taboos that were laid down in the Quran, those from Christian communities that became Protestant and, in much lower numbers, those that became Catholic after the second half of the nineteenth century do not follow these rules that separate 'pure' from 'impure' food. The fact that Muslim Batak students of the two Middle Schools in the Province of Northern Sumatra state that they adhere to the Quranic food regulations is surprising, because the large town of Pematang Siantar is quite modern in many respects and one might expect that new lifestyle trends, including nutritional habits, would invade and supersede traditional customs, just as many Jewish people in the United States do not follow Mosaic food rules. Indonesia, home of the world's largest Muslim population of more than 200 million people, has been successful, so far, in enabling a basically very peaceful coexistence of the many ethnic groups and their different religions. This is one of the cornerstones of the *Pancasila*, the political foundation of Indonesian society. Eating outside one's own home is very common and usually inexpensive, especially at the numerous food stalls (*warung*) on the sidewalks of cities. Rarely does one see 'halal' signs indicating that food in a particular stall or restaurant is prepared according to Islamic regulations. Yet, elsewhere, the culinary tradition of the food sold or served is often advertised, so that the customers know where they can obtain food, which is religiously, ethnically or otherwise appropriate for them.

Food Taboos of the Eipo

The Eipo, members of the Mek group of cultures and languages in the Star Mountains of Papua Province, Indonesia, lived, as it were, in a bubble of prehistory when interdisciplinary research began in July 1974 (Schiefenhövel 1976, 1983, 1991, 2014; Heeschen and Schiefenhövel 1983). Like all other Papuan and Austronesian peoples, they were and are pig breeders. At first sight, it thus seems surprising that there should have been a pronounced protein shortage. However, the pigs (*basam, Sus scrofa*) were very limited in number.

It is interesting that members of some of the clans were traditionally barred by taboo from eating pork (Koch and Schiefenhövel 1987) because their ancestor was the sacred pig (*kwemdina basam*); this kind of ancestor worship is common in Papuan societies. It is noteworthy that those who could not and did not eat pork did not show any signs of being less muscular or powerful, let alone show signs of malnutrition, compared to those who could enjoy the rare delicacy. The actual amount of pork per person per day was estimated to be around one gram; in other words, pork was not really an important source of animal protein. The culture could afford, as it were, the meat taboo for some of its members. It was also remarkable that there was no detectable envy on the part of those who were barred from eating delicious pork against those who could. Furthermore, there were (therefore?) also no reactions of disgust so common between different religious groups elsewhere in the world.

In 2008 workmen from Sulawesi erecting houses as part of a governmental programme bought a dog to supplement their normal diet of rice and tinned meat or fish. The Eipo were interested in this strange custom, but did not show much visible repulsion vis-à-vis this culinary act, even though they do not eat dog meat – probably because dogs, even though not always treated well, are seen as belonging to their families. This psychological reaction seems to be common in many cultures; it protects pets from being eaten by classifying them as taboo.

Discussion

Why, as Meyer-Rochow asks in his insightful article (2009), would people refrain from utilising perfectly good food? Why would they declare part of it 'impure' or improper? This could, as he points out, be the effect of political power by which some important food resources are taken away from the majority and reserved for a few others. This may have happened at times in the history of global food taboos, but does not seem to be a very common occurrence. Another avenue to explain why certain foods are rejected is to argue that these foods are either actually dangerous or otherwise detrimental for one's health or detrimental for the group's survival because rearing and feeding the respective animals means costs, which do not balance out with sufficient returns. This is the view of Marvin Harris (1974, 1979, 1985) who was inspired by Marxian ethnology and tried to explain the taboos on pork in the Jewish population as an ancient religious command not to invest in keeping pigs because they would not thrive in arid regions. Whereas this argument is correct (the pig is an animal of the sylvatic circle where it can find food in the forests), it is difficult to see why such an obvious fact would have to be fixed like cast iron in a religious law.

Sometimes people argue that a taboo against the meat of pigs is reasonable because it can contain specific parasites and can thus cause dangerous trichinosis in those who consume it. While this is biologically and medically correct, the pig would hardly have a chance to pick up trichinas in Palestine and the surrounding regions because the parasites are derived from rats and other animals typical in Northern Europe. In this explanation as well, the functionalistic approach does not have enough bite.

The same is true for Harris's (1985) argument that ancient Hindu settlers of India needed the cow to pull their ploughs and wagons, and that it would be counterproductive to kill them. Many cultures in the world, including those of Central Europe, demonstrate that both potential uses of this animal (for work and for food) can be very well combined, bearing in mind that this also includes cows being milked and thereby giving very valuable protein food for those who have lactase persistence. Again, no religious taboo would have been necessary. With regard to the Jewish and Islamic food taboos, a general functionalist interpretation must also be ruled out because, as has been demonstrated above, these taboos are so extremely detailed and obviously so arbitrary with regard to biological factors that no materialistic functions can be found for all or even a majority of them.

One could think that the avoidance of blood, so prominently present in both Islamic and Jewish law, might be a useful rule. Yet, blood, a very valuable protein, is consumed in various forms in many parts of the world without any negative effects (see Saucedo et al., this volume). Here, as in the case of other foods, an effective safeguard against possible harm from infected blood is that food containing blood (as indeed any food) should be properly heated. If disease avoidance were the main issue, one would expect the religions of our planet to specify clearly that people cook all their food long enough and with utmost care. However, this is not the case and speaks for a symbolic rather than a biological origin of food rules.

For a few issues in the long list of prescriptions and other rules, a functionalistic approach seems valid. The rules regarding milk could have their origin in the globally widespread fact that many populations do not have the genetic mutation that ensures high levels of post-weaning lactase. Yet, the Jewish rules to separate milk and meat seem a bit too far removed from this physiological mechanism. To avoid carcasses could be reasonable, but, as mentioned above, every sensible human would stay away from meat that smells extremely bad and is covered with parasites. Again, there is no need to formulate a religious taboo. With regard to alcohol, which is banned in the Islamic but not in the Jewish tradition (provided *kosher* production is ensured)[15] a functionalistic explanation is very sound: a lot of harm, physically, both mentally and socially, is caused by alcoholic drinks.

Mary Douglas' concept of a basically symbolic origin of the dichotomic conceptual structures in Halakhic dietary rules is somewhat similar to the one taken in this chapter, especially in her claim that a set of dichotomic imaginations ('clean' and 'unclean', in the case of the Halakha going back to God's command) is universal. She conducted anthropological fieldwork among the Lele of Congo, where, as everywhere, taboos regulate life, and she knew what she was writing about. She did not take biopsychological and ethological factors, such as the disgust reaction and the powerful effects of food taboos for cultural differentiation, into account: this comes as no surprise, as she was trained in sociology-oriented anthropology. The same can be said about the seminal work of Simoons, who also did not focus on the demarcating, contrast-enhancing effects of religiously stipulated dietary laws (for a further critique of these three approaches, see Hanke and Schiefenhövel 2008).

The human brain has an impressive propensity and capacity to structure the world into classificatory entities, creating, for example, complex botanic knowledge not inferior to that of our academic specialists (Hiepko and Schiefenhövel 1987). Like the 'hot'/'cold' schemes guiding nutrition and medicine in many parts of the world, these are often dichotomic, reducing complexity. This is how our ancestors managed in the bewildering magnitude of things and ideas. We still follow this heritage. What we eat is so closely related to ourselves – because it becomes part of us – that it is no wonder that thinking and worrying about food is so universal, so typical for all individuals and societies. Obviously, we are deeply imprinted (to use a Lorenzian term), from early infancy and most probably from foetal life onwards, to accept certain foods and to reject others (for a further exploration of these ideas, see Carter, this volume).

The most important effect of knowing about and respecting 'pure' versus 'impure' elements of nutrition is that it divides groups. The psychologically very powerful disgust reaction, neurobologically and physiologically closely linked to the vomiting reflex (Schiefenhövel 1997), is at the core of reacting to food (see also Rozin et al. 1993). Knowing that oneself belongs to the 'real' people who respect the 'right' kind of rules renders identity and belonging. The others are 'unclean' and different. Unfortunately, these days we also witness these reactions in their general, not necessarily food-related, dimension. A very interesting development, which is particularly strong in the United States these days is the possessiveness with which members of certain ethnic groups prosecute the 'usurpation' of 'their' foods and cuisine by members of other ethnic groups (*Die Zeit* 2016), a striking example of how 'political correctness' interferes with what most of us would probably have perceived as normal multiethnic reality.

For a tribal world, from which the Mosaic and Islamic sets of rules originated, such pseudospeciation (Erikson 1966) was useful and effective, as it helped to weld those people together who had the same strong, unshakeable convictions and prepared them for confrontation with others. It is an interesting question as to whether this biopsychological mechanism, dividing things and people into 'pure' and 'impure', is still active today. This might well be the case. The examples of the Batak and the Eipo, on the other hand, show that a peaceful coexistence of groups who follow different religiously grounded dietary rules is possible. There may be more disagreement and conflict among European vegans versus meat eaters than between the ones who can and do eat pork, and the ones who do not in the mountains of New Guinea or the northern half of Sumatra.

Wulf Schiefenhövel is Head of the Research Group in the Human Ethology Group at the Max Planck Institute for Biological Intelligence, Seewiesen, Germany.

Notes

1. All quotations of the Old Testament are from *The Bible, English Standard Version*, www.biblestudytools.com/esv (last accessed 1 November 2015).
2. https://en.wikipedia.org/wiki/Halakha (last accessed 1 November 2015).

3. https://en.wikipedia.org/wiki/Torah (last accessed 3 February 2023)
4. https://en.wikipedia.org/wiki/Kashrut (last accessed 1 November 2015).
5. http://www.britannica.com/topic/terefah (last accessed 2 November 2015).
6. Leviticus 11:9–12, http://www.biblestudytools.com/esv/leviticus/11.html (last accessed 2 November 2015).
7. For terms and rules concerning food, kitchen rules, slaughtering, etc., see https://en.wikipedia.org./wiki/Milk_and_meat_in_Jewish_law (last accessed 1 November 2015).
8. http://www.biblestudytools.com (last accessed 1 November 2015).
9. https://www.google.de/search?q=al-quran.info (last accessed 1 November 2015). This source was mainly used in relation to Islamic food rules.
10. http://www.etymonline.com (last accessed 1 November 2015).
11. http://www.al-islam.org/islamic-laws-ayatullah-ali-al-husayni-al-sistani/slaughtering-and-hunting-animals (last accessed 1 November 2015).
12. https://en.wikipedia.org/wiki/Dhabihah, 2015 (last accessed 1 November 2015).
13. Due to space constraints, only answers pertaining to the disgusting quality of food are reported here.
14. https://en.wikipedia.org/wiki/Islam_and_cats (last accessed 1 November 2015).
15. The Editors of Encyclopædia Britannica: Judaism. https://www.britannica.com/topic/kosher (last accessed 3 Feburary 2023).

References

Bateson, P. (1990) Konrad Lorenz, Obituary, *Ibis*, 132(2): 323–25.
Blume, M. (2009) The Reproductive Benefits of Religious Affiliation. In Voland, E. and Schiefenhövel, W. (eds) *The Biological Evolution of Religious Mind and Behavior*, Springer, The Frontiers Collection, Dordrecht, pp. 117–26.
Die Zeit (2016) Die Debatten-Polizei, 14 January: 63–64.
Douglas, M. (1966) *Purity and Danger: An Analysis of the Concepts of Pollution and Taboo*, Routledge & Kegan Paul, London.
Erikson, E. (1966) Ontogeny of Ritualization in Man, *Philosophical Transactions of the Royal Society London, B*, 251: 337–49.
Hanke, G. and Schiefenhövel, W. (2008) Jewish Dietary Rules: A Human Ethological Synopsis. In *Abstracts of the International Congress of the International Society for Human Ethology*, University of Bologna, Bologna, pp. 107–8.
Harris, M. (1974) *Cows, Pigs, Wars and Witches: The Riddles of Culture*, Vantage Books, New York.
_____. (1979) *Cultural Materialism: The Struggle for a Science of Culture*, Vantage Books, New York.
_____. (1985) *Good to Eat: Riddles of Food and Culture*, Simon & Schuster, New York.
Heeschen, V. and Schiefenhövel, W. (1983) *Wörterbuch der Eipo-Sprache. Eipo-Deutsch-Englisch*, Reimer, Berlin.
Heipko, P. and Schiefenhövel, W. (1987) *Mensch und Pflanze. Ergebnisse ethnotaxonomischer und ethnobotanischer Untersuchingen bei den Eipo, zentrales Bergland von Irian Jaya (West-Neuguinea), Indonesien*, Reimer, Berlin.
Koch, G. and Schiefenhövel, W. (1987) Eipo (West-Neuguinea, Zentrales Hochland) – Neubau des sakralen Männerhauses in Munggona. Publikationen zu wissenschaftli-

chen Filmen, Sektion Ethnologie, *Institut* für den *wissenschaftlichen Film, Göttingen, Sonderserie*, 7(9): 131–56.

McGrew, W.C. (2001) The Other Faunivory: Primate Insectivory and Early Human Diet. In Stanford, C.B. and Bunn, H.T. (eds) *Meat-Eating and Human Evolution*, Oxford University Press, Oxford, pp. 160–78.

Meyer-Rochow, V.B. (2009) Food Taboos: Their Origins and Purposes, *Journal of Ethnobiology and Ethnomedicine*, 5: 8–27.

Rozin, P., Haidt. J. and McCauley, C.R. (1993) Disgust. In Lewis, M. and Haviland, J. (eds) *Handbook of Emotions*, Guilford, New York, pp. 575–94.

Schiefenhövel, W. (1976) Die Eipo-Leute des Berglands von Indonesisch-Neuguinea: Kurzer Überblick über den Lebensraum und seine Menschen. Einführung zu den Eipo-Filmen des Humanethologischen Filmarchivs der Max-Planck-Gesellschaft, *Homo*, 26(4): 263–75.

———. (1983) Of Body and Soul – about the Concept of Man among the Eipo, Mek Language Group, Highlands of Irian Jaya (West-New Guinea), *Bikmaus: A Journal of Papua New Guinea Affairs, Ideas and the Arts*, IV(1): 87–93.

———. (1991) Eipo. In Hays, T.E. (ed.) *Encyclopedia of World Cultures, Volume II, Oceania*, G. K. Hall & Co, Boston, pp. 55–59.

———. (1997) Good Taste and Bad Taste: Preferences and Aversions as Biological Principles. In Macbeth, H. (ed.) *Food Preferences and Taste: Continuity and Change*, Berghahn Books, Oxford, pp. 55–64.

———. (2014) Human Ethological Perspectives on Prehistoric Adaptation and Dispersal in the Central Highlands of New Guinea. In Sanz, N. (ed.) *Human Origin Sites and the World Heritage Convention in Asia. World Heritage Papers 39*, UNESCO, Paris and Mexico City, pp. 235–54.

Schiefenhövel, W. and Blum, P. (2007) Insects: Forgotten and Rediscovered as Food. Entomophagy among the Eipo, Highlands of West-New Guinea, and in Other Traditional Societies. In MacClancy, J., Henry, J. and Macbeth, H. (eds) *Consuming the Inedible: Neglected Dimensions of Food Choice*, Berghahn Books, Oxford, pp. 163–76.

Schiefenhövel, W. and Voland, E. (2009) Introduction. In: Voland, E. and Schiefenhövel, W. (eds) *The Biological Evolution of Religious Mind and Behavior*, Springer, The Frontiers Collection, Dordrecht, pp. 1–7.

Simoons, F.J. (1961) *Eat Not This Flesh: Food Avoidances from Prehistory to Present*, University of Wisconsin Press, Madison.

———. (1991) *Food in China: A Cultural and Historical Inquiry*, CRC Press, Boca Raton.

Simoons, F.J. and Simoons, E.S. (1967) *A Ceremonial Ox of India: The Mithan in Nature, Culture, and History with Notes on the Domestication of Common Cattle*, Texas University Press, Austin.

Strungaru, C. and Schiefenhövel, W. (2001) Meat Preferences and Meat Taboos in a Multicultural Region of Sumatera – Anthropological and Evolutionary Perspectives. In Schultz, M., Atzwanger, K., Bräuer, G., Christiansen, K., Forster, J., Greil, H., Henke, W., Jaeger, U., Niemitz, C., Scheffler, C., Schiefenhövel, W., Schöder, I. and Wiechmann, I. (eds) *Homo – unsere Herkunft und Zukunft. Proceedings, 4. Kongress der Gesellschaft für Anthropologie (GfA), Potsdam, 25.–28. September 2000*, Cuvillier Verlag, Göttingen, pp. 111–16.

CHAPTER 3
FOOD AND ORDER: PURITY, DANGER AND THE BAYESIAN BRAIN

....

Mark Carter

Introduction

Mary Douglas' theories of classification, as outlined in her well-known work *Purity and Danger* (1966), revealed the fundamental importance of order, classification and 'purity' to human psychological development. Recent advances in neuroscience, particularly the Bayesian Brain theory (Friston 2005, 2010, 2013), highlight the imperative for the brain (and the mind engendered within) to impose order on experience and to keep the constructs used in this process in an ordered state. The links that Douglas initially made between her sociocultural observations and the psychological thinking of her time can be reappraised in relation to this contemporary approach. Douglas used food and the taboos surrounding them to illustrate her ideas – and food has also been a central element in psychology, including for Sigmund Freud and the field of psychoanalysis.

In this chapter, the connections between Douglas' approach to cultural classification systems and the work of Friston, Freud and other researchers are explored in relation to pure food. Douglas' ideas concerning mental representations are placed in the context of contemporary neurobiological approaches (Hopkins 2012), highlighting the necessity of ordering mental representations and internal mental states for the survival of organic life. Clinical discussion related to pure food is used to illustrate these ideas, with the story of The Gingerbread Man acting as a symbolic vehicle for articulating children's psychological and emotional states.

Mary Douglas, Pure Food and Mess

Douglas considered that a sense of order for individuals and social groups is generated by cultural classification systems, with reified concepts such as 'purity', in ordered relations and where contravention is disorder or 'dirt':

> ideas about separating, purifying, demarcating and punishing transgressions have as their main function to impose system on an inherently untidy experience. It is only by exaggerating the difference between within and without, above and below, male and female, with and against, that a semblance of order is created. (Douglas 1966: 4)

Food is an important focus for Douglas' illustration of her ideas. In the Old Testament Book of Leviticus, what may be eaten is juxtaposed by what is unclean and may not be eaten. Douglas' exposition of Leviticus is expanded to include other texts from the same tradition, placing the food laws in the context of holiness, where 'the dietary laws would have been signs at every turn inspiring meditation on the oneness, purity and completeness of God' (Douglas 1966: 58). She understands the ideas of holiness were given an external, physical expression in the 'wholeness of the body seen as a perfect container.' (ibid.: 52) The link she drew between wholeness and purity is central to the discussion of pure food in this chapter.

Douglas' approach to how culture helps to order an essentially messy human experience was based in ideas of how this order was created in the mind as described by F.C. Bartlett (1932). The Bayesian Brain theory has some general similarities with Bartlett's approach and so maps onto Douglas' thinking, but is a substantial contemporary development. It also has many links to Freud's work, including how it is situated in the approach of Hermann von Helmholtz (1821–94), where the brain is seen as an inference machine, inferring the world from its in-flowing sense data (Carhart-Harris and Friston 2010).

Feeling and Feeding States

A psychoanalytic perspective on food and feeding emphasises the physical and emotional experience of the infant in its primary relationship to its caregiver – generally, the breastfeeding mother, providing perhaps the ultimate pure food. For Freud (1991 [1905]), *orality* was the first stage in *libidinal* development. Libido is the primary internal drive for pleasure essential in the development of the ego, and could be loosely described as motivation. In early infant development 'surface' body experiences, such as feeding (Freud 1991 [1923]), are the infant's primary activity and interaction with the world. In a good feeding experience, libido becomes attached to mental representations of the experience and the mother (or caregiver), reflecting this primal feeling of goodness and pleasure. In this sense it is how the infant 'takes in' the world and is drawn towards the world as a good and safe place, where pleasure can be experienced.

In psychoanalytic theory, orality is a focus for pleasure and aggression for the infant. Melanie Klein (1977 [1952]) developed Freud's ideas further to describe how the infant's primary emotional state is unintegrated emotional ambivalence. This includes polar extremes, such as the deep pleasurable satisfaction of a good feed and the destructive rage when frustration is experienced, for example, if presentation of the breast is perceived as being late when the infant is experiencing hunger. Unalloyed good feeding experiences may form part of a deeper mental representational structure underlying the positive association of purity and food.

Holding extreme emotional positions, where we are not thinking in a holistic integrated way and not keeping other thoughts and feelings in mind, are commonly observed in children and adults. We can experience an internal 'mess', due to extreme emotional states where we struggle to comprehend what has caused us to feel this way due to the inherent difficulty of thinking clearly and coherently at these times (Fonagy and Luyten 2012) or due to the opacity of the external and internal world. The feeling that we are in a 'mess' itself causes us further anxiety (Holmes and Nolte 2019). Such internal difficulties represent a tremendous internal struggle that is essential for survival, particularly for a child due to the immaturity of self-regulating capacities (Fonagy and Target 2003), as such conscious and unconscious forces have the potential to wreak havoc in human behaviour (Damasio 2010).

Douglas understood the depth and breadth of concern about messiness in the human mind; as she states, 'reflection on dirt involves reflection on the relation of order to disorder, being to non-being, form to formlessness, life to death' (1966: 5). This assertion is prescient in the context of the contemporary Bayesian Brain formulations on the vital necessity of internal order for survival.

Our feelings are what motivate and guide us, warning us of threats to avoid or fight and drawing us towards what we need from our environment. They reflect our social, psychological and biological selves in relation to the current environment (Panksepp 1998; Damasio 2010). They are particularly helpful when there are limits on our knowledge in novel situations, and in this sense they are 'felt uncertainty' (Solms 2020), where we 'feel' our way through a new situation. Feelings are produced by the variations in our more basic neurobiological systems. Such systems have evolved to keep us alive, so they cover all the required internal states, which include, for example, hunger, thirst, fear and relational attachment. The systems receive data from the senses – either internal to the body or from the external environment – and when these data fall outside of the expected parameters, errors are generated. This process *feels like* something. The feelings generated in the mind vary depending on the system generating them and whether the errors are increasing, creating an unpleasant feeling, or decreasing, which is experienced as pleasant (Solms 2019, 2020; Holmes and Nolte 2019).

The Necessity for Order

Friston describes the central 'motivation' for organic life as 'resisting a tendency to disorder', something that strongly echoes Douglas' ideas. The Bayesian Brain theory provides us with the informational mechanism occurring within the brain's neurobiology, in the many levels of its hierarchy of multiple systems where 'bottom-up' stimuli are down regulated by 'top-down' predictions (gained from previous experience) about the internal and external world. The top-down predictions are compared to the information coming in bottom-up from the senses (sampling the external world and the senses monitoring the internal milieu of the bodily viscera) to see if the (internal and external) world is as predicted. If the sense data are not what is expected, then prediction errors occur (which *feels* like something, as described above) and these need to be resolved either through resampling the sense data (for example, doing a 'double-take'), or learning (changing the predictions) or taking action.

The aim of this system, both the neurobiology of the brain and the conscious and unconscious mind engendered within, is to keep all the neurobiological systems as quiet as possible, maintaining internal homeostasis. If our bodily nutritional stores are running low, for example, this will be registered via our internal senses as an error. The system subsequently sends further signals into the mind, which is *felt* as hunger. These hunger feelings can then focus attention and necessitate thinking and action to reduce the feeling. However, our feeling states are often not so straightforward, as they can be caused by intractable situations in the external world, cause us internal conflict, or they may feel overwhelming and when we experience high levels of feeling, our capacity to cognitively reflect becomes impaired (Fonagy and Luyten 2012).

It is during these times of internal chaos that we may need help from others, or use sociocultural products, such as fairytales, to comprehend this internal mess as Douglas describes, and begin to restore order to our internal mental state. If internal disorder were allowed to continue, it would pose a threat to the survival of the individual, impinging on their capacity to understand the world around them.

Cultural representations, as described by Douglas, have their place in the 'top-down' aspect of Friston's theory, contributing to how the world is seen (or predicted) and understood by the brain. These representations therefore have an ordering role through the classificatory system and the particular elements that are ordered in that structure, which helps to reassure the individual that their mess can be ordered as well as having a down-regulating role.

Fairy Tales and Food

Mental representations, built up from infancy as the child develops, are not just an individual internal learning experience, but one that is intertwined with the sociocultural environment (Frie 1997; Fonagy et al. 2002; Fotopoulou and Tsarkiris 2017). Henrietta Moore (2007) considers the early environment to be 'culturally constituted' and inhabited by social actors, which entails that internal fantasies and representations are both individual and social from the beginning. There is cross-disciplinary agreement that cultural products like fairytales help individuals to understand their world and their internal states (Bettelheim 1976; Obeyesekere 1990; Lurie 2003):

> This is ... how fairy tale depicts the world: figures are ferocity incarnate or unselfish benevolence. An animal is either all devouring or all helpful. Every figure is essentially one-dimensional, enabling the child to compre-hend its actions and reactions easily. Through simple and direct images the fairy story helps the child sort out his complex and ambivalent feel-ings, so that these begin to fall each one into a separate place, rather than being all one big muddle.

> As he listens to the fairy tale, the child gets ideas about how he may create order out of the chaos which is his inner life. The fairy tale suggests not only isolating and separating the desperate and confusing aspects of the child's experience into opposites, but projecting these into different figures. (Bettelheim 1976: 74–75)

Within a fairytale, a 'pure' food (such as that described in The Gingerbread Man) is a clear form with a positive emotional valence, free from contagion, disorder or dirt and mess. It is whole and safe, and stands in opposition to disorder and danger. These opposite poles together resonate with the child in an emotional mess, making it an attractive story to them.

Ideas about food and feeding lend themselves well to the top-down regula-tion as they are linked to physical experiences that are primary in the devel-opment of the psyche (Fotopoulou and Tsarkiris 2017) and common to all: 'biting someone's head off', for example, is a very evocative way to describe shouting at someone. The fact that a good feed for a baby is an extremely pleasurable experience with deep relational intimacy gives internal repre-sentations about food and feeding particular force to mentally represent extreme positive experiences (themselves generated by bodily based emo-tional systems).

In psychoanalytic psychotherapy with children, cultural figures, stories or nursery rhymes are often used by the child (as in everyday life) to try and articulate what they are feeling to themselves and to their therapist. Freud understood this well:

Freud ... chiefly drew on myth for his theories, he also invoked fairy tales in order to decipher the language of the unconscious and identify plots that illuminate the imperatives of desire – the drives to love and death. (Warner 2014: 116)

Whilst narratives such as fairytales have immediate appeal, they are, by definition, generalised, so the child can apply them further to their own specific situation. Such a thinking process is more effective if supported by another trusted person, such as a caregiver or a therapist (Fonagy et al. 2002; Bion 2007 [1967]; Callaghan and Tottenham 2016).

The Gingerbread Man: Examples from Psychotherapeutic Work with Children

Havsteen-Franklin (2016) describes how a relationally traumatised and emotionally abused child in a therapy session with her used the story of The Gingerbread Man as a way of expressing his fear of 'being tricked and eaten', which she linked to his worry about whether his therapist could be trusted at the beginning of the therapeutic work.[1]

The Gingerbread Man story generally starts with an older childless adult couple longing for a child, and so in the kitchen a gingerbread man is created and placed in the oven by the 'mother'. He comes alive (or is born, in a symbolic sense), but soon realises that everyone is out to eat him and so he swiftly runs away. The dire story follows him out into the social realm, where he encounters people and animals who all want to eat him. Whilst he is fast and proud of his prowess as he outruns all who chase him, taunting them as he goes, he is finally tricked and eaten by a clever fox.

There is much that is evoked by the uses of this story in psychotherapy, but for the current purposes the focus will be on food and feeding. Of central importance is the fact that the gingerbread man is 'born' sweet, desirable, whole and 'pure' in a safe place inside, and then embarks on an anxious yet omnipotent flight outside with no home or safety from persecutory figures, ending in the breakdown of form and death. The aliveness, wholeness, potency and goodness of the pure food are then contrasted with danger, disorder and death. Douglas' structuralist approach is apparent here in the story's simplified, compartmentalised and binary form.

These themes were evident when The Gingerbread Man story was also brought by another young child in the last few weeks of psychoanalytic psychotherapy in my clinic. In this instance, the therapeutic work had helped the young child work through his separation anxiety and resolve his regressive fantasies and wishes to merge with his mother after he felt he had lost her closeness and availability when he was an infant. When the therapist then introduced the end of therapy, with the accompanying loss and separation, the child was then exposed to a second loss and was angry at the

clever-fox-therapist who he felt had tricked him outside his merged relationship with mother, ending his reliance on regressive merger fantasy, and
he felt exposed to threatening external forces. The Gingerbread Man story
does not then have the same meaning for every child, but there are common
themes from the story that are appropriated differently by different children
to express an aspect of their internal state. In the first case the child's anxiety
is around establishing trust – the fear of being devoured if you trust another –
while in the second case the anxiety is that the trust that had been established
was in fact a dangerous trick, as a high level of negative feelings around separation are aroused by the news of the end of therapy.

In this particular clinical case the use of the representations of pure food
suggests that orality was an organising principle for both positive loving emotions and hateful angry feelings at a very primal level. The child's oral aggression towards the therapist may have meant that at an unconscious level, the
child wanted to eat the therapist, which would both destroy the therapist but
also keep himself or herself inside, and so denying the loss of separation. Also,
the child may have unconsciously wished to return to the warmth and pure
goodness of being back inside his mother, although this would have meant
the destruction of his own hard-fought individual self-identity and separation.
Through the story of The Gingerbread Man, the child found ways to express
some of his unconscious fears about his mother's own oral aggression and the
threat of feeling gobbled up by her and so compromising separation.

This child also defensively split off his good internal representations of
themselves, rendering them idealised, like the pure sweet and desirable food,
separate from the perceived threat of their aggressive feelings that appear
to the child to pose a risk that they will contaminate their sense of goodness
or even destroy all the good they have. The anger at the loss of their therapist is then projected onto the external world and perceived as persecutory
figures (Freud 1991 [1920]), as seen in the animals and people trying to eat
the gingerbread man. This polarised good and bad position is evident in The
Gingerbread Man story and is consistent with Douglas' structuralist approach.

The narrative of The Gingerbread Man captures something of these examples of complex, opposing, overwhelming and painful elements that constitute
the internal mess – the uncertainty and disorder in internal homeostasis.
It creates an ordered narrative in a way that resonates with Douglas' ideas
regarding the purity of form of animals as outlined in Leviticus, in contrast
to dirt and disorder. This story, when it resonates with the child's internal
experience, can help them to feel that there is order and to begin the process
of understanding themselves.

Discussion

The maintenance of internal informational order is an essential feature for
the survival of any self-organising system, such as human beings, and our

neurobiology – including the mental representations that are encoded within – functions to maintain this order. Mary Douglas, using the ideas of her time, observed how one of the functions of cultural representational structure is to order the representations that individuals use to make sense of their own experience. This chapter has suggested that these two perspectives, the neurobiological and the sociocultural, based on differing epistemologies, appear to converge around this idea of the ordering function of the representational milieu. The clinical presentation of The Gingerbread Man story has been used to illustrate this function for children in psychotherapy, utilising the ordering structure and the psychic 'potency' of the representations included within, notably a pure food. Whilst this does not establish that both perspectives are observing the same phenomena, it does suggest a link between these perspectives that may be a useful basis for further research.

As all human minds have limits on their capacity to manage extreme stimuli, and some minds more than others (with genetic differences or due to childhood adversity (McCrory and Viding 2015), it could be suggested that one of the functions of culture that has evolved is to produce and maintain representational resources that can be used to address (where possible) overwhelmed personal mental structures (Holmes 2020). The world does not respect our feelings, but our groups with their collective ideas are not so indifferent.

The clinical discussion in this chapter outlined elements that could constitute troubling internal mental states in children and illustrated how the story of The Gingerbread Man can be used by children to understand and express these mental states with themes of order and disorder. The use of a 'pure' food in the context of this fairytale may be linked to splitting and a lack of psychic emotional integration, but also contains the hope of returning to a stable ordered and predictable internal state where a greater emotional integration can be established. The dynamic of purity and danger in the narrative arc of the story informs the predictive processes of the brain, helping the downregulation of the mental state – a process further enhanced by conversations with trusted others, such as parents or therapists.

As the work of Friston and other researchers and therapists suggests, this is not the mere feelings of young children, but reflects a psychological internal struggle that has serious consequences for life in the physical world. The pure food of the gingerbread man can be a useful narrative component of psychotherapy. Such therapeutic treatment helps children with psychological and emotional difficulties to thrive in their environment, engaging with teachers, making friendships and concentrating on achieving in school – in other words, to live.

Mark Carter is Child Psychotherapy Operational Lead at the Anna Freud National Centre for Children and Families, London, United Kingdom. He is also Discipline Lead for Child and Adolescent Psychotherapy for Barnet CAMHS in the Barnet, Enfield and Haringey Mental Health NHS Trust, based at Edgware Community Hospital, London.

Note

1. For a further clinical example of the invocation of The Gingerbread Man story in therapy, see Afuape (2016).

References

Afuape, O. (2016) 'Run Run as Fast as You Can, You Can't Catch Me I'm the Gingerbread Man': An Assessment of Brothers in Care within the Context of 'Safe Therapy'. In Guishard-Pine, J., McCall, S. and Coleman-Oluwabusola, G. (eds) *Supporting the Mental Health of Children in Care: Evidence-Based Practice*, Jessica Kingsley, London and Philadelphia, pp. 63–72.

Bartlett, F.C. (1932) *Remembering: A Study in Experimental and Social Psychology*, Cambridge University Press, Cambridge.

Bettelheim, B. (1976) *The Uses of Enchantment: The Meaning and Importance of Fairy Tales*, Thames & Hutton, London.

Bion, W.R. (2007) [1962] *Learning from Experience*, William Heinemann, London and New York.

Callaghan, B.L., and Tottenham, N. (2016) The Neuro-environmental Loop of Plasticity: A Cross-Species Analysis of Parental Effects on Emotion Circuitry Development Following Typical and Adverse Caregiving, *Neuropsychopharmacology*, 41(1): 163–76.

Carhart-Harris, R.L., and Friston, K.J. (2010) The Default-Mode, Ego-Functions and Free-Energy: A Neurobiological Account of Freudian Ideas, *Brain*, 133(4): 1265–83.

Carter, M. (2012) The Robot, the Gangster and the Schoolboy: Intensive Psychoanalytic Psychotherapy with Luis, a Latency Boy in Search of a Father. In Malberg, T. and Raphael-Leff, J. (eds) *The Anna Freud Tradition: Lines of Development–Evolution in Theory and Practice over the Decades*, Karnac, London, pp. 235–52.

Damsio, A. (2010) *Self Comes to Mind: Constructing the Conscious Brain*, William Heinemann, London.

Douglas, M. (1966) *Purity and Danger*, Routledge, London.

Fonagy, P., Gergely, G., Jurist, E.L. and Target, M. (2002) *Affect Regulation, Mentalization, and the Development of the Self*, Routledge, London.

Fonagy, P. and Luyten, P. (2012) The Multidimensional Construct of Mentalisation and its Relevance to Understanding Borderline Personality Disorder. In Fotopoulou, A., Pfaff, D. and Conway, M.A. (eds) *From the Couch to the Lab: Trends in Psychodynamic Neuroscience*, Oxford University Press, Oxford, pp. 405–26.

Fonagy, P. and Target, M. (2003) *Psychoanalytic Theories: Perspectives from Developmental Psychopathology*, Whurr, London.

Fotopoulou, A. and Tsakiris, M. (2017) Mentalizing Homeostasis: The Social Origins of Interoceptive Inference, *Neuropsychoanalysis*, 19(1): 71–76.

Freud, A. (1993) [1936] *The Ego and the Mechanisms of Defence*, Karnac, London.

Freud, S. (1991) [1905] The Three Essays on the Theory of Sexuality. In *Sigmund Freud: 7. On Sexuality: Three Essays on the Theory of Sexuality and Other Works*, Penguin, London, pp. 33–69.

_____. (1991) [1920] Beyond the Pleasure Principle. In *Sigmund Freud: 11. On Metapsychology: Beyond the Pleasure Principle, the Ego and the Id and Other Works*, Penguin, London, pp. 269–338.

_____. (1991) [1923] The Ego and the Id. In *Sigmund Freud: 11. On Metapsychology: Beyond the Pleasure Principle, the Ego and the Id and Other Works*, Penguin, London, pp. 339–404.

Frie, R. (1997) *Subjectivity and Intersubjectivity in Modern Philosophy and Psychoanalysis: A Study of Sartre Binswanger, Lacan, and Habermas*, Rowman & Littlefield, London.

Friston, K. (2005) A Theory of Cortical Responses, *Philosophical Transactions of the Royal Society B, Biological Sciences,* 360(1456): 815–36.

_____. (2010) The Free-Energy Principle: A Unified Brain Theory? *Nature Reviews Neuroscience*, 11(2): 127–38.

_____. (2013) Life as We Know It, *Journal of the Royal Society Interface*, 10(86): 4–75.

Havsteen-Franklin, E. (2016) 'Can I Go Home?' Art Psychotherapy with Foster Children Returning to Their Birth Family. In Guishard-Pine, J., McCall, S. and Coleman-Oluwabusola, G. (eds) *Supporting the Mental Health of Children in Care: Evidence-Based Practice*, Jessica Kingsley, London and Philadelphia, pp. 88–101.

Holmes, J. (2020) *The Brain Has a Mind of Its Own: Attachment, Neurobiology, and the New Science of Psychotherapy*, Confer, London.

Holmes, J. and Nolte, T. (2019) 'Surprise' and the Bayesian Brain: Implications for Psychotherapy Theory and Practice, *Frontiers in Psychology*, 10(592): 1–13.

Hopkins, J. (2012) Psychoanalysis, Representation, and Neuroscience: The Freudian Unconscious and the Bayesian Brain. In Fotopoulou, A., Pfaff, D. and Conway, M.A. (eds) *From the Couch to the Lab: Trends in Psychodynamic Neuroscience*, Oxford University Press, Oxford, pp. 230–63.

Klein, M. (1977) [1952] Some Theoretical Conclusions Regarding the Emotional Life of the Infant. In *Envy and Gratitude and Other Works 1946–1953*, Dell, New York, pp. 61–93.

Lurie, A. (2003) *Boys and Girls Forever: Children's Classics from Cinderella to Harry Potter*, Chatto & Windus, London.

McCrory, E.J. and Viding, E. (2015) The Theory of Latent Vulnerability: Reconceptualizing the Link between Childhood Maltreatment and Psychiatric Disorder, *Development and Psychopathology*, 27: 493–505.

Moore, H.L. (2007) *The Subject of Anthropology: Gender, Symbolism and Psychoanalysis*, Polity Press, Cambridge.

Obeyesekere, G. (1990) *The Work of Culture: Symbolic Transformation in Psychoanalysis and Anthropology*, University of Chicago Press, Chicago.

Panksepp, J. (1998) *Affective Neuroscience: The Foundations of Human and Animal Emotions*, Oxford University Press, New York.

Solms, M. (2019) The Hard Problem of Consciousness and the Free Energy Principle, *Frontiers in Psychology*, 9: 1–16.

_____. (2020) New Project for a Scientific Psychology: General Scheme, *Neuropsychoanalysis*, 22(1–2): 5–35.

Warner, M. (2014) *Once upon a Time: A Short History of Fairy Tale*, Oxford University Press, Oxford.

CHAPTER 4
FROM CONCEPTS OF PURE FOOD TO A HEALTHY DIET IN GRECO-ROMAN ANTIQUITY

Amalia Lejavitzer

Introduction

When asked why we eat what we eat or why we don't eat everything that is biologically edible (Fischler 1995; Harris 2001), a complex range of ideas unfolds that imply 'eating' and 'food'. There is an enormous variety of possible responses, but all of them could be grouped into two large classes. The first class brings together explanations that emphasise the literal meaning of such concepts – i.e. what is edible and what nourishes is eaten. The second, on the other hand, refers to symbolic and, ultimately, ontological interpretations of those ideas: one eats what is accepted or permitted socially, and what identifies and confers identity both to a human group and to the individuals themselves, because food makes us what we eat, paraphrasing the famous aphorism of Brillat-Savarin: 'Dis-moi ce que tu manges, je te dirai ce que tu es' (Tell me what you eat and I'll tell you who you are) (1864: IV: 2). In this latter sense, the edible and, in particular, the dietary precepts that have to do with the 'pure' and the 'impure' refer to what food is permissible or taboo, which, defined by each culture (Fischler 1995), transcends the strictly nutritional and sensory properties of food.

In Latin, the adjective *purus* literally means 'Clean, free from dirt or filth, pure, unstained, undefiled' or, in a metaphorical sense, 'plain, natural, naked, unadorned, unwrought, unmixed, unadulterated, unsophisticated', and also 'unspotted, spotless, chaste, undefiled, unpolluted, faultless' (Lewis and Short 1991: 1494). That idea of 'pure' is linked to the sacred, the order, the cosmos, representing that which has no stain or defect, which has not been altered or adulterated by any fault and which presents no anomaly.[1] These semantic fields are made clear when speaking of 'pure food', as will be discussed below. For their part, Ernout and Meillet in their *Dictionnaire étymologique*

de la Langue Latine state that the adjective *purus*, 'sans tache, sans souil-
lure' (spotless, without contamination) also expresses something 'net, sans
mélange' (clean, without mixture), 'exempt de' (free from), which, above
all, is the meaning used in religious language and corresponds to the Greek
word καθαρός.[2] However, the verb *purare*,[3] derived from *purus*, has, since
historical times, been replaced by *purgare* (to purge) or *purificare* (to purify)
(Ernout and Meillet 2001: 546–47); the first of these was common in dietetics
and medicine, whereas the second was used in the areas of ritual and religion.

In the Roman world, there were two paths to purification. The first could
be achieved through rites called *lustrationes*[4] (religious acts that included
processions, sprinkling of water, sacrifices and offerings) and festivities, such
as the Lupercalia. The latter were rituals of purification and fertility, celebrated during February, 'the month of expiation', the name of which means
'to purify' (Lewis and Short 1991: 732), in memory of the Capitoline she-wolf
that fed Romulus, but also to purify the city (Shelton 1998), in order to return
it to order, after the chaos and excesses typical of the festivities of Saturnalia
at the end of the year. The other way to achieve purification was through diet,
that is, through feeding and purging, which is discussed below.

Thus, in this chapter, first some foods considered 'pure' by ancient Greeks
and Romans are discussed, as well as how they were characterised from a
culinary point of view, based on the testimony of the Latin recipe book *De Re
Coquinaria* (The Art of Cooking), attributed to Apicius.[5] Next, food prescriptions and the praise of frugality are discussed, as a lifestyle that allows one to
achieve purity (of body and spirit) as described in the treatise *De Abstinentia*
(On Abstinence) by Porphyry.[6] Finally, the link between pure food and a
healthy diet is analysed, using the word *diet* in the fullest sense of the Greek
word δίαιτα,[7] for which a general translation might be lifestyle.

Pure Foods: Olive Oil and Honey

When it comes to foods, what does 'pure' mean? To many, its immediate connotations are those of 'natural', 'fresh', 'unmixed' or 'uncooked'. It is clear
that in this case the adjective 'pure' refers to those foods that can be consumed
in their natural state with little or no preparation prior to their consumption.

Here I also mention Claude Lévi-Strauss, who in the first volume of his
Mythologiques[8] proposed the well-known 'culinary triangle' in order to
explain in a graphic way the antithesis between that which is raw, natural or
unelaborated and that which is cooked, cultural or elaborated (Lévi-Strauss,
1964, *Mythologiques I*).[9] He envisions an equilateral triangle in which each of
the three corners corresponds to one of the states in which foods exist: raw,
cooked and rotten. At the top of the triangle, he placed raw food, associated with the sphere of the natural world, since there is no step between its
procurement from nature and its consumption. On the other hand, on the

corners that form the base of the triangle and that are connected by a line, he placed the cooked on the left and the rotten on the right. Both states are the result of a transformation from the raw: through human action in the case of the cooked, and through a natural transformation in the case of the rotten (Lévi-Strauss 1968, *Mythologiques III*).

Authors of Greco-Roman antiquity commonly held a belief in the civilising value of the discovery of fire. For example, in his treatise *De Abstinentia*, Porphyry states that the change from the ancient diet of fruits to the consumption of meat was only possible thanks to the knowledge of fire. Fire allowed for the cooking of meat, since eating meat raw was considered to be a trait of the impious or of the uncivilised (Porphyry, *De Abstinentia*, I, 13). In fact, in the *Odyssey*, Homer sets up an allegorical paradigm about savagery when he describes the Cyclops as a monster, who does not appear human and does not eat bread (i.e. humans are bread-eaters, σιτόφαγοι[10] as described by Homer, *Odyssey*, IX, 190–91) or sow or cultivate fields, but who rather eats raw (and even human) flesh. The cooking of food thus becomes a symbol of civilisation.

In Apicius' recipe book, *De Re Coquinaria*, the concept of 'raw' is expressed by the adjectives *crudus* (raw), *recens* (fresh) and *viridis* (green). The first almost always refers to raw eggs, *ova cruda* (Apicius, IV, 2, 12–14; 17; 27; 28; 3, 5; VII, 7, 1; VIII, 7, 1; 8, 9; IX, 4, 2);[11] the second is associated with fruit (Apicius, I, 12, 4), where the connotation of 'recently picked' or 'fresh' is clear, as also with 'fresh meat' (Apicius, I, 8, 1)[12] or 'fresh cheese' (Apicius, IV, 2, 13); the third appears the greatest number of times, but is semantically the most narrow term, as it always applies to aromatic plants or leafy greens that are naturally that colour, and also to olives and their oil. In fact, when Apicius says 'green oil', *oleum viridem* (Apicius, I, 14; V, 2, 1–3; 3, 9; IX, 10, 2 and 10), he is alluding as much to its colour as to a specific type of oil, but he is likewise alluding to the qualities that are denoted by the term *viridis*, in this case fresh or recently squeezed.

In fact, oil, milk and honey are considered to be the symbols par excellence of the raw, the natural and (as a consequence) of the pure.[13] Of honey, Lévi-Strauss (1968) would say that it is 'more-than-raw'. Honey is a complete food in itself that can be eaten in a natural state without the need to cook it or mix it with other ingredients. From the beginnings of humanity, honey has been highly valued for its energising properties. It is thought to provide vigour and energy almost immediately upon consumption, since it is absorbed rapidly into the bloodstream, a fact that facilitates its use by the body. For this reason, it very quickly became the constant companion of travellers and pilgrims throughout their long journeys. In the first book of *De Re Coquinaria*, Apicius gives us testimony of this fact in a recipe for wine mixed with spices and honey (*conditum melizomum viatorium*). This wine is said to be meant especially for travellers, since 'it keeps forever and those who travel can use it during their journey' (Apicius, I, 1, 2).[14] Ancient medicine also made use of honey not only for its antiseptic and antibacterial properties, but also for its digestive and laxative properties. Honey is an ingredient in stomach medicines like the one that appears in the recipe book of Apicius, where it is recommended to drink water in which were boiled black beetroots along with wine and honey (Apicius, III, 2, 3 and 4).

One fact that might have influenced the belief about the purity of these foods is that the ancients considered both honey and olive oil to be divine gifts. Aristotle says that honey fell from the air because it was an exudation from the heavens, and as such its contact with the heavenly gods caused it to belong to a different category of food from anything else (Aristotle, *Historia Animalium*, V, 22–24). For his part, Pliny says that this liquid was the candy of the gods, a saliva emanating from the stars or a juice that air exudes during the process of its own purification (Pliny, *Historia Naturalis*, 11, 12).

The Greeks believed that Pallas Athena gave the olive tree to mortals and taught the inhabitants of Attica its cultivation and how to obtain its juice, olive oil. So the legend goes, Athena squared off with Poseidon for the rule of Attica; the gods then decided to resolve the conflict by granting victory to whoever gave the best gift to the inhabitants of the region. While Poseidon made a salt lake appear near the Acropolis, Athena caused an olive tree to grow near the Erechtheion, which gave her the victory (Grimal 1981). Moreover, certain olive trees were sacred in Athens, and if anyone dared to chop one down, they would be punished with death, as is mentioned in one of the speeches Lysias delivered before the judges of the Areopagus.[15]

Olive oil is the juice of the olive, 100 percent natural, which is pressed either by hand or mechanically to obtain it. There is no need to cook it in order to eat it or preserve it. In *De Re Coquinaria*, olive oil appears as a condiment for almost any dish including salad, but also as an additive for sweets and desserts. It was also used as a preservative. In ancient times, just as today, an equal mixture of olive oil and salt was the favourite dressing for greens,[16] whether cooked or raw. Carrots, for example, were seasoned 'with salt, virgin olive oil and vinegar' (Apicius, III, 21, 2).[17] In the book of Apicius, olive oil is not only called *hispanum* (referring to it being a product of Baetica[18] in Hispania), but it is also qualified by the adjectives *purum* ('pure') and *viridem* ('green'). In a strict sense, the latter term means the colour 'green', but it especially means 'fresh' in culinary language. When Apicius says *oleum purum*, it is likely that he is referring to olive oil which today would be called extra virgin, that is to say, the juice of the olive that is cold-pressed, with no defect, with no additives and without being subjected to any source of heat. These conditions were very difficult to obtain in antiquity. For this reason, it was common practice to fix any unpleasant odour or flavour of olive oil by adding salt, aromatic herbs or molten wax to create an oil of optimal quality (Palladius, *Opus Agriculturae*, XII, 19–21). As such, it was necessary to clarify that the olive oil was in fact 'pure'.

It was also necessary in medicine[19] and in cosmetics to clarify that the olive oil was in fact 'pure' to distinguish oils (*olei*) from unguents (*unguenti*). As Isidorus of Seville puts it:

Oil is *pure* and is unmixed with anything else. On the other hand, an unguent is anything which is prepared with common oil and enriched with a mixture of diverse spices. (Isidorus of Seville, *Origins*, IV, 12, 6)[20]

Purification through Food

Since ancient times, humans have maintained a direct relationship between the food they ate and the physical, moral and spiritual consequences of eating it. Adam and Eve were expelled from Paradise because they ate a forbidden food.

For this reason, many very different religions and philosophies had a serious preoccupation with the question of which foods to permit and which to prohibit, especially when it came to the daily diets of priests and philosophers. These various groups wrote many treatises with the goal of maintaining the purity of the soul. The rules of the Pythagoreans against the eating of beans are known[21] as are those of the Hindus about the eating of beef, as well as the rigorous dietary laws found in Leviticus that gave rise to the kosher kitchen among the Jews (Harris 2010).

In his *De Abstinentia* (IV, 3–7; 11–13; 15–17), Porphyry summarises the dietary practices and prohibitions of the Jews, Spartans, Egyptians, Syrians, Persians and Hindus, namely, all those peoples that prescribe either total abstinence from meat or abstinence from certain kinds of meat. Christians also adopted the practice of abstinence from meat in the form of fasting during Lent, but it was also chosen as a way of life by hermits and Cenobites (del Cerro Calderón 2000: 103–24). The book of Porphyry is essentially an apology for vegetarianism, since the author believes that eating meat is not recommended because it awakens the passions of the soul (Porphyry, *De Abstinentia*, I, 33, 1). On the contrary, 'a diet free of meat is both simple and easy to follow for anyone; it frees us and brings us salvation, since it grants peace to our judgment' (Porphyry, *De Abstinentia*, I, 47, 12–14).[22] According to the words of Porphyry, the observance of a dietary regimen has more to do with the moral sphere than with the food itself.

It is clear that the dichotomy between meat, greed and sin on the one hand and fruit, frugality and purity on the other hand does not belong exclusively to primitive Christianity and the early Patristic. Many peoples in antiquity considered moderation in eating as a necessary condition for a virtuous and moral life. The concept of the 'frugal diet' refers *sensu stricto* to a diet based on the fruits of the earth, that is, seeds, honey, plants and fruits, all those things that can be consumed in their natural state without need of admixture or cooking and were therefore considered pure, as we have said. However, frugality *sensu lato* alludes to a style of life guided by sobriety and a moderation of habits, including food. Therefore, since what is eaten has direct consequences for the body, both through the process of digestion and the stimulation of the senses (taste, sight, smell, touch and hearing), following a frugal regimen in all parts of daily life makes it possible to maintain the body within the boundaries of purity. As a consequence, a frugal diet played a significant role both in medicine and also in philosophy,[23] as well as in the religions of antiquity. Not only does such a diet aim at preserving bodily equilibrium in order to maintain health, but it also has a more transcendental goal: purity of spirit.

In sum, frugal eating leads to the purification of the body, to rapid digestion, to being light, to staying awake and to moderation. As such, it is considered morally good. On the contrary, eating meat stimulates the senses, causes slow digestion, and allows weight and drowsiness to take control of the body (Porphyry, *De Abstinentia*, I, 27–28). Therefore, frugality and abstinence from meat do much to make possible a release from material and bodily concerns with the goal of growing closer to the divine sphere (Porphyry, *De Abstinentia*, I, 54 and 57) and achieving purity of body and spirit (Porphyry, *De Abstinentia*, IV, 20). *Mens sana in corpore sano*,[24] said Juvenal (*Satura* X, 356), because health can only be achieved and preserved if one maintains the equilibrium between body, mind and spirit.

A Healthy Diet and Ancient Medicine

This chapter has already linked concepts of the purity of food to the purity of body and spirit. In this way, the preoccupation of humans with eating in a healthy manner and following diets in order to purify oneself is nothing new.

The modern meaning of the word *diet*, referring exclusively to what one eats and drinks, reflects only one aspect of the classical meaning of the term. As explained above, the Greek δίαιτα and the Latin *diæta* referred not only to what foods were eaten, but above all to one's entire way of life, especially in relation to how to live a healthy life, both physically and spiritually.

Leading a healthy lifestyle was an important part of this sense of the word 'diet'. This, of course, included healthy eating, but also frequent exercise, periods of rest, regular purges and baths. Above all, the role of the diet in ancient medicine was to stay healthy and to prevent sickness caused by upsetting one's internal equilibrium. Therefore, the diet had the goal of restoring an upset equilibrium, or otherwise of keeping that equilibrium from being upset by following an appropriate diet.

For Hippocrates, health was achieved by means of balancing the foods one ate and the physical exercise one carried out so that there would be no imbalance of these things, either excess or lack: 'In addition, if it had been possible to discover the appropriate measure of food for each nature, and the amount of exercise that was sufficient, without having either too little or too much, then health would have been found for every man with precision' (Hippocrates, *De Victu*, 1, 2, 3).

The treatises *De Victu* (On Regimen) and *De Victu Acutorum* (On Regimen in Acute Diseases), among other works that are included in the *Hippocratic Corpus*, reveal the importance that the doctor of Kos attached to diet. In *On Regimen*, one immediately notices the need the doctor has to understand the fundamental nature (δύναμις meaning power, faculty, ability) of each food and drink so as to know what effects each would produce in the patient, before prescribing any regimen intended to reverse the loss of equilibrium which had led to the sickness.[25]

In *On Regimen in Acute Diseases*, Hippocrates states that maintaining a simple nutritional diet founded on the continual consumption of medicinal drinks, such as a kind of mead, *hydromel* (Hippocrates, *De Victu Acutorum*, 55), and honey-vinegar, *oxymel* (Hippocrates, *De Victu Acutorum*, 58), will allow the patient to regain his health, even in the case of acute sicknesses (in other words, those that lead to death in most people) (Hippocrates, *De Victu Acutorum*, 5). Honey is an important ingredient in these drinks, as suggested by their Latin names.

In fact, diet is only one of the three parts of therapy for the ancient doctors. In the second century CE, Celsus summarises this fact in the following way: medicine 'is divided into three parts: one which cures via diet, another via drugs and the third which does it by hand. The Greeks call the first one *Διαιτήτικήν* (dietetics), the second one *Φαρμακευτικήν* (pharmaceutics) and the third one *Χειρουργίαν* (hands-on medical care)' (Celsus, *De Medicina, proemium*, 9).[26]

Meanwhile, Galen, for his part, put great emphasis on diet within his medical art.[27] He considered dietetics to be the foundation of therapy, since only through an adequate total life regimen, including food, exercise, baths and rest, could one maintain the ideal equilibrium of the bodily humours, and with it achieve and maintain one's health (Galen, XIX, 491 K).

Galen maintained the Hippocratic theory of four humours that conceived of the human body as composed of blood (characterised by heat), phlegm (characterised by cold), yellow bile (characterised by wetness) and black bile (characterised by dryness) (Galen, XIX, 485–86 K; I, 509–10 K). In the same way, foods and drinks had their own δύναμις, that is, their own power or ability to be hot, cold, wet or dry. As a consequence, it was of the utmost importance for the doctor to know the exact nature of each food so that he could include it in the diet in order that it might help to maintain the patient's bodily equilibrium, or to recoup it once it had been lost.

Baths also formed a part of the diet. Different kinds were prescribed depending on the needs of the patient, since each type had distinct properties.

There were salty baths to heat up the body and remove excess moisture; there were hot baths to lose weight if one was fasting, or otherwise to heat and hydrate the body if one was not fasting; and there were cold baths to impart heat and hydration if one was fasting, or otherwise to completely dry one out if one was not fasting (Hippocrates, *De Victu*, 2, 57). After all of this, in order to complete the treatment, it was recommended that one drink certain beverages such as the *apothermon*, made from semolina, wine and dried fruits, whose use after a hot bath explains the etymology of its name, transcribed from the Greek ἀποθερμον (ἀπὸ θερμοῦ, meaning after heat). Its use is referred to in Hippocrates when he prescribes 'that they bathe in hot water and drink *apothermon*' (Hippocrates, *De Mulierum Affectibus*, 1, 44; also in 2, 207 and 209). In *De Re Coquinaria*, there is the following recipe for its preparation:

> You will make *apothermon* like this. Spelt is boiled with pine nuts and peeled almonds soaked in water and washed with silvery chalk so that they turn more or less white. Into this you will mix in a raisin, cooked wine or raisin wine. Sprinkle cracked [pepper] on top and serve in a mug. (Apicius, II, 2, 10)[28]

In this recipe book there are also other recipes to drink *a balneo*, that is, 'after the bath'. One is 'boiled cuttlefish for after the bath. Put it in cold water with pepper, *laserpicium*, *garum*, and pine nuts, [add] eggs, and garnish to taste' (Apicius, IX, 4, 3).[29]

Such drinks or broths were well known for their laxative properties. Hippocrates refers to the natural purging quality of broths made with cuttlefish, octopus and other shellfish (Hippocrates, *De Victu*, 2, 48, 3). Among Roman authors, Celsus recommends cuttlefish ink to alleviate constipation (Celsus, *De Medicina*, 2, 29, 1–2), and Pliny adds that it should be cooked with oil, salt and flour to eliminate intestinal parasites (Pliny, *Historia Naturalis*, 32, 31, 100–1).

Another purging recipe for after the bath is also found in *De Re Coquinaria*, a sea urchin brine: 'Mix the best *garum* with salted urchin, and it will seem almost fresh, such that it can be consumed after the bath' (Apicius, IX, 8, 5).[30] Ancient medicine considered sea urchins (and the broth obtained from them) to be useful foods for relieving constipation (Celsus, *De Medicina*, 2, 29, 2).

All of these recipes constitute another of the elements integral to the diet (in the sense of δίαιτα); that is, the purges. Essentially, food, baths and purges were methods for cleaning and purifying the body through the evacuation of that which was unnecessary and harmful.

Conclusion

From what has been considered in the preceding pages, it can be said that, when referring to food, the concept 'pure' presents different nuances of meaning. First, it refers to food without admixture, being that which is legitimate, unadulterated or original, and precisely in this 'purity' is the guarantee of the quality of the product. Secondly, it refers to that food which is fresh, recently harvested or obtained, and has not been transformed by any process, either by fermentation or putrefaction, which alters its quality. Finally, pure food is that which can be consumed without any preparation or cooking, thus avoiding alteration of the product as well as preventing any forms of contamination that might be introduced into it through cooking (Douglas 1973).

For medical care in antiquity, purges were part of the diet, understood as a 'lifestyle', which, as explained above, also included food, rest and exercise. These purges were considered to be a way to recover any lost equilibrium, which had caused disease or any loss of health. The frugal diet, based on vegetarianism, and the purges helped to purify the body, to purify it of those polluting and impure elements that threatened order and endangered the individual (Douglas 1973). In short, in pure food and in purification through food, it is necessary to see not only the desire for a healthy lifestyle and a medical concern to restore the equilibrium that maintains health, but also the concept of leaving the profane behind in order to ascend to the divine, by refraining from consuming what, due to its impurity, impedes reaching the sacred (Caillois 1996 [1950]). It is a way of making the world sacred in order to recover the order of the cosmos (Douglas 1973).

In these ways, the dietary prescriptions associated with pure and impure foods represent a complex universe of meanings that cannot be interpreted exclusively from the points of view of hygiene or food safety, since they constitute a system of symbols that have deep spiritual, moral and, above all, identity implications (Costes 1987). Food is culture, as Montanari has pointed out, but also: 'The food system ... is the repository of the traditions and identity of the group. Therefore, it constitutes an extraordinary vehicle for self-representation and cultural change: it is an instrument of identity' (Montanari 2007: 153).[31]

Amalia Lejavitzer is a professor in the Department of Humanities and Communication, Faculty of Law and Human Sciences, Catholic University of Uruguay, Montevideo, Uruguay.

Notes

This chapter is based on the following article by the author: Lejavitzer, A. (2016). Dieta saludable, alimentos puros y purificación en el mundo grecolatino, *Nova Tellus*, 34(1), 109–21, http://dx.doi.org/10.19130/iifl.nt.2016.34.1.711. Accessed on 7 October 2022. It was translated into English by Luke Gorton; translations of the Greek and Latin quotations are by the author of this chapter.

 1. Some authors (Douglas 1973; Costes 1987) find in the concept of 'anomaly' the criterion that explains the apparently arbitrary classification of pure and impure food as stated in Leviticus.
 2. *Καθαρός*, meaning clean, unmixed, https://logeion.uchicago.edu/%CE%BA%CE%B1%CE%B8%CE%B1%CF%81%CF%8C%CF%82 (last accessed 7 October 2022).
 3. There remains a vestige of this verb in the verb *depurar* in Spanish (and other Romance languages) (Ernout and Meillet 2001: 546–47).
 4. From the verb *lustrare* (to purify), a synonym of *purificare*.
 5. This is the only recipe book that is preserved from Greco-Latin antiquity, dating from the end of the fourth century CE, but it comprises almost 500 recipes collected over the previous four centuries. The various compilers and cooks who contributed their preparations for the book remained anonymous; not so Apicius, to whom by tradition is attributed the authorship of the work or part of it. Yet, this is not totally appropriate because, although biographical data on him is scarce, it is known that he lived under the mandate of Tiberius (who ruled from 14 to 37 CE), of whom he was a relative. He also became known to posterity for his enormous fortune, his eccentricities in gastronomic matters and for his suicide.
 6. A neoplatonic philosopher and student of Plotinus; he was born in Tyre, Phoenicia, in 234 CE and died in Rome in c. 300 CE. *De Abstinentia* allows us to understand Plotinus' thoughts regarding the theory of souls, but also presents an exceptional justification and defence of vegetarianism and abstinence from meat in the diet.
 7. The Greek word *δίαιτα* is regularly translated into English as 'diet', which is derived from it, but *δίαιτα* had a far broader meaning of lifestyle, way of life, mode of living and customs, including dietary patterns, but not limited to them.
 8. *Mythologiques* is made up of four volumes; each of the first three bears a suggestive title related to food: *The Raw and the Cooked*, *From Honey to Ashes* and *The Origin of Table Manners*.
 9. Lévi-Strauss also offers a synthesis in *Mythologiques III* (1968), where he adds the opposing pair roasted/boiled, being fire as opposed to water.
10. Often translated as 'cereal eaters', but more literally 'wheat eaters'.
11. On only one occasion does Apicius refer to raw fish (IV, 2, 27).
12. Also in II, 2, 1: *adipes fasiani recentes*; IV, 2, 13: *echinos recentes* and *echinos recentiores*.
13. Nevertheless, this notion has been changing throughout history: in the sixteenth and seventeenth centuries, for example, it was thought that honey was a primary, untamed and crude form of sweetness, in contrast to those 'purer' and 'more civilised' forms, such as sugar (Fischler 1995: 271).
14. Apicius, I, 1, 2: *Conditum melizomum perpetuum quod subministratur per viam peregrinanti*.

15. This is the seventh discourse, titled *Defence in the Matter of the Olive Stump*.
16. The third book of *De Re Coquinaria* (The Art of Cooking), titled *Cepuros* (Related to the Garden), contains recipes which constitute an example of this.
17. Apicius, III, 21, 2: *sale, oleo puro et aceto*.
18. For the Romans, Baetica was a province in the Iberian peninsula that they called Hispania. It corresponds approximately with the Andalusia of today.
19. As Pliny says (*Historia Naturalis*, XXIII, 69–80), the ancients used it for its relaxing properties to improve the functioning of the digestive system, for the scarring of wounds, ulcers and burns, for the protection of the skin, and to help with muscle spasms and pains.
20. Isidorus of Seville, *Origins*, IV, 12, 6: *Oleum est purum nullique rei admixtum. Vnguentum vero est omne quod ex communi oleo confectum aliarum specierum commixtione augetur.*
21. For the prohibition against eating beans, cf. Empedocles (fr. 141 Diels-Kranz), Aristoxenus (fr. 25 Wehrli), Diogenes Laertius (8, 34 and 45), Callimachus (fr. 553 Pfeiffer), Cicero (*Div.*, I, 30, 62) and Aulus Gellius (*N. A.*, 4, 11).
22. Porphyry, *De Abstinentia*, 1, 47, 12–14: ἡ ἄψυχος καὶ λιτὴ τροφὴ καὶ πᾶσιν εὐπόριστος ἀφαιρεῖται ἡμᾶς, εἰρήνην παρασκευάζουσα τῷ τὰ σωτήρια ἡμῖν ἐκπορίζοντι λογισμῷ.
23. Philosophers such as Plato (*Phaedrus*, 270 b–c), Aristoteles (*Problemata*, 1, 2; 4; 13–15; 37; 48), Plutarch (*Moralia*, 2, 11: *De tuenda sanitate praecepta*; 12, 68: *De esu carnium*) and Iamblichus (*De Vita Pythagorica*, 16, 68; 24, 106–9), among others, discuss food and nutrition.
24. A healthy mind in a healthy body.
25. The catalogue of the properties of foods and drinks, one of the most lengthy and complete of which we know (consisting of Chapters 39–56 of the second book of *On Regimen*), begins with grains: barley, wheat and spelt (and the breads and drinks made from them); it continues with legumes, meats, bird, fish and seafood, eggs and cheese; finally, it concludes with drinks (water, wine, vinegar and honey), vegetables and fruits.
26. *Isdemque temporibus in tres partes medicina diducta est, ut una esset quae victu, altera quae medicamentis, tertia quae manu mederetur. Primam* Διαιτικήν secundam Φαρμακευτικήν tertiam Χειρουργίαν *Graeci nominarunt.*
27. The main works in which Galen discusses dietetics are: *De sanitate tuenda* [On the conservation of health] VI, 1-452 K; *De alimentorum facultatibus* [On the characteristics of foods],VI, 453-748 K); *De probis pravisque alimentorum succis* [On the good and the bad humours of foods], VI, 749-815 K; *De ptisana* [concerning hot drinks made with barley], VI, 816-831 K.
28. Apicius, II, 2, 10: *Apotermum sic facies. Alicam elixa nucleis et amigdalis depilatis et in aqua infusis et lotis ex creta argentaria, ut ad candorem pariter perducantur. Cui ammiscebis uvam passam, caroenum vel passum. Desuper [piper] confractum asparges et in boletari inferes.*
29. Apicius, IX, 4, 3: *Sepias elixas a balneo. In frigidam missas … cum pipere, lasere, liquamine, nucleis, ova [addes], et condies ut voles.*
30. Apicius, IX, 8, 5: *Echinis salsis liquamen optimum admisces, et quasi recentes apparebunt, ita ut a balneo sumi possint.*

31. *Il sistema alimentare ... è depositario delle tradizioni e dell'identitá di gruppo.*
Constituisce pertanto uno straordinario veicolo di auto-rippresentazione e di
scambio culturale: è strumento di identità.

References

Apicius, *De Re Coquinaria*. Edited and translated with an introduction and notes by
    André, J. (1987), Les Belles Lettres, Paris.
Aristotle, *Historia Animalium*. Translated by Pallí Bonet, J. with an introduction by
    García Gual, C. (1992), Gredos, Madrid.
Brillat-Savarin, J.A. (1864) *Physiologie du gout*, Furne, Paris. Published at: https://
    gallica.bnf.fr/ark:/12148/bpt6k5819426m/f22.item. Accessed on 24 December 2022.
Caillois, R. (1996 [1950]) *El Hombre y lo Sagrado*, Fondo de Cultura Económica,
    Mexico City.
Celsus, *De Medicina*. Edited and translated with an introduction and notes by
    Spencer, W.G. (1948), William Heinemann/Harvard University Press, London and
    Cambridge, MA.
Costes, A. (1987) Le pur et l'impur. Practiques alimentaires et religions, *Hommes et
    Migrations*, 1105: 54–63.
del Cerro Calderón, G. (2000) Condicionamientos de la Dieta Mediterránea en la moral
    patrística. In Pérez Jiménez, A. and Cruz Andreotti, G. (eds), *Dieta Mediterránea.
    Comidas y hábitos alimenticios en las culturas mediterráneas*, Ediciones Clásicas,
    Madrid, pp. 103–24.
Douglas, M. (1973) *Pureza y Peligro. Un Análisis de los Conceptos de Contaminación
    y Tabú*, Siglo XXI, Madrid.
Ernout, A., and Meillet, A. (2001) *Dictionnaire étymologique de la Langue Latine.
    Histoire des Mots*, Klincksieck, Paris.
Fischler, C. (1995) *El (h)Omnívoro. El Gusto, la Cocina y el Cuerpo*, Anagrama,
    Barcelona.
Galen, *Opera Omnia*. Edited by Kühn, C.G. (2001), Georg Olms, Hildesheim.
Grimal, P. (1981) *Diccionario de Mitología Griega y Romana*, Paidós Ibérica, Barcelona.
Harris, M. (2001) *Bueno para Comer*, Alianza, Madrid.
———. (2010) *Vacas, Cerdos, Guerras y Brujas*, Alianza, Madrid.
Hippocrates, *De Victu* (On Regimen). Edited and translated with notes by Jones,
    W.H.S. (1967), Harvard University Press/William Heinemann, Cambridge, MA.
———. *De Victu Acutorum* (On Regimen in Acute Diseases). Edited and translated
    with notes by Jones, W.H.S. (1967), Harvard University Press/William Heinemann,
    Cambridge, MA.
———. *De Mulierum Affectibus I–III* (On the Diseases of Women I-III). Edited by
    Littré, E. (1853), J.B. Bailliere, Paris. [CD-ROM, Thesaurus Linguae Graecae].
Homer, *Odyssey*. Translated as *La Odisea* by Pabón, J.M. with an introduction by
    Fernández Galiano, M. (1982), Gredos, Madrid.
Isidorus of Seville, *Origins*. In Isidoro de Sevilla, *Etimologías II*, edited and translated
    with notes by Oroz Reta, J. and Marcos Casquero, M.A. (1994), Biblioteca de
    Autores Cristianos, Madrid.
Juvenal, *Saturae*. Translated by Rudd, N. (1992), Oxford University Press, Oxford.

Lévi-Strauss, C. (1964) *Mythologiques I, Le Crut et le Cuit* (The Raw and the Cooked), Plon, Paris.

Lévi-Strauss, C. (1968) *Mythologiques III, L'Origine des Manières de Table* (The Origin of Table Manners), Plon, Paris.

Lewis, C. and Short, C. (1991) *A Latin Dictionary*, Clarendon Press, Oxford.

Montanari, M. (2007) *Il Cibo Come Cultura*, Editori Laterza, Bari.

Palladius, *Opus Agriculturae*. Edited by Schmitt, J.C. (1898) Corpus Scriptorum Latinorum, Leipzig. Published at: http://www.forumromanum.org/literature/palladius/agr.html. Accessed on 29 March 2023.

Pliny, *Historia Naturalis*. Edited and translated by Rackham, H. (vols. I–V, IX), Jones, W.H.S. (vols. VI–VIII), Eichholz, D.E. (vol. X) (1951, 1956, 1958–63). William Heinemann/Harvard University Press, London and Cambridge, MA, 10 volumes.

Porphyry, *De Abstinentia*. Edited and translated by Bouffartigue, J. and Patillon, M. (1977, 1979), Les Belles Lettres, Paris.

Shelton, J.A. (1998) *As the Romans Did: A Sourcebook in Roman Social History*, Oxford University Press, Oxford.

CHAPTER 5
EATING PURE: ETHNOGRAPHY AND FOOD IN 'FITNESS CULTURES'

....

Lorenzo Mariano and F. Xavier Medina

Introduction

In this chapter, our interest is focused on a very specific spectrum in relation to *pure food*: it relates to the construction of the body through sport and fitness cultures. Thus, we ask: what are the processes based on feeding the body only with what is the correct pure food? In this text we will address, through our research, the characteristics that we consider most important in this cultural system of clean eating, where the notions of body, purity, danger, transgressions, punishment and penance occupy a central place. 'Clean' and 'pure' are key concepts in the delimitation of an adequate diet for the configuration of a body and a sports lifestyle linked to fitness.

Fitness as a cultural phenomenon has attracted the attention of social scientists since the late twentieth century (Glassner 1989; Lloyd 1996; Lowe 1998; Volkwein 1998; Andrews et al. 2005). The first approaches, consistent with the epistemological trend of those years, gave a special role to physical culture and practices and personal meanings (Markula 1995; Moore 1997). The focus later turned to professional contexts, with special attention given to the culture of bodybuilders (Bolin 1992; Randall et al. 1992; Moore 1997; Volkwein 1998; Aksoy Sugiyama 2014). The literature on sports, gender and identity also increased during those years (Bunsell 2013; Johnston 1996; Klein 1993; Markula 1995; Randall et al. 1992). Finally, the research carried out led to macroreflections on postmodern Western societies (Maguire 2007), where the 'discourses about fitness are part of the cultural terrain of contemporary industrialised societies' (McCormack 1999: 156).

Although the bibliographic production on healthy lifestyles and physical activity has not stopped growing, work from a pathologising perspective has also addressed the phenomenon of what has now become known as 'reverse anorexia', muscle dysmorphia and other body image and related disorders (see Pope et al. 1993, 1994, 1997, 1999). The eating practices of these groups have also been analysed, sometimes serving as, in anthropological terms, 'merchants of astonishment', as Geertz memorably put it (2000: 60). For example, in the case of the bodybuilder culture, the need to take on as much protein and calories as possible becomes paramount, as Parasecoli (2008: 99) highlights: 'Translating grams and proteins into actual, available foods is not always easy. Eating is often viewed as refuelling.' That is why it is very common for bodybuilders to eat an average of thirty to forty eggs per day (cited by Aksoy Sugiyama 2014: 500). In the words of one bodybuilder cited by Andrews et al. (2005: 886):

> In the days right before a competition, daily intake in terms of diet can be reduced to 1000 kcal per day, with virtually no fat, while during 'bulking-up' season (increasing body mass), daily calorie intake can be over 5000 kcal (8 meals) per day.

In addition to these strict diets, eating practices include a variety of food supplements and, on occasions, the always controversial steroids.

Kuhn's work (2013) on cross-fitness, one of the most fashionable fitness practices, points out how the beginnings of this activity combined high-intensity exercise with a Palaeolithic-inspired diet (the Paleo Diet). This research aims to move away from the professional world of bodybuilding, with the analysis focusing on body-related practices and medical approaches. Beyond the competitive world, postmodern societies have aggressively embraced fitness in a myriad of different practices that currently seem to configure a healthy lifestyle. An increasing number of people follow a fitness regime (body and dietary practices for 'body fitness'). Today, fitness cultures offer a privileged space in which the convergence of postmodern discourses about the body, performative elements of self and identity, and the contemporary discussion of what is 'healthy' are analysed. It is a cultural context within, or even appropriated by, the capitalist discourse of the twenty-first century.

This chapter has been conceived mainly from the perspective of the anthropology of food, and we must bear in mind that the different sets of methods used from this field have their own characteristics, perspectives and applications (Hubert 2004; Macbeth and MacClancy 2004; Medina 2004, 2019; Messer 2004; López García, Mariano and Medina 2016). For this reason, in this research, an ethnographic approach employing a holistic and embodied methodology is adopted, derived from lived experience among the study's subjects (Tierney and Ohnuki-Tierney 2012), putting the focus very firmly on food and the phenomena related to it.

This chapter provides an ethnographic review of dietary practices framed within the fitness lifestyle. These are men and women aged between twenty and forty, who go regularly to the gym or engage in cross-fitness in Spain. They share knowledge and advice on social media sites or hire professional coaches that establish exercise and nutritional practices for them to follow so that they can attain the model body and level of 'fitness', which follows a story that combines both aesthetic and health concepts. Through the analysis of this amalgam of discourses and practices, we want the reader to delve into the culinary practices and their meanings, including the contradictions that define the identity of this group.

Although they also study or work, and have limited spare time, an increasing number of people are caught up in this culture, including those who fail at attempts to control and chisel their body. In other words, although this discourse manifests itself to differing degrees based on categories like gender, social class, education and income, it is a discourse that increasingly influences the postmodern individual, as manifested through the growing importance of the fitness industry and the huge proliferation of forums and websites devoted to this subject.

The Importance of Purity

A few decades ago in 1966, Mary Douglas defined *uncleanness* as 'matter out of place' (1966: 41). In this chapter, we focus on feeding practices – particularly the 'placed' and the 'out of place'– of a growing number of people in following what they call a healthy lifestyle in order to achieve a particular type of body. As they share ideas about body shape and exercise, and eating practices as well as forms of socialisation, it is possible to discuss them in terms of a culture or a subculture. We call them members of a *fitness culture* to distinguish the participants from *bodybuilders* – professionals with a different body model, framed within the context of competition or professionalisation – on which ethnographic research has focused on various areas, such as identity, gender and the anthropology of the body. This group includes women and men – as mentioned above, usually between the ages of twenty and forty – who spend between four and eight hours per week working out, while at the same time engaging in very particular eating practices, commonly known as *clean eating*.

'Clean eating' implies a total separation of certain 'pure' foods and sports supplements from foods that are 'impure' or 'dirty'. In order to be part of this culture, must one learn to eat in a particular manner, adopting popular rhetoric? Becoming an expert on this concept of purity is a central objective. For example, those who join this type of fitness culture know and describe the 'foods that are pure' (proteins, fats, etc.) per 100 grams, using scales to weigh every gram or surfing the internet to choose the most 'pure' foods. When deciding what they should eat, they exclude thoughts of pleasure or price in favour of the criteria of 'clean' and 'pure', which thereby become keywords for this emerging culture.

Along these lines, some of the practices of this group are the following:

- Eating food supplements daily (in this regard, protein powder, branched-chain amino acids (BCAAs) and/or creatine are the basic food supplements used, but other food supplements can also be used by long-term followers of this lifestyle).
- Implementing a rigorous assessment of what they eat and when they eat it.
- Employing portion control of serving sizes, which are always weighed and measured. Until very recently, aspects such as the taste of food and the pleasure of eating were marginalised or completely banished from consideration, with people eating 'the food that the body needs'.

Given this reality, what are these processes that are based on feeding the body with only that which is the *correct pure food*? The following is a brief description of the most important characteristics of this *clean eating* cultural system, where notions of purity, danger, taboos, transgressions or even punishment and penitence hold a privileged position. Thus, 'clean' and 'pure' are key concepts in the delimitation of *eating adequately* and are a central part of the configuration of a body and a lifestyle; colonising spaces like the gym, the supermarket or kitchen; and, ultimately, building an identity.

Searching Carefully for Purity

In April 2013, one piece of news spread like wildfire among gym regulars, fitness addicts and habitual consumers of sports supplements. The issue caused heated debate because it directly concerned the culinary practices of this group of individuals, who were accustomed to checking – and relying upon – the labels of food and products they eat. In a review of a series of the most widely used protein powder products, the 'purity' of each product was questioned. The analysis, documented on a specialist website,[1] alerted the public to a case of suspected fraud involving two products of one of the world's most popular and widely recognised protein powder brands. The following information could be read in the report:

In the case of ISO 100 Smooth Banana flavour, the product label claims that the protein content is 89 percent, but according to the results of the sample tested, the protein content was lower, 73.92 percent protein, offsetting the resulting deficit with an excess of carbohydrates. The carbohydrate content should be close to 2 percent according to labelling and, nevertheless, according to the results of the analyses, carbohydrate content was 22.99 percent.

For the subjects of our research, this is no minor issue, not only in terms of the fraud itself, but also in relation to review processes, i.e. those practices responsible for assessing the quality, the *purity*, of the food consumed. A distinguishing feature of this group of people is their deep concern about knowing exactly what it is they are eating (food composition, what is known as 'macros': the percentage of protein, carbohydrate and fat in a food or supplement) and adjusting the amount consumed throughout the day. This behaviour is not exclusive to this group, as a concern about 'labelling' is shared by people with orthorexia or those concerned with feeding themselves exclusively with organic products. Nevertheless, in the case of fitness addicts, the attention given is close to that of people with allergies, with the components or even traces of everything that they are going to consume being reviewed carefully. Accordingly, when they shop at the supermarket, these people take the time to review product labels, a selection process in which price is only a minor consideration. The important thing is the definition of 'clean': matter in place.

In the Spanish gyms where we carried out our research, some of the conversations revolved around the 'brands' of supplements that were reliable, although more expensive, while equally common was the recommendation of products that ended up in the pantries of a large part of this group, such as generic-brand oats from Mercadona, a popular supermarket chain: 'they are very good, at a great price'. Along these lines, one can find videos or websites recommending how to make fitness purchases in supermarkets.[2] In the choice between 'purity' and 'cost', there is always a winner: as pure as your pockets can afford. For example, in relation to consumption of protein – the most consumed food supplement and the one with which almost all those surveyed began – the market distinguishes two groups, separated by the percentage of 'purity' of isolated and concentrated protein. Huge jars of powder can be seen in some gyms and speciality stores; they contain whey protein of high biological value that is subjected to a process of more or less complex filtration to remove the lactose and fats. Isolated proteins have a purity of 90–95 percent, while the concentrated protein can be between 30 percent and 89 percent. The price varies significantly, so those who cannot afford to pay for the greatest amount of purity throughout the year choose to purchase it in isolated months of increased exercise, generally in the run-up to summer. For the purposes of our discussion here, one fact is essential: integrated into that culture is a learning process that involves distinguishing the purity and determining the appropriate price of a food or product based on that purity. Thus, it is not uncommon to hear about some product reviews extolling an intermediate equilibrium: 'It's not as pure as you would like [the protein], but the price is great. I use it in the winter, when you always wear more layers and it is not as noticeable [that you've gained a bit of weight].'

The question of the reliability of labels has a prominent place in forums and specialist websites. Thus, websites often cite scientific studies among other tactics to increase confidence in a particular product or food. Furthermore, social networks create a space for learning and facilitate discussions. However, there is also room for humour, as exemplified by a conversation on Twitter about one product bought in a supermarket that promises to have high protein content for less than one euro. The humorous tone arose when one person asked about the analysis of the product's amino acids (the aminogram!), using the character on the labels to laugh at the advertising as well as some group members' obsession with labels. In addition, this conversation allows us to appreciate the expert knowledge of the followers of this culture: this product is a 'rip-off', a way to cheat 'ordinary people', but not them and their careful and expert interpretation of the label. Accordingly, a classic example of the nature of the debate among fitness culture followers relates to the question of whether eating cornflakes for breakfast is healthy. Some advertisements have marketed cornflakes as a 'fitness' product, even as part of a healthy nutrition programme that helps one regain or attain a slender figure, a type of marketing aimed specifically at women. But after reviewing these products, they are found to have a high level of sugars, 'a high glycaemic index', and are therefore misleading and far from 'clean'. Thus, followers change cornflakes for oats, explaining this substitution with a 'scientific' discourse about their components or jokey comments about fraudulent advertising, remarking on the population's belief in 'healthy' power drinks and the purity of bottled juices.[3]

In general, this group is characterised by an obsession with being informed. As a result, they have specialist knowledge of what they eat, citing works published in scientific journals on nutrition so that they can adapt these findings to their personal food intake; incidentally, this differs significantly from one user to another. Some of them, who are more knowledgeable or with professional degrees, call upon or use as an argument the expert discourse of scientific publications, which they cite when voicing doubts or when a debate about nutrition arises. For many of them, this is a way of giving themselves an air of prestige and knowledge, sometimes to attract future clients: the scientist as an authority and 'tradition' and beliefs as powerful agents. In the majority of the gyms in which we carried out our work, these expert discourses are much more infrequent, but it is also possible to hear comments on a particular article, which call into question a fact hitherto taken for granted. In the words of one of our informants: 'Yes, I read that avoiding carbohydrates after six in the afternoon is a myth, there is research that says it does not matter.'

This obsession with food may cause people to stop eating out because, even if they order tuna or chicken salad, they are concerned about monitoring the preparation process, knowing the exact amount of nutrients and what they are really eating. This feature has been described as part of the pathological process of vigorexia (Glassner 1989; Lowe 1998), namely, difficult social interactions. This pathological element is not hard to locate among our informants: usually a dinner out with friends is permitted once per week, but they usually choose the healthiest dishes, without eating the chips or eliminating sauces, and do not consume alcohol. However, this is not regarded as a great loss. In the words of one individual:

> Yes, it is a sacrifice, but eventually you get used to it ... what happens to me now that it's not worth it ... to go out, get drunk, and work all week. I go out with friends, I have a Coke Zero, or dinner with water, and it's no problem.

In this regard, the process of building a diet, eating the right amounts, setting mealtimes and embracing taboos are part of the culinary everyday of *clean eating*.

Building a Diet: Some Basic 'Clean Eating' Notions

As mentioned above, the guidelines for organising a 'clean' diet must fit into a complex set of rules, including what foods should be eaten or not, which defines a complex culinary scene that adapts to different places and times of day. But it is important to note an idea that persists among the members of this culture: they do not 'follow a diet', at least not in the traditional way (e.g. a period of time of caloric restriction with a specific purpose, usually to get skinny). Following an 'Eat-Clean Diet' means embracing a lifestyle that includes a particular way of eating. The concept of purity in this sense has a very constitutional meaning: not only is it a lifestyle in terms of eating, it is also a lifestyle that revolves around the idea that it is 'healthy'. We now outline some of the characteristics of this 'pure' way to feed and clean the body and build the discourse of the healthy.

The Time Variable Defines a Changing Gastronomic Scene

The training schedule causes the idea of the 'right diet' to fluctuate over the course of the year. The specific Eat-Clean Diet used will be different if a hypertrophy-specific training programme is being carried out (which seeks to induce fast muscle growth and is usually characterised by hypercaloric and hyperproteic food intake) or if a muscle definition training programme is being followed (which seeks to increase fat loss without muscle loss and is also associated with hypocaloric and hyperproteic food intake). This way of conceptualising training and dietary requirements has been hegemonic for years and is still used in the majority of gyms where we carried out our work. The distinction between periods is constructed in relation to the degree of purity of the diet: during periods of bulking-up, it is possible to eat 'less clean', with the accepted 'capped' result, that is, coating the muscle with some fat. The idea is to maximise muscle gain. In the stages of muscle definition, the 'purity' of the diet becomes restrictive. As one personal trainer told us:

> At this time, although you think it's just a little, at the end of the day it's a lot. Today you miss raisins and *caffè macchiato*, you use sweetener instead of sugar … and you say, well, it wasn't so bad. But one day here, then another day and another day … in the end it all counts and you say screw it.

Weight fluctuations between the two periods can be up to 10 kg, and sometimes more. During definition periods, diets are respected gram by gram, and may include supplements known as 'fat burners', which promise to activate one's metabolism and reduce body fat. However, this training schedule based on two periods is now disappearing: these days, the recommendation is progressive, sustained and slow muscle gain, limiting fat gain. It is understood as a healthier model, which emphasises not diet, but lifestyle.

The diet should be adapted based on training and nontraining days and on the time of day the training is to take place (establishing the pre-workout and post-workout meal). It will matter if training takes place at 10 am, at 5 pm or 9 pm, and the same goes for nontraining days. Therefore, 'Eat-Clean' is not just a matter of choosing pure food; it is also important that this intake is done in the 'proper' way. The notion of purity, in this case, is also a matter of time, which is inevitably related to the training type and the load.

Banish Pleasure: A Utilitarian Use of Nutrition

'Eat-Clean' nutrition (the concept of 'purity') is almost tautological in nature; classical nutritional knowledge is dismissed and replaced by 'logic-based' nutrition in the struggle to reach a specific body shape (muscular type, in many cases wanting a fat percentage below 10 percent). Therefore, the search for 'pure' food displaces the social attributes of eating (as previously mentioned, those following this regime may stop eating out or with friends), the pleasure of eating, palatability, taste, etc. all being placed in a subordinate position. Research carried out on the bodybuilder culture has emphasised this same idea, understanding the food as 'fuel', as a means to an end (Aksoy Sugiyama 2014). The image of purity in this case requires a utilitarian definition and practice: what does the body you want to be living in need to eat? When should you eat those foods? This means, for example, eating listlessly, without desire, simply because it is what needs to be done. In the words of one informant:

> When you're bulking up, you have to eat a lot. And sometimes it's difficult, because you have to eat when you're not hungry. A couple of cans

of tuna or a tuna sandwich with rye bread … You eat because that's what the diet says you should do.

Although it is beyond the scope of this chapter, we should like to highlight here how modern fitness practices and ideologies try to fight against banishing flavour and pleasure, exploring culinary diversity in order to break away from the traditional monotony of 'tuna, rice and chicken', the classic fitness diet.[4]

Everyone in the group we studied is aware of the fact that training becomes meaningful only with proper eating habits. The right eating habits include a strict diet favouring a high amount of protein, a low sugar and fat intake, and supplemented with drugs. Without disciplining oneself in certain eating habits, the training itself becomes meaningless and, as one informant mentioned, 'a waste of time'. Because of the way in which our informants understand nutritional value, drugs are also treated as a kind of food, especially since they do not even pay attention to the taste of a food anymore (cf. Aksoy Sugiyama 2014).

The Purity of Nutrition: Complex Choices

Defining the 'right' diet is a complex issue. It is a phrase that never tires of being repeated, although there are some general recommendations that need to be customised to fit each person and circumstance. Although these individuals are all part of a community, each has his or her own diet. Many of these people – especially as they are immersed further and further into this culture and want to improve results – hire the services of professionals. Professionals lament this repeated intrusion and defend the need for an individualised and professional diet based on objectives, age, physical activity, etc.

However, there are many other possibilities, so as individuals delve deeper into this world and accumulate knowledge, they are able to design their own diets. In order to do this, there are general guidelines, food list components based on macronutrients, or even tutorials on the internet[5] and software.[6] The basic rule they follow, quoting scientific studies, is to calculate the macronutrient distribution (the 'macros') based on, as we previously commented, the training schedule and the day of the week (training or nontraining day). By way of an example, this table was taken from one of the Spanish reference websites:[7]

Muscle Definition Diet: 35–45 percent carbohydrate, 20–35 percent protein and 15–25 percent fat. Many people believe that to get muscle definition you must completely avoid fat; that's a mistake. Fat will help us in the muscle definition process (using mostly healthy fat).

Mass-Gaining Diet: 50–55 percent carbohydrate, 20–25 percent protein, 25–30 percent fat. Although lower percentages of protein intake are used, the total number of grams of protein intake for the three objectives usually remains stable (provided there is around 2 g per kg of body weight).

Weight Maintenance Diet: 45 percent carbohydrates, 35 percent protein and 25 percent fat. With this food distribution and an adjustment of caloric balance to daily requirements, we will keep our body fat index and muscle percentage as stable as possible.

Together with these recommendations, many web applications that are used to calculate the 'macros' of each food can be easily found on the internet, thus enabling Eat-Clean Diet followers to plan each diet based on the particular requirements.[8] Eating in a 'pure', 'clean' way then becomes a matter of arithmetic: if I have eaten 200 grams of pizza, which has a certain number of carbohydrates, proteins and fat, I'll have to base what I eat for the rest of the day on that and on what I want to get out of the macros.

Organisation as a Basis for the Borders of Purity

The ideology of fitness culture is based on certain cultural topographies, where the gym and the kitchen play a central role. They are built as almost sacred places, where it is understood that effort pays. However, it is not a matter of quantity but quality. To get into a fitness culture, it is not necessary, according to this rationale, to spend large amounts of time training and cooking. It is above all a matter of quality and organisation. There are ideas that are repeated like mantras ('abs [abdominal muscles] are made in the kitchen'), but the key concept is that it is important not to spend too much time and too many resources on this and to do what is required properly. In that sense, organisation plays a key role not only in training but also in nutrition. Many people choose to spend Sunday afternoons preparing food for the whole week ahead (of course, according to recommendations), which will be labelled and stored in several Tupperware containers, indicating the day and time they should be eaten, freezing the rest. This food may also be taken to work if it is impossible to eat it at home.

The progress of this 'fitness culture' can also be noted in the following matters: nowadays, it is possible to order (pure) fitness food from home, as there are companies[9] that deliver it perfectly labelled, describing exactly what is being eaten. These foods are received in packaged form, ready to eat or conserve, and with the company's confirmation that they meet the standards of purity demanded. Therefore, the food industry here provides yet another aid in a complex decision-making process, as it is a third party that either prepares the food or selects the best products from all those possible.

What to Eat: The Conversion of Food into the Sum of Its Components

As has been suggested before, 'clean' eating, attaining that definition of purity, is not just achieved by adding 'pure' products, but also through the complex sum of the components of all the food eaten. So, in theory, one can consume all types of food as long as it matches the requirements of macros, although the norm is not eating pizza and then adding or subtracting to compensate throughout the day. Unlike other diets, in which specific foods and grams are used, in this diet, foods are weighed to obtain the amount of carbohydrates, proteins and fat that is needed.

To continue with the idea of converting foods into the sum of their components, we are going to talk about one of the mantras related to the fitness food supply: the importance of the protein (about two grams per kilo of body weight per day) that must be consumed daily at each meal. That is why it is common for breakfast to include omelettes with egg whites or turkey, even though these omelettes are not a typical breakfast food in Spain. For several years, it has been commonly recommended by nutritionists to eat several meals a day, although within the wider society this is an idea that is starting to be dismissed in favour of the sum of the macronutrients taken daily. Here again we find a gap between the discourse of websites and social media networks, and the more traditional gym discourse.

Taboos and Risks

To finish this impressionistic review of the cultural understanding of pure food, we would like to point out that clean eating clearly rejects other gastronomic concepts that are 'out of place' and that we could say are 'impure'. As in other cultural groups, there is food considered taboo, food that goes against the cultural logic of the fitness culture. It is true that the modern rhetoric of adding macros emphasises the idea of 'eating everything', but in practice this is not so. There are 'impure' foods, those that have to be dismissed: the *taboos* in fitness. We can mention, for example, cold cuts like chorizo sausage, fried or frozen products that can be bought in any supermarket (pasties, fried squid rings, etc.) and cakes, among many others. Regardless, companies work on making similar products to these (such as protein cakes)[10] or fitness substitutes (like zero-calorie sauces).[11] As in ancient religions, one must do penance for excess. When one veers from purity, the path of virtue demands a very big effort be made – increasing the amount of workouts or even fasting – which once again echoes scientific research that supports the benefits of working out or tells us how to carry it out. In the world of fitness, sin also carries a punishment.

There also exist ritualised periods in which it is possible to 'sin'. This is akin to the indulgences of the Christian tradition, where sins are not forgiven, but are temporarily exempted from carrying penalties. This is known as the 'cheat meal', a meal (normally eaten once a week) that can be consumed during periods of hypertrophy. For those meals, the rules are relaxed and eating hamburgers, chips or pizza is possible. However, it is only one meal, and moderation is advised so as not to lose what has been achieved throughout the week. On this occasion, it is possible to 'sin' without being 'impure', though under restrained limits. The 'cheat meal' should be healthy, both for your body and your mind, as it breaks the monotony of the diet. However, this is very important: the cheat meal is excluded from the muscle definition periods.

In relation to risks, engaging in a fitness cooking lifestyle implies addressing and combating the challenges of veering from the path of purity – the dangers of, so to speak, 'falling into the filth'. This issue transfers discussions in the field of food and bodies to the realm of ideology and morality, constructing the ideological basis of fitness culture through attributes such as perseverance, strength and struggle. The principal aim, of course, is to control the emotional aspect of the individual, that part that wants to surrender to desires such as pleasure and attain the immediate reward. What is wrong is eating according to the wishes of the stomach (the short term and the emotional) instead of in search of the desired body (governed by reason and the long term). That is the way one of our informants, George, explained it:

> The problem is that for people who are not professionals (and even for them), our brain is always testing us because what our body likes is to be comfortable and to be given what it feels like having at the time. Things like … Well, I have accomplished this, so I am going to give myself a reward, or, I am fed up and I have no time, so I am going to skip my diet. I feel like doing that today, nothing will happen … Or: Why sacrifice myself so much if, in the end, I'm not going to get there, etc., etc.? It is not hard to improve little by little, but getting a muscular and defined body that gains admiration is difficult to get, not because we are not able to do it, not at all, but because we quit before pulling out all the stops.

And also:

> A day in which everything has been done brings us closer to our target and reinforces us both at a physical and mental level. Skipping a training session, not doing it to your full potential or skipping your diet weakens

you. The following day you don't usually feel very well and you do it the wrong way again because you get into what I call a destructive spiral, and although it is possible, you can go back to the right path after a few days, that time has made you go backwards. Well, we must look for a balance between what we want and what we are ready to give and be aware of it. As I told you, I had levels of 9–10 percent fatty tissue for years; now for years I've had a level of around 12 percent. Would I like to maintain the 9–10 percent? Of course, but I'm not prepared to give what is required to get it.

The dangers of falling into an 'impure' diet do not come just from eating forbidden food or falling prey to bodily desires, but also from not eating the right amount, and that concern appears clearly defined in the representations of catabolism and the fear of protein breakdown. Although this is a subject of debate, the idea is widespread that if you exercise intensively for more than an hour, or you do not eat proteins for several hours – such as during the night – the body starts to catalyse: to lose the muscle gained. This fear also has to do with the pure diet: in some cases, these people, mirroring the behaviour of professionals, even set an alarm during the night to get up and eat. However, the most common pattern is consuming proteins during dinner and in the morning and supplementing them with casein (protein-rich) shakes, which are supposed to be slow-release products.

Conclusion

We have seen some of the cultural rules of diet in fitness culture. Definitions of purity include a complex cultural structure where symbols, appropriations of the scientific discourse, the incarnation of postmodern discourse, mercantilist health and, because 'every person is a world unto himself', the eternal strategy of 'personalised' recommendations according to experience are mixed together.

As we proposed at the beginning of this chapter and despite showing that it is adopted differently depending on categories like gender, social class, education or income, this kind of discourse can increasingly be found in 'postmodern' individuals. This fact is made evident by observing the growing importance of the fitness industry or the growing proliferation of webpages, forums and social media sites dedicated to this issue. The focus is on becoming a kind of 'expert', surfing the internet to choose the most 'pure' foods and excluding thoughts of pleasure or price in favour of the criteria of 'clean' and 'pure', the keywords for this emerging culture. It is a diet that deeply separates purity from impurity, cleanliness from filth, transferring these distinctions from the dish – or the shake – to bodies and individuals.

Lorenzo Mariano Juárez is Assistant Professor in Anthropology in Faculty of Nursing and Therapy at the Universidad de Extremadura, Extremadura, Spain.

F. Xavier Medina is a Professor and Academic and Programme Director in the Food Systems, Culture and Society Knowledge Area of the Faculty of Health Sciences, Open University of Catalonia, Barcelona, Spain.

Notes

1. http://www.migimnasio.com/es_es/detectado-presunto-fraude-iso100-elite-whey-dymatise/ (last accessed 21 March 2013).
2. See https://www.youtube.com/watch?v=xAn_sWvOaj8 (last accessed 10 September 2021).
3. This is a recurring example among our informants. In online forums, this, like many other issues, is submitted for debate, with arguments that offer more particular points of view. See, for example: http://es.fitness.com/forum/threads/127532-cornflakles-malos (last accessed 10 April 2022). It is another feature of this group, where on social media sites the speed of discussion, and on many occasions the level of the arguments, is much higher than those among the users we spoke with.
4. Today it is possible to track on forums, websites or social media sites like Twitter or Instagram the effort to restructure the diverse and attractive aesthetic of fitness food from a culinary point of view, as well as the search for 'fitness' cakes or desserts, prioritising aesthetics over taste.
5. See e.g. https://www.youtube.com/watch?v=RP_vyRZUksk (last accessed 10 September 2021).
6. See e.g. *Nutrition Data* for Android devices.
7. http://nutritiondata.self.com (last accessed 10 September 2021).
8. See http://www.calorieking.com; http://nutritiondata.self.com (last accessed 4 April 2022).
9. See, for example: http://www.musclefood.com/, or in Spanish: http://fitfoodmarket.es/supermercados-fitness/ ((last accessed 22 February 2016).
10. http://www.myprotein.es/nutricion-deportiva/tortitas-de-proteina/10867261.html (last accessed 22 February 2016).
11. See https://www.nutritienda.com/es/walden-farms (last accessed 22 February 2016).

References

Aksoy Sugiyama, C. (2014) Bodybuilder's Life Style: The Diet and the Obsession with Body, *Ankara Üniversitesi Dil ve Tarih-Coğrafya Fakültesi Dergisi*, 54(1): 493–506.
Andrews, G.J., Sudwell, M.I. and Sparkes, A.C. (2005) Towards a Geography of Fitness: An Ethnographic Case Study of the Gym in British Bodybuilding Culture, *Social Science and Medicine*, 60: 877–91.

Bolin, A. (1992) Appeal, Food and Fat: Competitive Bodybuilding, Gender and the Diet. In Moore, P.S. (ed.) *Building Bodies*, Rutgers University Press, New Brunswick, NJ, pp. 184–208.

Bunsell, T. (2013) *Strong and Hard Women: An Ethnography of Female Bodybuilding*, Routledge, Abingdon.

Douglas, M. (1966) *Purity and Danger: An Analysis of the Concepts of Pollution and Taboo*, Psychology Press, Hove.

Geertz C. (2000) *Los Usos de la Diversidad*, Paidós, Barcelona.

Glassner, B. (1989) Fitness and the Postmodern Self, *Journal of Health Behaviour*, 30: 180–91.

Hubert, A. (2004) Qualitative Research in the Anthropology of Food: A Comprehensive Qualitative-Quantitative Approach. In Macbeth, H. and MacClancy, J. (eds) *Researching Food Habits: Methods and Problems*, Berghahn Books, Oxford, pp. 41–54.

Johnston, L. (1996) Flexing Femininity: Female Body-Builders Refiguring 'the Body', *Gender, Place and Culture*, 3(3): 327–40.

Klein, A.M. (1993) *Little Big Men: Bodybuilding Subculture and Gender Construction*, State University of New York Press, New York.

Kuhn, S. (2013) The Culture of CrossFit: A Lifestyle Prescription for Optimal Health and Fitness, *Senior Theses – Anthropology*, Paper 1. Published at: http://ir.library.illinoisstate.edu/sta/1. Accessed on 7 October 2022.

Lloyd, M. (1996) Feminism, Aerobics and the Politics of the Body, *Body and Society* 2(2): 79–98.

López García, J., Mariano, L. and Medina, F.X. (2016) Usos y Significados Contemporáneos de la Comida Desde la Antropología de la Alimentación en América Latina y España, *Revista de Dialectología y Tradiciones Populares*, 71(2): 327–70.

Lowe, M. (1998) *Women of Steel: Female Body Builders and the Struggle for Self-Definition*, New York University Press, New York.

Macbeth, H. and MacClancy, J. (2004) Introduction: How to Do Anthropologies of Food. In Macbeth, H. and MacClancy, J. (eds) *Researching Food Habits. Methods and Problems*: Berghahn Books, Oxford, pp. 1–17.

Maguire, J.S. (2007) *Fit for Consumption: Sociology and the Business of Fitness*, Routledge, New York.

Markula, P. (1995) Firm But Shapely, Fit But Sexy, Strong But Thin: The Postmodern Aerobicizing Female Bodies, *Sociology of Sport Journal*, 12(4): 424–53.

McCormack, D. (1999) Body Shopping: Reconfiguring Geographies of Fitness, *Gender, Place and Culture*, 6(2): 155–78.

Medina, F.X. (2004) Tell Me What You Eat and You Will Tell Me Who You Are: Methodological Notes on the Interaction between Researcher and Informants in the Anthropology of Food. In Macbeth, H. and MacClancy, J. (eds) *Researching Food Habits: Methods and Problems*, Berghahn Books, Oxford, pp. 52–62.

_____. (2019) Food Culture: Anthropology of Food and Nutrition. In Ferranti, P., Berry, E. and Anderson, J. (eds) *Encyclopedia of Food Security and Sustainability*, Elsevier, Amsterdam, pp. 307–10.

Messer, E. (2004) Food, Culture, Political and Economic Identity: Revitalising the Food Systems Perspective in the Study of Food-Based Identity. In Macbeth, H. and

MacClancy, J. (eds) *Researching Food Habits: Methods and Problems*, Berghahn Books, Oxford, pp. 181–92.

Moore, P. (ed.) (1997) *Building Bodies (Perspectives on the Sixties)*, Rutgers University Press, New Brunswick, NJ.

Parasecoli, F. (2008) *Bite Me: Food in Popular Culture*, Berg, New York.

Pope, H.G. Jr., Gruber, A.J., Choi, P., Olivardia, R. and Phillips, K.A. (1997) Muscle Dysmorphia: An Unrecognized Form of Body Dysmorphic Disorder, *Psychosomatics*, 38: 548–57.

Pope, H.G. Jr., and Katz, D. (1994) Psychiatric and Medical Effects of Anabolic-Androgenic Steroid Use: A Controlled Study of 160 Athletes, *Archives of General Psychiatry*, 51: 375–82.

Pope, H.G. Jr., Katz, D. and Hudson, J. (1993) Anorexia Nervosa and 'Reverse Anorexia' among 108 Bodybuilders, *Comprehensive Psychiatry*, 34: 406–9.

Pope, H.G., Jr., Olivardia, R., Gruber, A.J. and Borowiecki, J. (1999) Evolving Ideals of Male Body Image as Seen through Action Toys, *International Journal of Eating Disorders*, 26: 65–72.

Randall, A.J., Hall, S.F. and Rogers, M.F. (1992) Masculinity on Stage: Competitive Male Bodybuilders, *Studies in Popular Culture*, 14: 57–69.

Tierney, R.K. and Ohnuki-Tierney, E. (2012) Anthropology of Food. In Pilcher, J.M. (ed.) *The Oxford Handbook of Food History*, Oxford University Press, Oxford, pp. 117–134.

Volkwein, K.A.E. (1998) Introduction: Fitness as Cultural Phenomenon, in Volkwein, K.A.E. (ed.) *Fitness as Cultural Phenomenon*. Wasman Publishers, Münster, pp. ix–xxiii.

CHAPTER 6

'PURE FOOD' IN CATERING FOR PUBLIC INSTITUTIONS: POLICIES AND ASPIRATIONS IN THE CITY OF LIVERPOOL, ENGLAND

Lucy Antal

Introduction

From obesity and diet-related ill-health to food insecurity and waste, climate change and loss of biodiversity, declining prosperity and social dislocation, food is not only at the heart of some of our greatest problems of today, but is also a vital part of the solution. This chapter will consider the topic of 'pure food' in relation to the procurement of food for public institutions and the legislation that is beginning to change its provision and sourcing to be aimed at reducing or even omitting processed ingredients. For the purposes of this chapter, I am defining 'pure food' as 'relating to or concerned with the promotion of food that is free from preservatives, colouring or other additives or cultivated without the use of chemical fertilizers'.[1]

The primary focus for this chapter is the provision of foods for different public institutions in the city of Liverpool in northwest England as regards health and education. Specifically, the catering tenders issued for the Royal Liverpool University Hospital (RLUH) and how inclusions of clauses within those tenders lean towards a 'pure food' approach will first be considered. The chapter will then discuss school meals with information on food procurement and staff training, so that any school catering company is encouraged towards the ethics of 'pure food' for the food it serves to approximately 42 percent of Liverpool's schools. I shall refer to legislation, both new and existing within these sections, and then finally I shall write about food provision for children where I believe there should be consideration given to mandatory regulations regarding food provision and sourcing.

The chapter is based on my work with Liverpool Food People and its successor organisations, and on field research undertaken as part of 'The Procuring Food for the Future' project.[2] This was an exploration of the role that anchor institutions (organisations that in addition to their main function can also make a strategic contribution to the local economy, such as universities, schools and hospitals) can play in creating a better food system – one that underpins local food economies and the health of the earth's ecosystems.

The City of Liverpool

Liverpool is in the northwest of England and in the 2021 census had a population of 501,935 people.[3] Known for football, shipping and a particular pop group, it is a multicultural city and its status as a port has long contributed a wide mix of peoples, cultures and religions to the population. Liverpool is home to the oldest Chinese and Black African communities in the United Kingdom, and it housed England's first mosque, established in 1889. As a port city, it amassed great wealth in the eighteenth and nineteenth centuries and was commonly referred to as the Second City of the Empire (after London) due to its involvement in shipbuilding and freight transport.[4] However, the massive decline in shipping and industry and the advent of containerisation during the mid- to late twentieth century had the effect of creating some of the highest unemployment rates in the United Kingdom during the early 1980s, as the docks and traditional manufacturing industries went into sharp decline. In recent years, Liverpool has reinvented itself as a destination for tourism, fuelled by regeneration projects such as the Albert Dock, the creation of the new retail shopping centre, Liverpool One, and excellent cultural attractions and events, including being awarded the title of Capital of Culture 2008, as well as a burgeoning student population who attend Liverpool's three universities.

Whilst this is all good news and a welcome return to more prosperous times, Liverpool also still has a legacy of ill health and early mortality that can be attributed to high levels of unemployment (in some cases intergenerational), poor-quality housing, the decline of food-related skills, loss of access to fresh food in certain areas, and a density of fast-food and convenience stores, all of which has led to what can be referred to as 'food deserts' and swamps. It was calculated that in March 2021, 15.6 percent of households in Liverpool were in fuel poverty and 28 percent of the children were in low-income families. In comparison with 317 English local authorities nationwide, Liverpool was deemed the third most-deprived local authority as regards 'health deprivation and disability' in Britain.[5]

Furthermore, in Liverpool life expectancy for both men and women is lower. There are disproportionately high early death rates from heart disease and stroke in Liverpool, with the male mortality rate from cardiovascular disease before age of seventy-five at 478 per 100,000 deaths in 2021.[6] It has also been calculated that around 80 percent of premature heart disease is preventable through changes in lifestyle (e.g. Wald and Law 2003). In Liverpool, rates of adult 'healthy eating', smoking and physical activity are worse than the average for all of England.[7] The effects of COVID-19 have added to these problems and the mortality rate.

The Sustainable Food Places Network and Liverpool Food People

According to its own website, the Sustainable Food Places Network (SFPN) is 'a partnership programme led by the Soil Association, Food Matters and Sustain (SFPN), the alliance for better food and farming, which is funded by the Esmée Fairbairn Foundation and The National Lottery Community Fund'. It 'brings together pioneering food partnerships from towns, cities, boroughs, districts and counties across the UK that are driving innovation and best practice on all aspects of healthy and sustainable food'.[8]

In this way, the SFPN helps people and places share challenges, explore practical solutions and develop best practice on key food issues. The SFPN approach involves developing a cross-sector partnership of local public agencies, businesses and non-governmental organisations (NGOs) committed to working together to make healthy and sustainable food a defining characteristic of where they live. As of 2015, the key aims that the SFPN champions, from addressing food poverty to tackling the climate emergency, were being addressed within the Liverpool City Region by a diverse grouping of NGOs, businesses, community organisations, the health sector and local government under the name Liverpool Food People, which was established in 2011 and dissolved in 2018. This role has subsequently been taken up by Feeding Liverpool.[9]

Food and Better Public Health Strategies in Liverpool

Recently, health authorities in Liverpool have been seeking to adjust the way in which healthy living is encouraged within the city. The Clinical Commissioning Group (CCG) of the National Health Service (NHS) has been spearheading a change in healthcare by focusing on prevention rather than treatment. They want to spend more money upfront on encouraging better, healthier living through physical and mental activity in order to have a positive effect on wellbeing and thus lead to a healthier population. Funding is being made available to deliver activities such as projects for growing healthier foods and running cooking courses. The Liverpool NHS CCG has also played a key role in the changes made to the one catering tender made for the RLUH.

Liverpool Food People produced a food action plan that detailed its aims and ascribed particular actions. Procurement of foods was one of its important themes. Liverpool Food People judged that it was incumbent upon public institutions in Liverpool to consider the quality and provenance of the food that they were supplying to the population that used their services. In particular, key organisations such as hospitals and schools have a role to play in the promotion and supply of 'pure food' as part of their educational brief.

Strategies for Hospitals in Liverpool

In this chapter the strategies for the RLUH, as a key public institution in the city, are used to exemplify relevant actions that can be taken – in particular, how making changes to their procurement requirements makes a difference to the sourcing of food and, in this way, not only provides healthier and fresher food, but also sets an example for patients, staff and visitors.

In recent years, the hospital has undergone an extensive rebuilding programme and was officially reopened in January 2023. An opportunity arose in 2014 for Liverpool Food People to offer advice to the sustainability and catering managers at the RLUH as they prepared the catering tender for the new building. Also, those administering the Liverpool NHS CCG were keen to see social value principles and sustainable food embedded within the contracts. In this connection, recommendations had been published by the national government regarding the procurement policies for hospitals, called the Balanced Scorecard (BSC), which sets out mandatory requirements for hospital food standards, including the following priorities:

- *Health and Wellbeing* – the differing nutritional needs of consumers and understanding consumer behaviours to ensure uptake of nutritious healthy food at different life stages, e.g. to help a child concentrate at school or help an elderly patient recover more quickly.
- *Supply Chain Traceability* – to ensure the integrity of food supply chains (avoiding any repeat of the horse meat scandal).[10]
- *Seasonality & Variety* – better uptake of seasonal food to reduce the negative impact of environmentally inappropriate production methods such as wrong climate for production of a given food (tomatoes in December).
- *Food Safety and Hygiene* – exploring the long-term impacts of routine use of antibiotics in livestock production and concerns over animal welfare.

(Department for Environment, Food and Rural Affairs 2014)

At the same time, the Soil Association,[11] which campaigns on healthy, humane and sustainable food, farming and land use, and that champions organic food, has created a 'catering mark' called Food for Life. This catering mark provides an independent endorsement that meals are fresh, healthy, sustainable and meet the nutritional element of the Government Buying Standards (GBS).[12] A request was made for the bidders for the new contract to apply for this catering mark and to achieve at least the Bronze Award standard as soon as possible, which includes the following mandatory requirements:

- At least 75 percent of dishes are freshly prepared from unprocessed ingredients.
- Meat is from farms that satisfy UK welfare standards.
- Eggs are from cage-free hens.
- Menus are seasonal and in-season produce is highlighted.
- Catering staff are supported with skills training in fresh food preparation and the Catering Mark.
- No fish is served from the Marine Conservation Society 'fish to avoid' list.
- Information is on display about food provenance.[13]

If we look at these recommendations in the context of 'pure food', we can see how applying both the GBS and the Food for Life catering mark[14] to the specifics of the catering tender can make a difference to the quality and nutritional value of the food served within the hospital.

The catering tenders were written with a request that the bidders incorporate both the GBS analysis and a request for a Silver Food for Life catering mark to be achieved within twelve to eighteen months of the opening of the new hospital. In order to comply with this requirement, bidders would need to look at the feasibility of establishing a Central Processing Unit within the wider Liverpool City Region; this would be in contrast to the previous catering system, where food was prepared and sourced in southeast England and transported by road to Liverpool. This also fitted in with Liverpool Food People's aspiration to connect producers to consumers, supporting local procurement routes and relationships that reflect sustainable food ethics, by reducing carbon miles, creating jobs locally and supporting local growers and producers in northwest England.

In addition to the catering tenders, Liverpool Food People recommended that the RLUH should look towards creating a food and drink strategy that laid out the expectations of the hospital trust regarding *all* the food and drink sold on their premises, including those in the retail units, through each contract. This followed the Hospital Food Standards Panel's report on standards for food and drink in NHS hospitals, which was published in August 2014[15] and clearly states that hospitals should meet the challenges of providing nutritional food to support patients' recovery, supporting healthy food choices for staff and visitors, including social responsibility and sustainability within food procurement. This dovetailed with the concerns of the clinicians, nutritionists and dieticians working in the hospital, who had been uncomfortable with the current status quo, whereby they were advising on diet and lifestyle changes to improve health, while working in a hospital where foods high in sugar and fat content were provided as well as promoted and sold in the retail outlets onsite – for example, the prominent display of sugary drinks on special offer and the less prominently displayed 'healthier' options.

A food and drink strategy was prepared by the managers responsible for hotel services, health and wellbeing, and sustainability with input from Liverpool Food People, and was taken to three RLUH trust groups – the Patient Meal Experience Group, the Health and Wellbeing Group, and the Sustainable Development Steering Group – for monitoring and approval.

The new catering contract was awarded to the incumbent caterers ISS. This is a ten-year contract with a further two-year extension. The service provided by ISS to the RLUH is an a la carte selection menu called Eat Well, which supplies a wide range of options for patients, including dietary, culturally and religiously appropriate choices.[16] The plans for the replacement hospital impacted the catering tenders as the new building does not have full commercial kitchens, but instead ward prep kitchens where already plated and prepared food can be heated and served. The argument for this is both one of cost and also service. The hotel services team (who cover food provision, portering and cleaning) have chosen the a la carte heat and serve option on the grounds of offering patients a wider choice of meals than could be managed via a central kitchen and also a preference for diverting staff resources towards patient support – so each ward has a catering team dedicated to ensuring the patients are fed at a time appropriate to their needs and appetite rather than a rigid schedule. There are pros and cons to this approach, but the new design of the hospital means it is the way in which future catering contracts will be managed.

Strategies in Schools in Liverpool

In 2015 in Liverpool, school food was not controlled centrally; each school was able to make its own decision on its own catering provision, with many choosing to outsource it rather than prepare it inhouse. The Office for Standards in Education, Children's Services and Skills (OFSTED) Common Inspection Framework requires OFSTED to inspect how 'children and learners keep themselves healthy, including through healthy eating' (OFSTED 2015). As part of this, inspectors will look at 'the food on offer and visit the canteen to see the atmosphere and culture in the dining space and the effect this has on pupils' behaviour' (ibid.). Inspectors will also look at the 'breadth and balance of the curriculum, of which practical cookery is now a part' (ibid.)

The Transforming School Food Strategy (TSFS), evaluated by the University of Wolverhampton, demonstrated that Liverpool schools that had provided school food 'in house' reported major benefits (Jopling et al. 2011). Interestingly, the focus groups conducted by the research team had revealed that the biggest barrier to improving school food and nutrition was the school environment. Relevant factors included small dining areas and lack of cooking facilities in which to learn about food and nutrition (ibid.).

One school catering company worked hard to ensure students are fed a 'pure food' diet and procure their raw materials as sustainably and ethically as possible. Food For Thought Liverpool[17] was established in 2003 by a group of six local headteachers who had become disillusioned with the poor quality of food served in their schools and formed a not-for-profit school meals company that is owned and managed by all its partner schools. As of 2021, Food For Thought comprised eighty-three schools (approximately 42 percent of Liverpool's schools) and freshly prepared 2,000,000 meals per annum. It did not impose portion control, allowing pupils to choose the food they feel they need. Care about food sourcing was very important to Food For Thought. Fresh organic, free range and sustainable local foods were chosen wherever possible.

Also, all the school cooking staff were trained, and in some cases retrained, to cook using fresh ingredients with a minimum of food waste. Lunch menus are published on the website each day so that parents are made aware of what their children are eating. Liverpool Food People and its successor organisations are very supportive of all that Food For Thought is achieving and highlighted it as an example of best practice for school meal provision as part of the Healthy Family strategy. It had been Liverpool Food People's goal to see more schools follow this style of catering provision. Between 2015 and 2021, Food For Thought significantly increased its operations, more than doubling the number of schools it supplied. It also added food growing to more school spaces, allowing pupils to really understand where their food comes from.

Liverpool Food People carried out research into procurement to enable broader and better understanding of the legislation about food provision within UK public services. Surprisingly, as of 2022, there is as yet no mandatory requirement about food to be served to preschool children in a nursery or childcare setting. This seems to be a striking omission, since OFSTED also inspects nurseries and childcare settings, and yet, unlike for its school inspections, OFSTED does not include food and nutrition provision as part of its assessment.

A paper commissioned by Liverpool Public Health and published in May 2011 had the objective of exploring nutrition and food provision in preschool nurseries in Liverpool in order to develop interventions to promote healthy eating in preschool settings. This report concluded that nurseries required support on healthy eating at policy, knowledge and training levels as the period before a child starts primary school is one of the most critical times for their growth and development (Parker et al. 2011). It is the contention of Liverpool Food People and its successor organisations that this needs to be addressed and that mandatory regulations regarding the provision of food to early years need to be introduced. For many children attending nursery, all of their daily meals will be eaten in that space and thus this is a critical time for the development of bone density and palate, and the setting-up of healthy eating patterns for life. Liverpool Food People made recommendations to the Liverpool City Region Child Poverty and Life Chances Strategy Refresh 2015–18[18] regarding this and suggested that the local authorities need to develop a toolkit (or utilise any that already exists) that sets out strong guidelines for preschool food provision in the Liverpool City Region that will include advice on reducing processed food and salt content, and the nutritional requirements for under-fives.

Conclusions

The provision of food by public institutions such as hospitals and schools has an important bearing on the health of the population they serve. They also have a significant educational function for the wider population too. It is therefore critical to ensure that the food that is provided within their premises is as healthy as possible, something that is a product of a partnership between the institutions themselves, local authorities, central government and – as in the case study outlined here – local community groups and NGOs. This chapter has offered exemplars of aspiring best practice in food procurement in the city of Liverpool and has highlighted areas that require more attention. It has set the practicalities and challenges associated with ensuring that healthier forms of food are served by public sector bodies, in line with the recommendations of governments and nutritionists, and dovetailing with the dietary aspirations of many in the general population – as outlined elsewhere in this book – to eat more 'purely'.

Changing the public procurement landscape is not an easy task: central purchasing, perceptions around what can be considered value for money, big business interests and a food culture that has lost its way with regard to understanding seasonality and values convenience over ethics are all barriers to overcome. But there are glimmers in the gloom. If the RLUH has succeeded in influencing its catering contractors to embrace fresher, healthier and more ethical sourcing of purer foods, it will make other hospital caterers within the region consider how they operate. Similarly, this chapter has demonstrated how a partnership approach to school catering can ensure that healthier food is provided to younger generations. Organisations like Liverpool Food People and Feeding Liverpool are reflective of wider societal concerns in relation to food trends in the Western world, stemming from a desire to pursue healthier and 'purer' forms of living. The fact that this is now recognised by governments and public institutions is a source of hope; however, the proof will, of course, be in the (hopefully fat and sugar-free!) pudding.

Acknowledgements

I wish to thank Paul and Helen for their help and encouragement.

Lucy Antal is Senior Project Manager at Feedback Global's Regional Food Economy and BBC Food & Farming Community Champion 2021, based in Liverpool, Merseyside, United Kingdom.

Notes

1. www.lexico.com/definition/pure_food (last accessed 14 April 2022).
2. Collaborating in this research were University of Leeds, Lancaster University, Food Futures and FoodWise Leeds. A report by Marshall et al. (2020) has been published at https://foodfutures.org.uk/wp-content/uploads/2020/11/FF-Procurement-Report-Final-November-2020.pdf (last accessed 13 March 2023).
3. https://www.ukpopulation.org/liverpool-population/ (last accessed 14 April 2022).
4. https://en.wikipedia.org/wiki/Second_city_of_the_United_Kingdom (last accessed 14 April 2022).
5. https://liverpool.gov.uk/council/key-statistics-and-data/headline-indicators/deprivation/ (last accessed 14 April 2022).
6. https://liverpool.gov.uk/council/key-statistics-and-data/headline-indicators/deprivation/ (last accessed 14 April 2022).
7. https://www.liverpoolccg.nhs.uk/media/1072/the-blueprint.pdf (last accessed 14 April 2022).
8. https://www.sustainablefoodplaces.org/about/ (last accessed 14 April 2022).
9. https://www.feedingliverpool.org/ (last accessed 14 April 2022).
10. https://www.liverpoolecho.co.uk/news/liverpool-news/horsemeat-scandal-abattoirs-deal-take-3322451 (last accessed 14 April 2022).
11. https://www.soilassociation.org/?gclid=EAIaIQobChMIi8zCjNbZ9gIVl-vtCh3rHAjJEAAYASAAEgL9SvD_BwE (last accessed 14 April 2022).
12. https://www.gov.uk/government/collections/sustainable-procurement-the-government-buying-standards-gbs (last accessed 14 April 2022).
13. https://www.foodforlife.org.uk/~/media/files/criteria%20and%20guidance/893-00-ffl-criteria_layout-final-(2).pdf (last accessed 14 April 2022).
14. https://www.sustainweb.org/sustainablefishcity/inspired_food_for_life/ (last accessed 14 April 2022).
15. https://assets.publishing.service.gov.uk/government/uploads/system/uploads/attachment_data/file/523049/Hospital_Food_Panel_May_2016.pdf (last accessed 14 April 2022).
16. https://www.rlbuht.nhs.uk/departments/trust-support-services/hotel-services/ (last accessed 13 April 2022).
17. https://foodforthoughtschools.co.uk/ (last accessed 14 April 2022).
18. https://www.knowsley.gov.uk/knowsleycouncil/media/Documents/liverpool-city-region-child-poverty-and-life-chances-strategy-refresh-2015-18.pdf (last accessed 14 April 2022).

References

Department for Environment, Food and Rural Affairs (2014) *A Plan for Public Procurement: Food & Catering Balanced Scorecard for Public Food Procurement*, DEFRA, London.

Jopling, M., Coleyshaw, L. and Whitmarsh, J. (2011) *Evaluation of Liverpool's Transforming School Food Strategy: Final Summary Report*, Centre for Developmental and Applied Research in Education, University of Wolverhampton.

Marshall, R., Antal, L., Clayton, A., White, R., Woodcock, S., Boyle, N., Corvaglia, M.A., Ryland, D., Morgant, E. and Selviaridis, K. (2020) *Procuring Food for the Future*, A Report of N8 Agrifood Programme, Leeds and Lancashire.

OFSTED (2015) Ofsted – School Food Plan. Published at: www.schoolfoodplan.com › Report › Ofsted. Accessed on 20 March 2022.

Parker, M., Lloyd-Williams, F., Weston, G., Macklin, J. and Mcfadden, K. (2011) Nursery Nutrition in Liverpool: An Exploration of Practice and Nutritional Analysis of Food Provided, *Public Health Nutrition*, 14(10): 1867–75.

Wald, N.J., and Law, M.R. (2003). A Strategy to Reduce Cardiovascular Disease by More Than 80%, *British Medical Journal*, 326(7404): 1419.

CHAPTER 7
BLOOD USED IN FOOD: WHEN, WHERE AND WHY NOT?
···

Gabriel J. Saucedo Arteaga, Claudia A. Flores Mercado and Paul Collinson

Introduction

In some countries, horse, cow or pig blood is consumed as food, often combined with meat, fat, cereals and/or milk; examples include black pudding, blood sausage, the Korean dish *soondae*, *blodplättar* from Scandinavia and the Irish *drisheen*. Some of these are foods eaten in times of scarcity or by poorer people. Blood may be cooked in many different ways or, in some communities, consumed raw from the neck of the live animal. In contrast, from other cultural perspectives, blood is considered dirty, nasty, dangerous and subject to a religious ritual or taboo. These latter cultural attitudes are particularly strongly expressed among Jews, Muslims and Greek Orthodox Christians; they were also described in the Bible (Douglas 1973, 1999).

Never forgetting that food is the basis of nutrition, choices of what to eat usually have a cost-effective nutritional relationship, and yet foods also acquire symbolic, economic or social values, separate from those related to their nutritional properties (Flandrin 1987; Garine and Garine 1998). A food system not only nourishes, it is also a set of practices and techniques, full of social and symbolic meaning that provides emotional satisfaction; it is a means of both social and cultural construction (Harris 1999). As well as the gustatory sensations of sweet, salty, sour, bitter and umami (i.e. reactions on the tongue), there are the other physical sensations of textures and of olfaction (flavours and odours), upon which cultural codes have been imposed. Traditional social anthropological analyses of this topic stem from the observance of opposite or complementary concepts, such as hot-cold or raw-cooked-rotten, as expounded initially by Levi-Strauss (Levi-Strauss

1966; Gómez 1993; Garine and Garine 1998). Notions of purity and impurity are fundamental to these ideas:

> Each culinary system is adapted to social and environmental conditions with food variations having ecological or economic reasons. Food should nourish the collective stomach before feeding the collective mind. Selected culturally, customs contain a core of collective wisdom, ecologically correct, economically efficient and safe food. (Harris 1995: 162)

From a philosophical perspective, we can define that which is pure as something that has not been mixed with anything else. In this sense, pure also means that no changes or processes have been applied. Thus, impure means diverse, mixed and dialectic. When talking about the impure, there is a lot to say: it is rich in its diversity (Jankelevitch 1990; MacClancy, this volume). Food is usually diverse and mixed, and is part of a dialectic and historical process (Toussaint 1992). Therefore, analysing food as pure or impure is not only a subjective but also an ideological endeavour.

Mary Douglas (1973) provided a fundamental contribution to the debate concerning pure and impure food based on an analysis of the books of the Old Testament, a Durkheimian vision, and with the book *Leviticus as Literature* (1999), which demonstrated the symbolic boundaries contained within them. Our approach here is closer to historical and dialectical materialism; the objective is to analyse and describe the use of blood as food, where it is used, in which contexts and why it is not used. The methodology we have used is a cross-sectional study among urban and rural Mexican populations, together with a literature review, participant observation and extensive ethnography.

Blood: Ancient Rites and Popular Beliefs

For much of our history as *Homo sapiens*, we have been hunter-gatherers and, for even longer, opportunist scavengers. Whether scavenged or hunted, the nutritional benefits of the consumption of meat are considered to have been crucial in human evolution, in addition to cooking and the diversification of foods (Leonard 2002). Many nonhuman animal predators and scavengers primarily attack an animal's abdominal area to eat their prey's blood-rich liver, kidneys, heart, spleen and other vital organs first. It is assumed that this pattern developed due to the nutritional benefits of consuming these organs, which are also easier to chew, swallow and digest than other parts of the animal; of the latter, bone marrow is also prized, which is full of red and white blood cells and platelets. All meat consumed includes blood, even though blood is not commonly discussed as part of meat eating. So, there is practically no population in human history that has not consumed blood as part of their diet or used it in their rituals. In ancient literature, in old and modern cookbooks, in the ethnographic record, and in contemporary daily eating habits, references to hematophagy[1] – using blood as a food source – can be found. Blood is nutritious, being high in amino acids (Ofori and Yun-Hwa 2014), glucose, fatty acids and vital minerals, not least of which is iron in the easily digested haem groups within red blood cells. We will return to the nutritional qualities of blood later on.

In cultural terms, blood also has an ambiguous meaning that stimulates the imagination; its loss equates with weakness, with paleness suggesting illness and ultimately death. Yet, the converse is also true, in that blood can be identified with strength and life. Furthermore, it can cause fear and revulsion too. These last associations are compounded by the fact that blood is also a potential source of pathogens, allergens and disease (Spittler 2016). In structuralist terms, blood is also 'marked out' in lots of different ways, as its loss cuts across the boundary between the self and the outside world; it therefore potentially undermines the purity of the self. The strong taboos around menstruation exemplify this and, although the situation is changing in some countries, remain prevalent in all human cultures to greater or lesser degrees. Thus, blood can, at the same time, be considered a pure and an impure substance.

Clearly there is diversity between human societies in their access to specific kinds of foods, and for meat-eaters access to different animals. Furthermore, there can be cultural differences in choices of parts of any animal that might be preferred; even within families, there can be a differentiated distribution of highly valued foods between members. Except perhaps in the most economically advanced societies of today, foods that are indigenous to an area tend to have become the most common foods that are consumed. Local animals were originally hunted, but in due course some species became domesticated, to be fed, slaughtered and eaten. In this way, people acquired a better understanding of those animals and put them to a wider range of uses, after which many still became food.

Thus, food supply and human nutrition is strongly related to the environment, the means of production and social organisation. Food can acquire cultural and ideological values that can find expression in conflicts between different groups. Through this, one can understand the differences in the use and consumption of animals, and the possible differences in their social, symbolic or economic value. Some of the practices and customs relating to food among earlier civilisations remained only in the same areas, whereas others were adopted in other regions and cultures. In other words, food is part of a materialistic, dialectical and historical process, which necessarily involves sociocultural change and transformation (Toussaint 1992; Diamond 1998).

In ancient history, several blood rites have been recorded that may have different meanings but that generally associated blood with a special power, as a substance that gives life or energy. Some civilisations attached several attributes to blood depending on the animal from which it was extracted. The most common beliefs surrounded notions of purification, protection, power, energy, virility and fecundity.

The principal world religions have contributed to the spread of a series of ideas relating to the consumption of or prohibition of blood. In some rites, blood – as a purifying agent – is reserved for God, because it is seen as life-giving and therefore divine. A specific example of blood used in this sense is found in certain Jewish rituals, while the use of blood as a protective agent was a practice of earlier Semitic Hebrew and Phoenician nomadic peoples (McCarthy 1969). In the Bible God tells Abraham that he shall not eat meat with blood because 'blood is life': 'if the blood of goats and bulls sanctifies, how much more, then, will the blood of Christ…' (Hebrews 9:13). The Quran prohibits the consumption of the 'blood and the flesh of swine' (Al-Baqara, Chapter 2, Verse 73) and says that Allah 'has created man from a [blood] clot' (Al-Alaq, Chapter 96, Verse 2). There is a parallel here with ancient Chinese medicine, which holds that blood contains the soul, as described in the Huang Di Nei Ching text, *The Yellow Emperor's Classic of Medicine* (Ni 1995; see also Curran 2008). Livestock sacrifice was often used as an offering to the gods because of the symbolic, cultural and economic value of the slaughtered animal (Butt 2007; Ramos 2018). In Spain, during the Roman Taurobolium rituals of the second and third centuries CE, in which a Cybelene priest was baptised, the priest would stand under a wooden platform with holes drilled into it; a bull would then be slaughtered upon the platform and its blood would stream down, soaking the priest's clothes, head and body (Özkaya 1997).

In ancient Greece and Rome, blood was apparently used to restore a woman's virginity, to induce chastity and immunity from sexual temptation (Reck and Benkato 2018), to restore the intellect (Berens 2009) or as a remedy for tuberculosis (Iglesias Vázquez 2013). Egyptian pharaohs reputedly used to be bathed in blood as a restorative practice or as a preventative treatment against leprosy or elephantiasis (Righi 2012). In Greece, Spartan warriors would drink a 'black soup' made of blood, as they were convinced that it would give them great strength (Ekroth 2002; Park 2018). In ancient Rome, drinking uncooked blood was thought to provide strength, vigour and courage, especially if it was drunk directly from the neck of a great gladiator (Tucker 2011); blood consumed in this way was also thought to cure diseases such as epilepsy, a belief that endured through the Middle Ages and beyond[2] (Sugg 2011, 2015). Drinking blood was considered an act of identity and a means of filial bonding, of brotherhood (Lennon 2011: 143). The Hungarian countess Erzsébet Báthory – a character in a popular tale – was said to bathe regularly in the blood of young women, which she would also drink to prevent tuberculosis and to preserve her beauty (Murillo-Godínez 2010; Radford 2014; Klimczak 2016: 37). The idea of blood drinking to restore youthfulness was also promoted by the influential humanist scholar Marsilio Ficino in the fifteenth century (Tucker 2011). In medieval Europe, drinking the blood of pregnant animals was thought to cure infertility (Bustle.com 2022). Blood consumption was also considered deadly in certain cultures and was sometimes used as a means of committing suicide (Ogden 2001: 255; Ekroth 2002).

In the present day, members of some ethnic groups drink animal blood to increase their strength and other attributes, as well as for health reasons. African pastoralist communities such as the Nuer of South Sudan and the Maasai of Kenya and Tanzania use bovine blood, extracted from the jugular vein of a living animal, to feed a sick or weak person (Evans-Pritchard 1953; Nestel 1989; Cortés López 2001; Garine 2017). In Barcelona, Spain, and Yucatan, Mexico, until relatively recently, poor people would form a queue at slaughterhouses to drink the fresh blood of the slaughtered livestock (Góngora 2005). In parts of Ethiopia, raw blood from ruminants is widely consumed as part of a dish consisting of blood mixed with a local drink, *chaka* (Kussia and Ayano 2018). Among the Inuit of Canada and Alaska, seal's blood is drunk for its nutritional and health-giving properties (Borré 1991). In Vietnam, pig's blood is widely consumed in a dish known as *tiet canh* during family celebrations, particularly weddings; people view it as medicinally beneficial (Huong et al. 2014). In countries where bullfighting is practised, some people used to drink the blood of the defeated animal (McCormick 2009: 24). Another contemporary belief in some countries is that drinking blood might be helpful for patients receiving chemotherapy (Davidson 2006).

Traditional Consumption of Blood in Mexico and New Alternatives

Although blood from a number of different animals is consumed in Mexico, there is a preference for the consumption of pig's blood. It is possible that pigs were not highly regarded or valued by ancient cultures, perhaps for not being a local animal but an alien one as in Judeo-Christian ideology. However, nowadays it is an animal that is consumed almost worldwide and is one of the principal sources of animal protein for humans (Miller and Ullrey 1987; Etim et al. 2014). Pig's blood is cheap and can be viewed as a health food thanks to its nutritional qualities and the fact that it can prevent or reduce the risk of anaemia. Comparing the macronutrients and micronutrients in pig's blood with other types of food demonstrates that its protein and iron content is significant (e.g. Okanović et al. 2010); it is also low in calories, cholesterol and carbohydrates (e.g. Fankal.com 2022). Moreover, the health risks of consuming pig's blood are likely to be practically the same as eating pork, the safety of both being dependent on cooking.

Although the social and cultural context has changed over the centuries, some fears, stigmas and religious connotations remain extant regarding the consumption of blood in Mexico, but it is still consumed nonetheless. Significant differences can be observed in the attitudes to blood consumption of indigenous or *mestizo*[3] rural and urban populations, which seem to stem from the different relationships that people have with animals. It is still common for rural people to breed, feed and care for animals, but also to slaughter and consume them – that is, they are part of a comprehensive food system. By contrast, urban dwellers have hardly any contact with live animals and very rarely slaughter them. Thus, their food system is highly segmented and they are consumers of selected and standardised parts of animals. Also, many parts of the animals are no longer available for sale or they have been eliminated by the market – that is largely the case with blood. A very general explanation may be that from 1970, the Mexican population rapidly changed from being predominantly rural to being predominantly urban (the Mexican population today is 75% urban) and, with this, food access, culinary practices and diet also changed.

Pozole is a Mesoamerican dish that was traditionally prepared with corn kernels, canine meat, chilli and sometimes blood, while today it is prepared with beef or pork. *Red mole* is another Mesoamerican dish that might represent blood, but it in fact does not contain any. In colonial times, the pork sausage was brought to New Spain, which, after being adapted to the Mexican context, has remained in the traditional Mexican diet as *moronga* (pork, lamb or beef blood prepared with spices, chilli, mint and a few pieces of fat, stuffed into pig's intestines and cooked in boiling water). This dish can be found in restaurants for the middle class, traditional markets, supermarkets or street food stalls, mainly in the centre and south of the country. In *mestizo* and indigenous rural villages, it is possible to find dozens of recipes using the blood of pig, goat, lamb, turkey, beef, chicken or even, in coastal areas, turtle. For example, during festivals, the Tarahumara Indians prepare a dish with goat blood called *ramáli*,[4] which is a broth of cooked blood, with shredded meat, mixed with beans. Participants in these festivals also consume the blood of chicken, beef, venison or pork.

In a Mexican rural community, there is an indigenous pagan ritual that fuses several historical, religious, social and cultural aspects of blood consumption described in the previous paragraphs. As part of our research, some people from the community explained the ritual to us and we witnessed it on two occasions: once on a mountain and once in a cave by a river. The ritual is performed for the entire community, by a family or individually, with a traditional priest conducting the ceremony. During the ritual, adult men and women dance around a table every day for five days, each one carrying a stone idol in one hand and, in the other, a bottle of beer. They place the idols on the table and pretend to give them some beer, and then leave the empty bottles cluttered around them. The idols are dressed in white and wear a cap covering their heads. Each day, the participants sacrifice an animal of a different species. Two adult men smear the fresh blood of the slaughtered animals on the face of the idols. They also put a piece of cooked meat close to them and act as if they were feeding the idols. The blood of birds is poured on the ground, while that of large animals is collected to be cooked and consumed later at home.

This ritual is performed twice a year: in May to ask for rainfall and good crops, when the community's members also irrigate their farmlands with blood to 'fertilise' them; and in January, when the purpose of the ritual is to prevent any problems arising between members of the community and to ask for peace within it.[5] The centrality of blood in the ritual demonstrates its symbolic importance to the people of this rural area as well as its perceived nutritional (and fertilising!) value. These notions are increasingly disappearing in other areas of the country, particularly in urban areas, where blood consumption has greatly reduced in recent years.

Reasons for and against the Consumption of Raw or Cooked Blood

The nutritional properties of blood are well known. Blood plasma contains amino acids, carbohydrates, lipids and vitamins. However, the most important nutrients in blood are iron and the amino acids that form the albumin protein[6] and the beta-globulin protein.[7] A very important function of beta-globulin in the red blood cells is to transport iron into the tissues where it is required. Although there are several types and causes of anaemia, the most common one is the lack of iron-rich foods in the diet, whether because the body is unable to process them or because of the way the food is cooked, causing the iron to be used inefficiently or to be lost. Iron-deficiency anaemia has consequences for human health: it reduces children's mental and physical capacity, it may lead to delayed growth and it is relevant in hypothermia. In pregnant women, it increases the risk of miscarriage or premature birth, or it may cause the baby to have a low birth weight. In adults, it raises the heart rate and produces arrhythmia or tachycardia. In general, anaemia causes fatigue, dizziness, paleness, immunosuppression, headache and brittle nails that facilitate the spread of infections on the fingers (Martínez et al. 2008).

Anaemia is one of the most widespread health problems. The World Health Organization estimated in 2005 that it affected approximately 1.62 billion people worldwide, mostly preschool children, pregnant women and women of reproductive age in Africa, India and Latin America (cited in Iglesias Vázquez et al. 2019). In urban Mexico, the prevalence of iron deficiency anaemia is 23 percent for preschool children, and more than 15 percent for pregnant women and also for older adults. It also affects school-age children and teenagers – 10 percent and 5 percent respectively – whilst up to 50 percent of the population of rural areas may also suffer from anaemia (Gutiérrez et al. 2013).

On the other hand, most people who live in urban areas probably think drinking blood is an animalistic behaviour. A common phrase used is 'I'm not a vampire'. Among Christians, who may remember that God forbade consuming blood, it may be considered something unholy, filthy and disgusting, especially when the blood is uncooked and warm, or is consumed directly from an animal. Finally, more educated people are likely to be aware that raw blood can transmit disease, bacteria or viruses; as one of our informants put it, 'a higher accumulation of [them] can be present in blood; if eating meat can be dangerous, drinking blood should be even more so'.

Conversely, cooked blood is deemed a nourishing food when consumed in the form of meat or any of the savoury dishes known to contain blood, such as blood sausage. Although heating meat or other foods containing blood at normal cooking temperatures (62°C and above) generally destroys any pathogens within the blood, this is not true for other meat-borne pathogens, such as the prions causing bovine spongiform encephalopathy (BSE) (commonly known as mad cow disease) or the Beta-2 agonist from clenbuterol contamination, which cooking at normal temperatures does not destroy (Rose et al. 1995). In 2007 in Mexico City, 500 people were hospitalised because of acute clenbuterol poisoning. For this reason, Mexico's Health Minister warned against eating viscera, causing blood and viscera consumption to reduce significantly in urban areas (e.g. BBC.co.uk 2011; Flores 2011; SGS.com 2012). Further cases of clenbuterol poisoning in Mexico occurred in 2011 and 2020 (see also Deraga, this volume).

Much of the blood produced from meat processing in Mexico today is wasted. For cattle, pigs and sheep, between 3 percent and 4 percent of an animal's weight is blood; for goats and chickens, it is between 6 percent and

Table 7.1. National production of livestock and blood, by species (live) in Mexico, 2016 (data compiled by the authors, taken from Galiano (1993), Madrid (1999) and SIAP_SAGARPA 2016)

Species	Blood per unit (litre)	Average per unit (litre)	Blood percentage by weight	National production of livestock (units of livestock)	National production of blood (litres)
Birds	0.16	0.16	7.0%	1,676,865,981	268,298,557
Bovine	7.5–24	15.5	3–4%	7,957,971	123,348,551
Porcine	1.8–4.8	3.50	3–4%	16,793,865	58,778,528
Ovine	1.4–2.7	1.90	4–4.5%	3,014,314	5,727,197
Caprine	1.86	1.80	6.2%	2,311,804	4,161,247
					Total: 460,314,079 (authors' elaboration)

7 percent. We have calculated that the total amount of blood produced in Mexico in official slaughterhouses from poultry, cattle, pigs, sheep and goats in 2016 was over 460 million litres. Poultry accounted for the largest proportion – approximately 268 million litres – while cattle and pigs produced approximately 123 and 59 million litres of blood respectively (see Table 7.1). In Mexico City alone, 48 million litres of blood were produced in the same year. However, from the total blood produced, only around 10 percent is used as food; 90 percent is poured down the drain, something approved by the government's health protocols. Given the prevalence of anaemia in Mexico, a public health campaign extolling the benefits of blood consumption might go some way towards reducing this waste.[8]

Conclusion

In the history of human societies, blood and blood consumption has been consistently associated with highly variable attitudes and meanings. The symbolic, religious and spiritual connotations of blood both reflect and belie its potential as a nutritional resource, something that applies as much today as it did in ancient civilisations. Blood is an inherently ambiguous substance provoking contradictory cultural associations, which vary considerably across time and place. It is at once both pure and impure – a notion that finds expression in differing attitudes towards its consumption, such as those we have described in Mexico.

In the collective imagination there are some romantic ideas (which are not necessarily true) about the essence of nature and purity:

1. People in rural areas are more 'natural' and therefore 'purer' than those living in urban areas.
2. People living in rural areas are indigenous, speak an ancient language and live in isolation, and are therefore 'more natural' and 'purer' than others.
3. Living more 'naturally' means living with more 'purity'.
4. Being 'closer to nature' means being more 'pure'.
5. Living further away from urban areas means being less 'polluted'.

Exploring these ideas further is beyond the scope of this chapter, but what seems certain and objectively demonstrable is that, in rural areas, most indigenous people and peasants possess a holistic food system: they are both producers and consumers. Their production chains are short: they usually know what animals eat; they feed, slaughter and cook them. Therefore, they use animals as a resource in a broad environmental context. By contrast, urban dwellers are largely consumers outside of an environmental context and have no knowledge of most parts of the production chain: they do not feed the animals they eat, nor do they slaughter them. Not only do they never see the whole animal, but they also buy and consume selected parts, which are processed in industrialised settings and often sold as ready-to-eat foods. Rituals such as those observed in rural Mexico can reveal much about how blood is conceived in local communities, in which there is little bifurcation between the production and consumption of food, whilst the distancing of food production and consumption is one explanation for the notions of disgust surrounding the consumption of blood in urban Mexico. Nevertheless, even here it is still possible to eat black pudding or blood sausage and – on some special occasions – take a sip of raw blood.

Gabriel J. Saucedo Arteaga is a research anthropologist in medical sciences at the National Institute of Medical Sciences and Nutrition, Salvador Zubirán, Mexico City, Mexico.

Claudia A. Flores Mercado is a researcher at the Technological University of Mexico, Mexico City, Mexico.

Paul Collinson is a social anthropologist with interests in the anthropologies of food, conflict and development in Europe and Africa. He is a Visiting Research Fellow and former lecturer at Oxford Brookes University. He also works as a senior conflict analyst for the UK government.

Notes

1. Hematophagy, a word generally used for insects and invertebrates that feed off blood, is applied here to humans.
2. In Bolivia, blood from bats is reportedly still widely consumed as a treatment for epilepsy, but ironically exposes people to other diseases (Maron 2018).
3. Meaning someone of mixed European and indigenous descent.
4. This has an interesting resemblance to the black soup of the Spartans.
5. Jimenez-Lopez, J., personal comunication (2006).
6. Human serum albumin is a protein made up of a single polypeptide chain of 585 amino acids
7. A beta-globin protein is made up of 146 amino acids. It binds a haem group, the small molecule containing the important iron atom.
8. A new trend is to prepare sweet food or desserts such as ice cream, lollipops, meringues and cakes with blood, because a type of flour can be obtained from blood from industrial processes. These alternative uses are seen as an option to provide protein and iron to children with egg allergies in Denmark, Spain, Italy and Switzerland (Davidson 2006).

References

BBC.co.uk (2011) Five Mexico Players Test Positive for Banned Substance. Published at: https://www.bbc.co.uk/sport/football/13719472. Accessed on 11 March 2022.

Berens, E.M. (2009) *The Myths and Legends of Ancient Rome*, MetaLibri, Amsterdam.

Borré, K. (1991) Seal Blood, Inuit Blood, and Diet: A Biocultural Model of Physiology and Cultural Identity, *Medical Anthropology Quarterly*, 5: 48–62.

Bustle.com (2022) How We've Talked about Infertility Through History. Published at: https://www.bustle.com/articles/76161-how-infertility-was-talked-about-through-out-history-because-to-fight-a-taboo-you-need-to. Accessed on 11 March 2022.

Butt, K. (2007) ¿Deben los Cristianos 'abstenerse de sangre?'. Published at: http://www.gbasesores.com/sangre/sangre_abstenerse.html. Accessed on 29 September 2021.

Cortés López, J.L. (2001) *Pueblos y Culturas de Africa*, Mundo Negro, Madrid.

Curran, J. (2008) The Yellow Emperor's Classic of Internal Medicine, *British Medical Journal*, 336: 777.

Davidson, A. (2006) *The Oxford Companion to Food, Second Edition*, Oxford University Press, Oxford.

Diamond, J. (1998) *Armas, Gérmenes y Acero: Breve Historia de la Humanidad en los Últimos Trece Mil Años*, Random House, Madrid.

Douglas, M. (1973) *Puerza y Peligro*, Fondo de Cultura Económica, Mexico City.

———. (1999) *Leviticus as Literature*, Oxford University Press, Oxford.

Ekroth, Gunnel (2002) *The Sacrificial Rituals of Greek Hero-Cults in the Archaic to the Early Hellenistic Period*, Presses Universitaires de Liège, Liège.

Etim, N.N., Offiong, E.E., Williams, M.E. and Asuquo, L.E. (2014) Influence of Nutrition on Blood Parameters of Pigs, *American Journal of Biology and Life Sciences*, 2: 46–52.

Evans-Pritchard, E.E. (1953) The Sacrificial Role of Cattle among the Nuer Africa, *Journal of the International African Institute*, 23(3): 181–98.

Fankal.com (2022) Pork Blood Nutrition Facts. Published at: https://www.fankal.com/en/foods/324-pork-blood.html. Accessed on 12 March 2022.

Flandrin, J.-L. (1987) Historia de la Alimentación: por una Ampliación de las Perspectivas, *Revista d'Historia Moderna*, 6: 7–30.

Flores, J. (2011) El clembuterol y los tacos de chorizo. Published at: https://www.jornada.com.mx/2011/06/14/opinion/a03a1cie. Accessed on 1 September 2021.

Galiano, Y. (1993) Los Subproductos Procedentes de los Animales del Avasto, *Eurocarne*, 17: 61–68.

Garine, I. de (2017) Drinking in Northern Cameroon among the Masa and Muzey. In Garine, I. de and Garine, V. de (eds) *Drinking: Anthropological Approaches*, Berghahn Books, Oxford, pp. 51-65.

Garine, I. de and Garine V. de (1998) Antropología de la Alimentación: Entre Naturaleza y Cultura, *Actas del Congreso Internacional de Alimentación y Cultura*, 1: 13-34.

Gómez, P. (1993) Lo Crudo, lo Cocido y lo Podrido. De las Estructuras Mitológicas a las Culinarias, *Anthropologica. Revista de Etnopsicología y Etnopsiquiatría*, 13: 91–111.

Góngora, R. (2005) La Sangre en la historia de la humanidad, *Revista Biomédica*, 16: 281–88.

Gutiérrez, J.P., Rivera-Dommarco, J., Shamah-Levy, T., Villalpando-Hernández, S., Franco, A., Cuevas-Nasu, L., Romero-Martínez, M. Villalpando, S. and Rivera-Dommarco, J.Á., (2013) *Encuesta Nacional de Salud y Nutrición 2012. Resultados Nacionales*, Instituto Nacional de Salud Publica, Cuernavaca, Mexico.

Harris, M. (1995) *Nuestra Especie*, Alianza Editorial, Madrid.

———. (1999) *Bueno para Comer: Enigmas de la Alimentación y Cultura*, Alianza Editorial, Madrid.

Huong, V., Hoa, N., Horby, P.W., Bryant, J.E., van Kinh, N., Toan, T. and Wertheim, H. (2014) Raw Pig Blood Consumption and Potential Risk for Streptococcus Suis Infection, Vietnam, *Emerging Infectious Diseases*, 20(11): 1895–98.

Iglesias, R.L. (2013) Tuberculosis: Raising Awareness through Research. Published at: https://everyone.plos.org/2013/03/25/tuberculosis-raising-awareness-through-research/. Accessed on 12 March 2022.

Iglesias Vázquez, L., Valera, E., Villalobos, M., Tous, M. and Arija, V. (2019) Prevalence of Anemia in Children from Latin America and the Caribbean and Effectiveness of Nutritional Interventions: Systematic Review and Meta-analysis, *Nutrients*, 11(1): 183.

Jankelevitch, V. (1990) *Lo Puro y lo Impuro*, Taurus, Madrid.

Klimczak, N. (2016) Deities or Vampires? Hecate and Other Blood-Drinking Spirits of Ancient Times. Published at: https://www.ancient-origins.net/history-ancient-traditions/deities-or-vampires-hecate-and-other-blood-drinking-spirits-ancient-times-020865. Accessed on 29 September 2021.

Kussia, G.G. and Ayano, A.A. (2018) A Habit of Raw Farm Animal Blood Consumption and Public Awareness about Associated Health Risks in Konso District, *Anatomy and Physiology*, 5(6): 350–55.

Lennon, J. (2011). Carnal, Bloody and Unnatural Acts: Religious Pollution in Ancient Rome. MPhil thesis, University of Nottingham. Published at: http://eprints.nottingham.ac.uk/12550/1/546504.pdf. Accessed on 5 March 2022.

Leonard, W.R. (2002) Food for Thought: Dietary Change Was a Driving Force in Human Evolution, *Scientific American*, 287: 106–15.

Lévi-Strauss, C. (1966) *The Raw and the Cooked: Introduction to the Science of Mythology 1*, Penguin, London.

Madrid, A. (1999) *Aprovechamiento de los Subproductos Carnicos*, Mundi-Prensa, Madrid.

Maron, D.M. (2018) Bats Are Being Killed so People Can Suck Their Blood, *National Geographic*, 7 December. Published at: https://www.nationalgeographic.com/animals/article/killing-bats-for-their-blood. Accessed on 12 March 2022.

Martínez, S.H., Casanueva, E., Rivera, D.J., Vitieri, E.F. and Bourges, R.H. (2008) La Deficiencia de Hierro y la Anemia en Niños Mexicanos. Acciones para Prevenirlas y Corregirlas, *Boletín Médico del Hospital Infantil de México*, 65: 86–99.

McCarthy, D.J. (1969) The Symbolism of Blood and Sacrifice, *Journal of Biblical Literature*, 88(2): 166–76.

McCormick, J. (2009) *Bullfighting: Art, Technique and Spanish Society*, Transactions, New Brunswick, NJ and London.

Miller, E.R., and Ullrey, D.E. (1987) The Pig as a Model for Human Nutrition, *Annual Review of Nutrition*, 7(1): 361–82.

Murillo-Godínez, G. (2010) La sangre, consideraciones históricas e ideologías relacionadas. Published at: https://www.portalesmedicos.com/publicaciones/articles/2150/1/

La-sangre-consideraciones-historicas-e-ideologias-relacionadas.html. Accessed on 24 December 2021.

Nestel, P.S. (1989) Food Intake and Growth in the Maasai, *Ecology of Food and Nutrition*, 23(1): 17–30.

Ni, M. (1995) *The Yellow Emperor's Classic of Medicine: A New Translation of the Neijing Suwen with Commentary*, Shambhala Publications, Boulder, CO.

Ofori, J.A. and Yun-Hwa, P.H. (2014) Issues Related to the Use of Blood in Food and Animal Feed, *Critical Reviews in Food Science and Nutrition*, 54(5): 287–97.

Ogden, D. (2001) *Greek and Roman Necromancy*, Princeton University Press, Princeton.

Okanović, Đ., Ristić, M., Kormanjoš, Š., Nježić, Z., Lilić, S., and Grujić, R. (2010) Chemical and Nutritional Quality of Slaughter Pigs By-products, *Quality of Life*, 1(1): 5–15.

Özkaya, V. (1997) The Shaft Monuments and the Taurobolium among the Phrygians, *Anatolian Studies*, 47: 89–103.

Park, J. (2018) Vampires, Alterity, and Strange Eating. In Shahani, G.G. (ed.) *Food and Literature*, Cambridge University Press, Cambridge, pp. 270–86.

Radford, B. (2014) Vampires: Fact, Fiction and Folklore. Published at: https://www.livescience.com/24374-vampires-real-history.html. Accessed on 29 September 2021.

Ramos, M.M. (2018) La Sangre: Testimonio y Simbolismo, *Prolijia Memoria. Segunda Época*, 2(1): 21–38.

Reck, C. and Benkato, A. (2018) 'Like a Virgin': A Sogdian Recipe for Restoring Virginity and the Sanskrit Background of Sogdian Medicine, *Written Monuments of the Orient*, 4(2): 67–91.

Righi, B. (2012) *Vampires through the Ages: Lore & Legends of the World's Most Notorious Blood Drinkers*, Llewelyn Worldwide, Woodbury, MN.

Rose, M.D., Shearer, G. and Farrington, W.H. (1995) The Effect of Cooking on Veterinary Drug Residues in Food: 1. Clenbuterol, *Food Additives and Contaminants*, 12(1): 67–76.

SGS.com (2012) Clenbuterol – Contaminated Meat Hits China, Mexico and Sports. Published at: https://www.sgs.com/~/media/Global/Documents/Technical%20Documents/Technical%20Bulletins/Scoop/sgs-cts-cc-food-clenbuterol-feb-2012-en-p4.pdf. Accessed on 11 March 2022.

SIAP_SAGARPA (2016) *Anuario pecuario, Resumen nacional, producción, precio, valor, animales sacrificados y año.* Published at: http://infosiap.siap.gob.mx/anpecuario_siapx_gobmx/ResumenNacional.do. Accessed on 29 September 2021.

Spittler, L. (2016) Is Animal Blood a Safe Ingredient? *Food and Nutrition*, July–August. Published at: https://foodandnutrition.org/july-august-2016/animal-blood-safe-ingredient/.

Sugg, R. (2011) The Art of Medicine: Prescientific Death Rites, Vampires, and the Human Soul, *The Lancet*, 377(9767): 712–13.

———. (2015) *Mummies, Cannibals, and Vampires: The History of Corpse Medicine from the Renaissance to the Victorians*, Routledge, Abingdon.

Toussaint, S.M. (1992) *A History of Food*, Blackwell, Oxford.

Tucker, H. (2011) Blood Lust: The Early History of Transfusion, *Scientific American*, 12 July. Published at: https://blogs.scientificamerican.com/guest-blog/blood-lust-the-early-history-of-transfusion/. Accessed on 24 April 2022.

CHAPTER 8
PURE FOOD, FOOD TOURISM AND THE MYTHOLOGISING OF WESTERN IRELAND

Paul Collinson

Introduction

Visit any reasonably sized bookshop in Ireland and you will invariably be confronted by an array of travel guides, travelogues and place memoirs on the country, most of them focused on its western and southern counties. Some of these are glossy photo books, capturing Ireland's stunning natural beauty, colourful pub and shop fronts, or perceived Irish 'eccentricities', such as flocks of sheep or horse and carts blocking main roads, with perhaps a tourist bus crawling behind them – and often all three together. Along with the standard, factually based guides published by well-known brands, there are also likely to be historical studies and natural histories, personal or biographical accounts of rural childhoods, descriptions of road trips (or glorified pub crawls), of which there are a bewildering array for Ireland's relatively small size, and immersive, quasi-anthropological studies of particular areas of the country. Juxtaposed with these, there is often a section devoted to religion, spirituality, mysticism, folklore, 'Celtic wisdom' and other themes, perhaps more general in geographical focus, but usually containing a number of books on Ireland and Irish traditions. Not far away will be a cookery section where, nestled between the popular hardbacks by often British 'celebrity chefs', there will invariably be a large choice of Irish cookery books focused on the country's rich culinary heritage.

In this chapter, I wish to explore the relationship between these thematic areas in relation to food tourism in Ireland. It is my contention that the foodscapes presented in the marketing of Irish food to tourists form part of a long, and broader, tradition surrounding the cultural construction of western Ireland, reified, in part, in the juxtapositions seen in the modern Irish bookshop. In this way, I seek to draw a parallel between notions of cultural and environmental 'purity' and the purity of food, something that is implicitly and explicitly utilised in the marketing of Ireland as a tourist destination.

In the first section, I explore how western Ireland[1] has been mythologised over the years and highlight some of the essential elements of this. The second section presents an overview of food tourism and highlights its growing importance to the sector as a whole. I then go on to discuss food tourism in western Ireland, arguing that the way in which food is packaged and presented is part of an overall marketing strategy that seeks to imagine and construct the region in a highly distinctive way. In evidence, I draw on qualitative content analysis from three main online tourist websites: Discover Ireland.com, the Irish state's primary outward-facing tourism portal; the Wild Atlantic Way website, promoting a driving route along the west coast; and Ireland.com, run by Tourism Ireland, which is responsible for marketing Ireland abroad as a holiday destination. I draw parallels between these modern conceptions of western Ireland and the way in which the region was mythologised in the past. I then place the preceding material in a theoretical framework based on ideas concerning the postmodernist society and commodification of culture, before drawing the chapter together with some tentative conclusions and suggestions of avenues for possible further research.

The 'Myth' of Western Ireland

Western Ireland has long been a locus of cultural construction, something flowing from the earliest travel writings of the seventeenth and eighteenth centuries, through the nationalist movements of the nineteenth and early twentieth centuries, distilled in more recent decades in popular literature, film and music, and continuing today in the information age in a myriad of different media and cultural forms (cf. Gibbons 1996). And, as we shall explore later, it is also apparent in the way in which Ireland has been and continues to be promoted to tourists.

For the Irish literary revivalists of the latter part of the nineteenth century, western Ireland was the repository of a Gaelic culture that had been displaced by, above all, British colonialism and the invasion of the modern world, and thus stood in stark contrast to the increasingly Anglicised, industrialised Ireland of Dublin and the east. It was seen as a 'pure' and primordial representation of what Irish identity ought to be, despite the fact that a number of the mostly Anglo-Irish founders of the Gaelic Revival, as it came to be known, had little direct knowledge of its inhabitants (McCarthy 1988: 162). The project was to preserve and revitalise what was left of this autochthonous Ireland of the past (e.g. Watson 1979; Pierce 2002: 12; Khasawneh 2013). As the poet W.B. Yeats, the key figure in the movement and one member who did know western Ireland well, stated: 'Wherever the old imaginative life lingers it must be stirred to more life, or at the worst, kept alive, and in Ireland this is the work of the Gaelic movement' (1962: 208–9). In Yeats' *Fairy and Folk Tales of the Irish Peasantry* (1888), *Stories from Carleton* (1889) and *Celtic Twilight* (1893), Douglas Hyde's *Beside the Fire* (1890) and *The Love Songs of Connacht* (1904), and Lady Isabelle Augusta Gregory's *Gods and Fighting Men* (1903) and *A Book of Saints and Wonders* (1906), among many others, the focus was on preserving the oral Gaelic culture of the west (Russell 2014). As the founders of the Abbey Theatre stated in their pamphlet *Irish Plays*:

> This life is rich in dramatic materials, while the Irish peasantry of the hills and coast speak an exuberant language and have a primitive grace and wildness due to the wild country they live in which gives their most ordinary life vividness and colour unknown in more civilized places. (Quoted in Clark 1982: 121)

Anthropology had a minor role in the mythologising project too. The early ethnographic research of Arthur Court Haddon and Charles R. Brown on the Aran Islands in 1891–93, which represented some of the earliest anthropology conducted anywhere at the time, was focused primarily on establishing a physical link between the inhabitants and 'negroid races' in line with the evolutionist paradigm of late Victorian academia. The results were published in the *Proceedings of the Royal Irish Academy* in 1893. Three years before arriving on Aran, Haddon, a professor of zoology at the College of Science in Dublin, had undertaken his first expedition to the Torres Straits in Melanesia (ten years later he would lead the famous expedition there from the University of Cambridge) and it would be reasonable to suppose that he saw a parallel between the islanders living off the coast of County Galway and the 'primitive' islanders of the Pacific. Despite his and Brown's main concern being anthropometric study, their documentation of the everyday life of the people was echoed in the western Ireland promoted by the Gaelic revivalists and, according to Walsh (n.d.), is likely to have had an influence upon it – partly through magic lantern tours that Haddon undertook afterwards to display the photographs that had been taken of his subjects.

Although the extent to which Haddon and Brown's work was an influence on the playwright John Millington Synge – who visited Aran in three separate trips between 1898 and 1901, on the advice of his friend W.B. Yeats – is unknown, it is highly likely that he was aware of it. If anything, Synge's *The Aran Islands* (1907) is a far superior work of ethnography than Haddon and Brown's own paper, and has certainly aged better. More than simply an extended journal, the everyday lives of the population and the folk tales that he heard on the islands are presented in vivid and evocative detail, and in the manner of a documentary film-maker (Gerstenberger 1990: 8) as he records the 'spirit of the west of Ireland, with its strange wildness and reserve' (Synge 1966: 123–24). Synge essentially acted as a participant observer on the islands, almost twenty years before Malinowski invented the central methodology of the discipline. Both in its own right and as the basis of Synge's most celebrated plays, particularly *Riders to the Sea* (1904) and *Playboy of the Western World* (1907), *The Aran Islands* had a profound impact on the Irish Literary Revival and its view of peasant Ireland (Green 1994: 20).

Anthropologists who came subsequently were also drawn primarily to the west. Whilst it is a stretch to suggest that the anthropology of western Ireland had a major influence on the way in which the region came to be portrayed (or imagined) in popular discourse over the course of the past century or so, the parallels are certainly evident. Perhaps the most obvious of these is the notion that the rural west – its landscape as well as its inhabitants – is somehow more 'authentically' (or more 'purely') Irish than other areas of the country, which is one of the reasons why urban Ireland has been relatively neglected in the Irish ethnographic record (cf. Curtin et al. 1996). And this is a notion that has definite echoes in the way in which the region is marketed to tourists today, notably in relation to its food, as we will explore below.

There are many important variations in the way in which western Ireland has been mythologised, imagined and invented by writers, poets, artists, songwriters, marketeers and (perhaps) anthropologists over the course of the last century and a half, and the way that these have been utilised instrumentally by political agitators, governments and politicians, all of which have been well rehearsed in the literature and are beyond the scope of this chapter. However, and at the risk of gross over-abstraction, there are certain key features common to this project that can be drawn out.

First, it is a place in which 'community' is central, albeit perhaps an imagined one in Andersonian terms (Anderson 1991), where family and society blend almost into one and where the lives of its inhabitants are largely bound up with and determined by the social forces of the locale rather than by those seeping in from the nebulous outside world. The history of the country and the (sometimes harsh) reality of rural life often fades into the background, in favour of an unchanging, idealised present. In this portrayal, western Ireland is imbued by a degree of primitivism – something that was obviously especially evident in the work of the early anthropologists and was discernible in the work of some of their descendants as well (Donnan and Wilson 1996). It is a place to find the 'simple life', where ancient traditions and beliefs live on, and that has yet to be fully subsumed into industrialised and postindustrialised society. It is a romantic place: wild, certainly, but also sensual, where people are in touch with their inner thoughts and feelings and are at one with them, and in which the shackles formed by the social mores of everyday life in the 'modern' world can perhaps be loosened a little and new possibilities explored (a theme very much to the fore in Synge's writings and plays). It is somewhere in which nature and humanity exist in a state of harmony and balance, where the unadulterated, pristine environment shapes the lives of everyone living there; their economic system, modes of living, subsistence, cuisine and even attitudes and behaviour. Finally, it is a healthy, life-giving place, where the purity of the land and sea is reflected in the purity of the body and mind – a connection articulated partly through its food.

With these themes in mind, I will now turn back to explore food tourism in Ireland and how the 'Myth of the West' finds echoes in contemporary tourist marketing.

Food Tourism Overview

Some Definitions

The close relationship between tourism and food is now well established in virtually all Western countries and in many other areas of the world. Food tourism has been defined as 'visitation to primary and secondary food producers, food festivals, restaurants and specific locations for which food tasting and/or experiencing the attributes of specialist food production regions are the primary motivating factor for travel' (Hall and Mitchell 2001: 308). There is a related category of 'culinary tourism', which is 'any tourism trip during which the consumption, tasting, appreciation or purchase of [local] food products is an important component' (Smith 2007: 100, quoted in Hall and Gössling 2016: 7).

These definitions highlight the fact that food tourism is motivated by a desire to sample foods that are specific to a particular place or region, something that therefore excludes the 'all-inclusive' package holiday in which the opportunity to eat (and drink) as much as possible may be a significant consideration for holidaymakers, even though the types of foods on offer in the hotel are often the same as those that are consumed at home. It is quality, not quantity, that is important. Food tourism often dovetails with other categories of tourism, including cultural, ethical and ecotourism, and is also related to wider societal trends, such as the increasing interest in environmental issues and sustainability, and the rise of the Slow Food movement worldwide.

It is widely recognised that food tourism is now an important and distinct category of tourism overall. The ability of food tourism to stimulate local food economies is enhanced by the reportedly greater spending power that food tourists have in comparison to other types of tourist (OECD 2012). Marketing strategies surrounding food tourism usually emphasise local and regional produce and cuisine in the context of the cultural heritage and identity of an area, with 'traditional', 'artisanal' and 'handmade' modes of production to the fore (e.g. Boyne et al. 2003; Bowen and de Master 2014; James and Halkier 2014). There is a symbiotic relationship here too that operates beyond the mere economic, with food tourism both stimulated by and nurturing local food cultures and foodscapes (e.g. Ilbery et al. 2005; Everett and Aitchison 2008; Sims 2009, 2010; Cavicchi and Santini 2011; Hall and Gössling 2016; Timothy

2016). Thus, the intrinsic qualities of the food itself are combined with the culture and traditions of the locale to further emphasise its 'purity'.

Food Tourism in Western Ireland

These observations are germane to food tourism in western Ireland, where the way in which food is promoted to visitors is an integral component of an overall marketing strategy that seeks to construct a specific identity for the area (how integral is revealed by a simple search for 'food' on the Discover Ireland website, which returns no fewer than 2,135 hits).[2] It is one centred on nature, natural beauty and historical continuity, emphasising the characteristics of the landscape as an unspoilt rural paradise on the edge of Europe. The culture of the inhabitants of western Ireland is explicitly tied to this, the richness of their traditions and their welcoming nature portrayed as stemming directly from the environment in which they are born and raised. Thus, the literature, storytelling, poetry, music, song, 'friendliness' – and cuisine – of the western counties of the country are part of a holistic cultural package in which place, nature and community are intrinsically interrelated and symbiotically nurture one another.

These themes are especially evident in relation to the promotion of the Wild Atlantic Way, a 2,400 km driving route running down the western seaboard from County Donegal in the north to County Cork in the south, which was established in 2014 (see Figures 8.1 and 8.2). Using evocative photography and video, traditional Irish music and clips of local people talking about the area and their lives, various websites present a powerful sales pitch for the transformative potential of the west coast:

Wild, rugged, unspoilt, untamed. Where land and sea collide … stretching 2,400 kilometres along Ireland's coastal seaboard. It is a journey … defined by the native Irish that enrich this unique region. In this wilderness, the Irish have long worked and played and you can join and share with them, in their creativity, their history and native Irish language, in their pastimes, in their independence, born of the land and sea. This is a journey to and through the Ireland you imagined. This is the wild, magnificent Ireland of your dreams. Join us for a journey that will stay with you for ever.[3]

[Woman 1]: 'It is wild, it gives you the feeling of being somewhere far away.'

[Woman 2]: 'There is something about being close to the ocean, we are a line in a long history. The elements are working away even without us, creating very beautiful spaces for us to look at.'

[Man 1]: 'I love just being able to escape the madness of the world.'

[Woman 1]: 'You can take the whole area where you live in, the air, the pasture, the salt from the sea and make it into something beautiful.'

[Woman 2]: 'The natural beauty that surrounds us on this west coast.'

[Woman 1]: 'There is always something new down there, it's local, it's wild, it's just beautiful.'[4]

Unforgettable moments

It's easy to feel the wild that defines this coastline; it's everywhere, from sheer cliffs that plunge into crashing Atlantic waves to remote, weather-beaten islands. But the west of Ireland is about more than that, it's about moments of connection. It's the chat from locals, the warmth of a fire-lit pub, the tapping feet of a traditional music session. From the elemental weather to the oak-smoked salmon, the essence of the Wild Atlantic Way runs deep.[5]

It is notable, in passing, the number of times 'wild' is invoked in these quotations; 'wild(ness)' was also a key descriptor for Synge in describing not only the Aran Islands themselves, but also their inhabitants, particularly the women (Gibbons 1996: 30).

Food in western Ireland is promoted as 'pure' in several different ways. Most obviously, it is often claimed to be unadulterated: organic food is an extremely important feature of the food promoted to tourists, and most restaurants and food producers highlight this aspect of their produce. Localism is another key feature: the shorter the distance between field and fork, the better. There is an emphasis on the artisanal aspects of food production, with traditional techniques passed down the generations still being applied in small farmhouse kitchen-scale enterprises. Leading on from this is a sense of 'authenticity', with food seen as pure in the sense of being wholly indigenous and unsullied by outside influences:

The tang of salty sea air on your lips, jaw dropping cliffs views and endless gourmet delights: a trip along Ireland's Wild Atlantic Way is sure to give you an appetite. Experience our culinary trail where you can taste the seafood fresh from the boats, engage with local artisan producers, and enjoy the atmosphere of well-loved establishments along the Wild Atlantic Way. From smoked salmon in County Donegal, Michelin stars in the City of Tribes to island eateries and famous puddings along the Kerry and Cork coast, savour our suggestions on this stunning stretch of coastline.[6]

> Seafood is where the Wild Atlantic Way meets Ireland's unique culture. It's about lobster and crab, salmon and mackerel, oysters and mussels plucked fresh from the heaving ocean. But it's also about the men and women who mix tradition and 21st-century techniques to bring it from tide to table, to serve it just a few miles (or in some cases, just a few feet) from where it's caught.[7]

> Clean Atlantic waters, a mild climate and lush green fields; the geography of Ireland and its food are inseparable. On the Wild Atlantic Way, Ireland's natural larder is visible at every turn. From grazing fields to fishing boats, it's not uncommon for food to go from 'farm to fork' or 'tide to table' within hours – if not minutes. Supplying the tasty treats on your plate are the artisan food producers and sustainable farmers whose fields dot the coast, and they have long-seated relationships with the hands that feed you. As you dine along the west coast of Ireland, you can also meet the makers. Stay on farms, take part in food festivals and learn traditional skills, like foraging and fishing. It's not a formal affair; ask in the bakery, at your table, on the quayside or at the bar about your food and how it has travelled, to really get a sense of the place.[8]

As the second extract above suggests, food is also marketed as an 'experience' in which consumption can be combined with other activities, with specific 'food experiences' featuring prominently on tourist websites. Sometimes the link between food and culture is explicitly combined into one experience:

> Private Dining with an Artistic Twist

> Prepare for a night of taste explosions and quality entertainment in Broc House at the Yeats Dining Experience. Foodies Damien Brennan and Paula Gilvarry pair fine foods with poetry, with Paula serving up a feast of local dishes while Damien feeds the soul between courses with some of WB Yeats' best-loved poems.[9]

Of the various types of food activities on offer, foraging is one that has grown in importance in recent years in Ireland (as well as other places in Europe). Various restaurants, hotels and other small enterprises offer tourists the opportunity to participate in guided foraging trips to gather wild food, usually in woods, forests and along the seashore, and then cook it themselves in cookery schools or have it cooked for them, usually in high-class restaurants. Little could be purer, it seems, than something that has been collected by one's own hands and potentially cooked by them as well. It is also seen as a purifying experience for body and soul; in the words of one foraging guide, quoted in the *Irish Times* in 2019:

Foraging is such a holistic thing to do: you're exercising and connecting with nature in the outdoors, which does your psyche and your emotions the world of good. (Darach Ó Murchú, quoted in *Irish Times* 2018)

One type of food that has become increasingly popular as a foraged product in Ireland's coastal regions in recent years is seaweed. It is also packaged and sold as a healthy snack, a food additive, an alternative to pasta or a skincare product; according to Bord Bia, the Irish Food Board, 40,000 tonnes of seaweed are harvested in Ireland each year. The way in which seaweed is marketed by the various producers in Ireland is illuminative for our discussion, with the following examples being typical:

All of our seaveg is hand harvested by our team in Kilcar, Co. Donegal along the Wild Atlantic Way. All of our seaweed products are organically certified and 100 percent naturally grown.[10]

Wild Irish Seaweeds Ltd have been harvesting wild organic seaweed from the west of Ireland for over 100 years. All our seaweed comes from the pristine nutrient rich waters of the Atlantic Ocean off the west coast of County Clare. We have kept the same hand harvesting techniques handed down over 4 generations.[11]

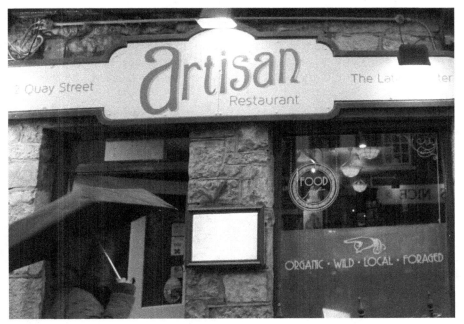

Figure 8.1. Restaurant in Galway, western Ireland. © Paul Collinson

There are also a number of spas along the west coast of Ireland offering seaweed treatments and baths, promoted as the ultimate destressing experience. Seaweed is thus a pure food par excellence: it can be easily collected along the seashore; it is intrinsically organic; it is purportedly extremely healthy and rich in nutrients; it can be used as a detoxifier or destressor; and it is a traditional product, processed for subsistence for hundreds of years.

So what does all this mean in theoretical terms?

Theoretical Considerations

Self-evidently, the marketing of Ireland and Irish food in the way we have described is a response to the demand of visitors to Ireland themselves. Voluminous amounts have been written about the essential characteristics of the postmodern society, centred on the atomisation of familial and social relationships, the lack of rootedness to the locale, the fast-paced and fleeting nature of everyday experiences, the temporality and anxiety surrounding paid work, and the superficiality of many modern forms of cultural communication and production, among other characteristics. As Mary Douglas herself was quoted as saying:

> Every year the progress of advanced capitalist society makes our population consist of more and more isolates. This is because of the infrastructure of the economy, especially electronic communications.[12]

In this context, it is no surprise that somewhere that is perceived as offering a more rooted, culturally rich and 'authentic' experience, as well as being at the same time potentially exotic and exciting (and a place where one may

Figure 8.2. Pure food *par excellence*: seaweed products on sale in western Ireland. © Paul Collinson

not even get a phone signal!), is highly appealing to a certain type of contemporary Western tourist who is concerned about cultural diversity and, potentially, their environmental footprint. In this conception, the 'purity' of food is partly a function of its sustainability, as measured against several criteria: it is derived from renewable sources; it is not mass-produced using industrialised processes; it has not been adulterated by the addition of artificial additives; it has not been transported hundreds of miles before reaching the consumer; and it does not use wasteful packaging (among other considerations). It is also a function of its perceived 'authenticity', a correlation that also applies in reverse – the purer a food is, judged across several different criteria, the more likely it is held to be 'authentic'. Thus, the marketing of food as organic, sustainable, handmade, artisan, etc. both fuels and is fuelled by an expectation on the part of the food tourist that this is how local foods that they have come on holiday to seek out *ought to be* – and, indeed, as a result, they usually are.

Over two decades ago, Graham (1999) distinguished between three different types of authenticity in relation to Ireland: 'Old Authenticity' typified by Yeats' work and the Gaelic Revival; 'New Authenticity', such as the contemporary marketing of the country's heritage; and 'Ironic Authenticity', with the example being a commercial for beer. Whilst this formulation is helpful, I would suggest that the distinction is less clear-cut than Graham made out. Rather, we have argued here that there is a continuity in the discourse surrounding and portrayal of western Ireland as 'authentically Irish', which connects the revivalists of the late nineteenth and early twentieth centuries with the marketeers of today. Indeed, in a sense the former could be viewed as marketeers as well: through their publications, lectures, exhibitions, etc., they were appealing to the Irish population to take note of their Gaelic heritage and culture and to embrace it in order to create a new, distinctive and, importantly, unadulterated national identity. They were constructing and selling western Ireland in line with their own vision, albeit to a domestic audience rather than a predominantly foreign one.

The packaging of Irish culture in this way, which today includes its cuisine and culinary traditions, is a stark example of what Jean Baudrillard called the 'commodification of anything and everything'. In *The Consumer Society*, Baudrillard stated that: 'We have reached the point where "consumption" has grasped the whole of life', characterised by 'the consumption of human relations, of solidarity, reciprocity, warmth and social participation' (1998[1970]: 29; 162). There is, of course, a certain performative aspect to this as well, in the sense that an 'authentic', 'indigenous' (and 'pure') culture is a product of negotiation between internal and external forces, between the observed and the observer, and between reality and imagination (Bourdieu 1986; Harris 2013: 12; Herzfeld 2016).

More prosaically, the following quotations from the Ireland.com website encapsulate these ideas rather well:

Seafood chowder by the fire in a wind-whipped coastal pub. Traditional Irish stew in the surrounds of an 18th century market. Afternoon tea in a castle overlooking a misty lough. Food in Ireland isn't just about the taste; it's about the place, the experience, the land and sea, and the people who created it.

Food is an integral part of contemporary culture on the island of Ireland – from buzzing farmers' markets, to incredible local ingredients, craft brewing and distilling, and innovative chefs who celebrate the rich connection between place and plate – and it shows.[13]

Conclusions

In this chapter, I have drawn a parallel between cultural and food purity and have attempted to demonstrate the way in which the two are connected in the mythologisation of western Ireland. I have argued that the relationship between 'purity' and 'authenticity' in the way in which culture is perceived can also be applied to food and that the relationship is mutually reinforcing: the more 'authentic' a food is held to be, the 'purer' it is, and vice versa. I have also suggested that there is a continuity between the marketing campaigns of today and the way in which western Ireland has been constructed in the past.

One might argue that, in structuralist terms, what is presented to the tourist – food, culture, experience – is founded on a series of binary oppositions, whereby traditional Irish culture, however defined, is implicitly contrasted with 'fast-paced', modern life in industrialised societies:

Tradition: Modernity
Wild: Tame
Authentic: Inauthentic
Rural: Urban
Natural: Unnatural
Unchanging: Dynamic
Slow: Fast
Hidden: Known
Community: Atomisation
Inclusive: Alienating
Sensual/Sexual: Frigid
Remote: Familiar
Simple: Complex
Synchronic: Diachronic

These are also reflected in the promotion of food:

Organic : Inorganic
Healthy : Unhealthy
Sustainable : Unsustainable
Hand-made : Mass-produced
Home-cooked : Factory-produced
Raw : Processed
Artisanal : Automated
Local : Distant
Fresh : Stale
Tasty : Bland
Warm : Cold
Pure : Impure
(Adapted from Collinson 2017)

An interesting avenue for further research would be to examine how resonant such a schema is to both tourists and marketeers, and the ways in which it is reified in the locale. By so doing, the nature of the communication processes between visitors and hosts, between tourist marketing and consumption, and between cultural construction and the reality of lived experience may be teased out in order to more fully understand the dynamic interplay between these different spheres. In scratching the surface here, we have hopefully demonstrated that food – and the ways in which it is made, promoted, understood, experienced and consumed – is a useful vehicle for delving further into some of these complex issues.

Paul Collinson is a social anthropologist with interests in the anthropologies of food, conflict and development in Europe and Africa. He is a Visiting Research Fellow and former lecturer at Oxford Brookes University. He also works as a senior conflict analyst for the UK government.

Notes

1. Whilst western Ireland is an amorphous geographical concept, it is generally held to be centred upon the western seaboard counties of Donegal, Sligo, Mayo, Galway, Clare, Kerry and Cork, with perhaps other neighbouring inland counties such as Leitrim, Roscommon and Limerick included as well.
2. Search conducted on 20 September 2017.
3. Transcribed from Ireland's Wild Atlantic Way promotional video: https: thewildatlanticway.com/ireland's-wild-atlantic-way/ (last accessed on 20 April 2020).

4. Transcribed from Wild Atlantic Way – Shaped by the Sea – Tastes promotional video. https: thewildatlanticway.com/shaped-by-the-sea/ (last accessed 18 October 2018).
5. https://www.ireland.com/en-gb/destinations/experiences/wild-atlantic-way/ (last accessed 12 February 2021).
6. https://www.discoverireland.cn/en-in/articles/tripideas/flavours-of-the-wild-atlantic-way/ (last accessed 12 February 2021).
7. https://www.burrensmokehouse.com/blog/taste-the-atlantic-experience (last accessed 12 February 2021).
8. http://www.wildatlanticway.com/stories/food/food-stories-of-the-wild-atlantic-way (last accessed 12 February 2021).
9. https://www.discoverireland.cn/en-in/articles/tripideas/flavours-of-the-wild-atlantic-way/ (last accessed 12 February 2021).
10. https://organicseaweedireland.com/organic-seaweed/ (last accessed 12 February 2021).
11. https://wildirishseaweeds.com/ (last accessed 12 February 2021).
12. This quote is widely attributed to Mary Douglas, but whether it ever actually appeared in print is unknown. See https://www.brainyquote.com/quotes/mary_douglas_237125 (last accessed 29 September 2021).
13. https://www.ireland.com/en-gb/things-to-do/themes/food-and-drink/food-and-drink-in-ireland/ (last accessed 12 October 2021).

References

Anderson, B. (1991) *Imagined Communities: Reflections on the Origin and Spread of Nationalism*, Verso, London.
Baudrillard, J. (1998 [1970]) *The Consumer Society: Myths and Structures*, Sage, London.
Bourdieu, P. (1986) The Forms of Capital. In Richardson, J. (ed.) *Handbook of Theory and Research for the Sociology of Education,* Greenwood, New York, pp. 241–58.
Bowen, S., and DeMaster, K. (2014) Wisconsin's Happy Cows? Articulating Heritage and Territory as New Dimensions of Quality Production, *Agriculture and Human Values*, 31(4): 549–62.
Boyne, S., Hall, D. and Williams, F. (2003) Policy, Support and Promotion for Food Related Tourism Initiatives: A Marketing Approach to Regional Development, *Journal of Travel and Tourism Marketing*, 14(3-4): 131–54.
Cavicchi, A. and Santini, C. (2011) Brunellopoli: Wine Scandal under the Tuscan Sun, *Tourism Review International*, 15(3): 12–24.
Clarke, B.K. (1982) *The Emergence of the Irish Peasant Play at the Abbey Theatre*, UMI Research, Ann Arbor.
Collinson, P.S. (2017) Consuming Traditions: Artisan Food and Food Tourism in Western Ireland. In Medina, F.X. and Tresserras, J. (eds) *Food, Gastronomy and Tourism Social and Cultural Perspectives*, University of Guadalajara, Guadalajara, pp. 31–48.
Curtin, C., Donnan, H. and Wilson, T.M. (eds) (1996) *Irish Urban Cultures*, Institute of Irish Studies, Belfast.
Donnan, H. and Wilson, T.M. (1996) *The Anthropology of Ireland*, Routledge, Abingdon.

Everett, S. and Aitchison, C. (2008) The Role of Food Tourism in Sustaining Regional Identity: A Case Study of Cornwall, South West England, *Journal of Sustainable Tourism*, 16(2): 150–67.

Gerstenberger, D. (1990) *John Millington Synge, Revised Edition*, Twayne, Boston.

Gibbons, L. (1996) *Transformations in Irish Culture*, Cork University Press, Cork.

Graham C. (1999) '… Maybe That's Just Blarney': Irish Culture and the Persistence of Authenticity. In Graham C. and Kirkland R. (eds) *Ireland and Cultural Theory*, Palgrave Macmillan, London, pp. 7–28.

Greene, D.H. (1994) J.M. Synge: A Reappraisal. In Casey, D.J. (ed.), *Critical Essays on John Millington Synge*, G.K. Hall, New York, pp. 15–27.

Haddon, A.C. and Browne, C.R. (1893) The Ethnography of the Aran Islands, Co. Galway, *Proceedings of the Royal Irish Academy*, 3(2): 768–830.

Hall, M.C. and Gössling, S. (2016) From Food Tourism and Regional Development to Food, Tourism and Regional Development: Themes and Issues in Contemporary Foodscapes. In Hall, C.M, and Gössling, S. (eds) *Food Tourism and Regional Development: Networks, Products and Trajectories*, Routledge, Abingdon, pp. 3–53.

Hall, C.M. and Mitchell, R. (2001) Wine and Food Tourism. In Douglas, N., Douglas, N. and Derrett, R. (eds) *Special Interest Tourism: Context and Cases*, Wiley, London, pp. 307–29.

Harris, M. (2013) Emergent Indigenous Identities: Rejecting the Need for Purity. In Harris, M, Carlson, B. and Poata-Smith, E.S. (eds) *The Politics of Identity*, University of Technology Sydney ePRESS, Sydney, pp. 10–25.

Herzfeld, M. (2016) Culinary Stereotypes: The Gustatory Politics of Gastro-Essentialism. In Klein, J.L. and Watson, J.A. (eds) *The Handbook of Food and Anthropology,* Bloomsbury, London, pp. 31–47.

Ilbery, B., Morris, C., Buller, H., Maye, D. and Kneafsey, M. (2005) Process and Place. An Examination of Food Marketing and Labelling Schemes in Europe and North America, *European Urban and Regional Studies*, 12: 116–32.

Irish Times (2018) Foraging Dinner, Fresh from an Irish Rock Pool, 10 February.

James, L. and Halkier, H. (2014) Regional Development Platforms and Related Variety: Exploring the Changing Practices of Food Tourism in North Jutland, Denmark, *European Urban and Regional Studies*, 23(4): 831–47.

Khasawneh, H. (2013) An Aestheticising of Irish Peasantry, *Journal of Franco-Irish Studies,* 3(1): 143–59.

McCarthy, P.A. (1988) Synge and the Irish Literary Renaissance. In Kopper, E.A. Jr. (ed.) *A J.M. Synge Literary Companion*, Greenwood Press, Westport, CT, pp. 161–74.

OECD (2012) *Food and the Tourism Experience. The OECD-Korea Workshop*. Published at: http://www.oecd.org/publications/food-and-the-tourism-experience-9789264171923-en.htm. Accessed on 7 October 2017.

Pierce, D. (2002) Cultural Nationalism and the Irish Literary Revival, *International Journal of English Studies*, 2(20): 1–22.

Russell, E. (2014) The Celtic Twilight: Folklore and the Irish Literary Revival, *Journal of Publishing Culture*, 2: 1–16.

Sims, R. (2009) Food, Place and Authenticity: Local Food and the Sustainable Tourism Experience, *Journal of Sustainable Tourism*, 17(3): 321–36.

——. (2010) Putting Place on the Menu: The Negotiation of Locality in UK Food Tourism, from Production to Consumption, *Journal of Rural Studies*, 26: 105–15.

Smith, S.J. (2007) Leisure Travel. In McCarville, R. and Mackay, K. (eds) *Leisure for Canadians*, Venture, State College, PA, pp. 93–102.

Synge, J.M. (1966) *Collected Works II (Prose)*, ed. Alan Price, Oxford University Press, Oxford.

Timothy, D.J. (2016) Introduction: Heritage Cuisines, Foodways and Culinary Traditions. In Timothy, D.J. (ed.) *Heritage Cuisines: Traditions, Identities and Tourism*, Routledge, Abingdon, pp. 1–25.

Walsh, C. (n.d.), 'The Aran Islands … the Most Remarkable Islands I Have Come Across Anywhere'. Alfred Cort Haddon 24th July 1890. Published at: https://ballymaclinton.wordpress.com/2015/07/24/the-aran-islands-are-in-many-respects-the-most-remarkable-islands-i-have-as-yet-come-across-anywhere-alfred-cort-haddon-24th-july-1890/. Accessed on 6 February 2021.

_____. (2013) Charles R. Browne, the Irish Headhunter, *Irish Journal of Anthropology*, 16(1): 16–22.

Watson, G. (1979) *Irish Identity and the Literary Revival*, Croom, London.

Yeats, W.B. (1962) *Explorations: Essays and Plays*, Macmillan, New York.

CHAPTER 9
BIOETHICS AND PURE FOOD: THE CONSUMERS'
DILEMMA IN WEST MEXICO

Daria Deraga

Introduction

This chapter concerns concepts of pure food in West Mexico and the different viewpoints between different sectors of the population, according to age group and to general socioeconomic aspects. The term 'pure food' in Spanish – *alimento puro* – itself provoked few comments. However, whereas frequently for the older generation the phrase meant food only with no additional items associated with it, for many of the younger members of the population it meant organic food, or for those who knew the terms, foods without any modification, such as in their genetic or chemical make-up. So, from their perspective, *food purity* is considered to be that which has avoided being contaminated or unhealthy, and so is used in a similar sense to *food safety.*

Although there is no doubt about the importance of bioethics in our time of technological development and advances in medicine and agriculture, there is a discrepancy in the ways in which people are influenced on this subject by mass media through the internet, television and popular publications, which are not always scientifically oriented. Bioethics in this discussion is related to agriculture, food safety and food security, and how people in West Mexico respond to the public media information on the bioethical discussions and criticisms of food products, the most notorious being transgenic or genetically modified organisms (GMOs),[1] but also the claims for organic foods. The question is how this information is perceived by adult consumers, and the criteria, according to scientific or popular beliefs, used for the rejection or acceptance of these products. For many people in West Mexico, *food security* means having food on the table and not going hungry, and so, for these people, it is seldom, if ever, connected to healthy or unhealthy properties of the foods. However, the term *food safety* among people in West Mexico would refer to foods that are healthy, avoiding contaminated or unhealthy products. For the sake of this discussion, unless otherwise stated, the definition by the Food and Agriculture Organization (FAO) is used for the term food security: 'Food security exists when all people, at all times, have physical and economic access to sufficient, safe and nutritious food that meets their dietary needs and food preferences for an active and healthy life'.[2] Of relevance here is the fact that there is a 'right to food' law for inhabitants of Mexico City,[3] but not in rural areas.

The study used in this chapter is related to bioethics in West Mexico and several areas of concern were discussed. What are some of the problems facing people in their quest for organic products and non-GMOs? What confidence can consumers have in the marketing of food products labelled as organic? What is the future for consumption of cultured, *in vitro* meat?[4] Can *in vitro* meat be considered safe, pure, organic or even suitable for vegetarian consumption? Young adults are now concerned – they question health and food safety, as well as food security, and many try to select uncontaminated products in this area of Mexico. One of the problems these young adults face is the economic ability to purchase a strict selection for consumption of food products that are considered pure, healthy or organic, as sold in specialised markets.

Discussions with Consumers

The information in this chapter is based on interviews. People interviewed varied in age and gender, and the main divisions were based on age, economic, educational, rural or urban status. To begin with, discussions conducted in a conversational manner with young to middle-aged adults pertaining to the low-income rural sector show a lack of concern or knowledge about transgenic products, and the idea of organic food made no sense to most, and even less to those who were vegetarian. They eat what they can get; their diet is generally very simple. As an example, products such as yoghurt are basically unknown or rarely consumed. Whenever possible, much of the food is produced in their rural habitat in a very natural way. As such, the bioethical questions being asked by this study, along with the related concerns, had very little impact on their concepts of food consumption.

It is amongst the middle economic range of consumers, especially university students, where more opinionated viewpoints were evident about the pros and cons of organic and transgenic products. In fact, a heated debate occurred when a group of students were asked what they considered to be healthy food. Some were vegetarian and defended their position strongly, being very adamant about the dangers of transgenic products and their concern about animal welfare. Conversely, others were neutral, claiming that everyone should consume whatever they want. There were several students who strongly defended transgenic products, stating that they are a way of providing food to many, due to their longer shelf life, reduced crop loss and accessible prices, thereby aiding food security. Others were pro-organic food and, when questioned on how to judge the validity of the *organic* origin of each item and any guarantees about the production methods, they defended their opinions through conversations they had conducted with friends who produce such products. But a number of these students were indecisive about choices of food products, claiming that the high cost of organic products made them unattainable. Furthermore, they noted the issue of not really knowing which foods being sold in the markets are transgenic or GMOs. The selection method for most was based on visual appeal, whereas a few became very opinionated and argued that pretty-looking tomatoes are very likely to be transgenic, insisting that one cannot select by whether something *looks* better. None of the students could present a scientific explanation of their criticisms.

The arguments presented among university students demonstrated a great concern about contaminated foods. This is one of the main reasons for selecting organic food as an option. Chemicals in fertilisers and insecticides were the most common factors mentioned. Older generations were not as adamant on this subject as young adults. This could be due to younger generations being more connected to social media and information through electronic devices in general, whereas older generations are more connected to their rural background and the experience of losing crops due to plagues of insects or of farming soils with nutrient deficiencies. Therefore, the latter do not condemn the use of insecticides or chemical fertilisers. Also, many of this older age group did not have the advantage of a complete education during their childhood, thus making it harder for them to comprehend concepts of possible health-related problems due to contamination or GMOs.

Contamination of Food Products

In Mexico, there have been serious food contamination problems, but in the past, many cases did not receive significant attention. However, from 1991 to 2001, there was an epidemic of the bacterium *Vibrio cholera* (cholera) in Mexico, following which a new public health system was developed across many aspects of life and the environment, which had a significant impact on public health (Sepúlveda et al. 2006). This was followed in 2013 by another cholera outbreak.[5] The bacterium's genetic profile was different from that of the 1991–2001 outbreak, but showed a 95% similarity to a strain first seen in Haiti (Diaz-Quiñonez et al. 2016), from which it was presumed to have been introduced into Mexico by transmission from Caribbean countries (Moore et al. 2014). Whereas the infection is usually mild or without serious consequences if treated properly, it was clearly a social health problem. Apart from the original transmission from abroad, its cause and that of other diarrhoeal diseases (see e.g. Contreras et al. 2020) were associated with untreated sewage water being used for irrigation of food crops, especially problematic for those food plants that grow close to the ground such as lettuces, strawberries and herbs. Recognition of this led to advice to wash these products well before consuming them, but this advice was not always taken very seriously. Fortunately, due to exposure at an early age, those who had survived infancy had some natural immunity to these pathogens. On the other hand, Gutiérrez et al. (1996) had demonstrated that in Mexico, mortality from diarrhoeal diseases among those aged under five was greater during the months of highest temperatures and rainfall between May and September, months associated with harvesting these foods. They also showed the gradual decrease in infant mortality from these causes from 1978 to 1993. Waste water issues continued to be studied in Mexico (see e.g. Caucci and Hettiarachch 2017) and are still important in relation to food safety in some regions today.

As well as such cases of contamination through the use of sewage in the irrigation of food plants, there have been cases of other contaminations researched and considered in academic journals, such as finding organochlorine pesticide residues in fish (Mora et al. 2001) or in butter (Waliszewski et al. 2003). However, a more serious issue in the public media was the excessive use of hormones in growing livestock. In 2001, the use of the beta-2 agonist clenbuterol (sometimes spelt in Spanish as clembuterol) on livestock,[6] with its anabolic-like effects,[7] became a significant topic of popular concern. Clenbuterol was used to create fast and abundant muscle growth, producing maximum weight in cattle and pigs destined for slaughter. Canada and the United States at that time permitted this product to be used in small doses; so, in Mexico where the importation and use of clenbuterol in livestock was permitted, cattle ranchers decided that given the fact that a small amount creates faster growth, by doubling the dose, young cattle would obtain the desired weight twice as quickly. The outcome was drastic, in that the overdosing of the young animals destined for slaughter caused a concentration of the substance in their liver. People who consumed liver from these animals became very ill. The discovery of the cause precipitated a big scandal, as a result of which clenbuterol was banned from importation and for use in cattle and pigs. But soon it was being reproduced illegally in local laboratories within Mexico, and consequently its use continues on a more discreet level, evading detection by the authorities. An article in the local *Público* newspaper of Guadalajara in June 2001, entitled 'Vacas Que Se Nutren como Fisicoculturistas' ('Cows That Are Fed as Physico-culturists') gave the situation a rather light touch, but needless to say, the consumption of liver plummeted after this article was published. In this case, people did react due to the seriousness of the health problems caused by consuming liver, perhaps because the media portrayed it as alarming news (Deraga 2008: 156).

At that time, the concept of pure or healthy food was not an important issue for the public and the problem was simply blamed on the cattle ranchers. However, since then things have been changing. Nowadays, due to more widely accessible information on health issues through local, national and international news media, one can observe that these past experiences with contaminated foods available on the market have influenced consumers by making more people aware of what they are eating, and therefore making them more selective. In summary, articles in the public media about such situations in Mexico have affected people's views about risks to food safety, and in this way have been unevenly altering the public understanding of the purity of the food they are willing to consume, and, as a consequence, a new interest in how foods are described and labelled has emerged.

The Validity of Labelling Food Products

In recent years, confidence surrounding the labelling of products as 'organic', 'healthy' or 'suitable for vegetarians', for example, has increasingly been questioned by some consumers in Mexico, although not by the majority. Again, in the ethnographic studies in this chapter, this topic was more readily discussed among the university students than among the older generations. This shows that among the younger educated population, there is a growing concern about the validity of information on food products.

A discussion began when one student in a group questioned the labelling of products as organic, while others said that the producers had to say how it was grown or prepared so that it could be labelled as organic and truly organic. Again, no one questioned or raised the fact of noninspection and a lack of official proof of the claims made by the producers or retailers for the labelling as organic. So, even here, there seemed to be an absence of scientific questioning or researching the validity of labelling of these products concerning healthy, uncontaminated food. But there is hope, in that among the younger adult generation, one can see a tendency towards being much more critical of claims made in marketing food products. This lack of confidence in marketing claims among some of the students had already stimulated an interest in permaculture and home-grown vegetables, which are now coming to be viewed as an alternative to purchased organic food. For example, two young twenty-year-old female interviewees grow some vegetable products in their home gardens for personal use, stating that the reason is so that they can be confident that there is uncontaminated food on the table. Also, a young male informant, who works as a waiter and studies industrial design, plans to begin a project of hydroponic production to obtain healthy, uncontaminated, non-transgenic vegetables for sale. This shows that some of the younger generation in West Mexico are concerned about health and food products and are spending time researching food safety and food selection for consumption.

In addition, the fact that more young people are becoming concerned about the validity of labelling is a very important factor for the future credibility of those products considered healthy, organic or natural.

A young woman interviewed, who sells organic foods, gave an interesting example of the change in the concern for products being called organic, natural and safe. She has been involved in the creation of a new official organisation called the Red Mexicana de Tianguis y Mercados Orgánicos[8] (Mexican Network of Organic Food Markets and Street Venders). This organisation has a committee for inspection in the fields and animal farms, documenting and advising the farmers on the conditions under which their products are being grown or raised. Furthermore, the organisation gives a certificate for those products that reach their specified standards, so that the products can justifiably claim to be organic. These products, showing their certification, are then taken to the local open markets or the more commercial retail outlets selling organic foods.

Cultured Meat

Another topic covered in the research used in this chapter was the future consumption of cultured *in vitro* meat. Yet, in West Mexico, most people are not aware of the laboratory process of producing cultured meat, and it was necessary to explain and give a short definition of lab-grown, cultured or *in vitro* meat:

> Lab-grown meat is an alternative to conventional meat. It is cultivated in labs through the culture process, wherein a biopsy is taken from a live animal and stem cells are separated from the muscle cells. These stem cells are cultured in a medium that provides them with the nutrients needed for proliferation. The stem cells multiply and transform into muscle cells and fat cells, eventually forming meat.[9]

Yet the idea of *in vitro* meat for human consumption is not completely new. When writing about culturing meat, Ford (2010) includes examples of earlier discussions of the possibility, citing even a suggestion by Winston Churchill.

Bhat et al. (2015: 241) describe the *in vitro* meat production system (IMPS) as 'the production of meat outside the food animals by culturing the stem cells derived from farm animals inside the bioreactor by using advanced tissue engineering techniques'. They go on to comment on the world's first hamburger cultured from bovine skeletal muscle stem cells. According to them, 30 billion cells forming 10,000 muscle fibres were used to create the hamburger. The cost of production was US$300,000. The people who tasted this hamburger said it was recognisable as meat, but the flavour and dryness indicated the need for fat tissue to be added. It was concluded that cultured meat had a long way to go before becoming a common consumer's product.

Datar and Betti (2010: 13) propose that the IMPS could be 'a humane, safe and environmentally beneficial alternative to slaughtered animal flesh as a source of nutritional muscle tissue'. They cite earlier articles on the research into the process and the patents, outlining several of the problems encountered, but they see the IMPS as a viable response to the increasing demand for meat in an environmental situation of reducing resources for animal husbandry. Yet, they also identify some flaws in the concept at present because certain nutrients, naturally in meat from animals, are not formed in the IMPS process.

In his editorial to a series of articles, Jean-François Hocquette (2015) considers whether *in vitro* meat could be beneficial for humanity faced with such serious contemporary issues as the protein demands of an ever-increasing global population as well as land degradation in many areas due to human activities and livestock pasturing. However, he goes on to explain that one challenge for cultured meat is to mimic traditional meat in terms of sensory quality at an affordable price in order to become acceptable for future consumers. Yet, beyond these technological and economic aspects, he argues that citizens and consumers might one day be convinced that artificial meat will bring both personal (taste, safety and healthiness) and societal benefits (food security, no environmental degradation, better animal wellbeing, etc.), but that this is uncertain. Nevertheless, discussion of the demand for meat in the context of contemporary environmental conditions, including climate change and the need to reduce the carbon footprint of producing meat, is expanded by Aurélie Hocquette et al. (2015). Their study is based on a survey of the views of 'educated French people' and 'educated people worldwide' about *in vitro* meat, including questions concerning expected taste acceptability, environmental concerns and animal welfare. Sharma et al. (2015) also discuss the concept of an IMPS, including some of the drawbacks for the acceptability of *in vitro* meat due to losses of components that affect flavour and even colour. They then include some results about its acceptability from polls in different countries.

For the purposes of the study used in this chapter, the topic of cultured *in vitro* meat was introduced into the interviews in West Mexico, but many people were confused; it is still not common knowledge that this is possible. Even when presented with the above information, urban adults thought that *in vitro* meat was way too futuristic to consider. Then, a group of biological anthropology students from the University of Guadalajara were asked whether or not *in vitro* meat could be considered as a solution to any of the issues outlined above, and whether it could be considered in any way purer compared to conventional livestock products. Also, could this method provide healthier meat products for human consumption? What about vegetarians? Can *in vitro* meat be considered as a production method that is less harmful to the environment? They were more open-minded and interested in possibilities of feeding more people in a safer way. They were then asked if *in vitro* meat could be a solution for achieving a 'pure food' and although they became interested in the concept, their arguments were initially directed towards a concern for contamination due to unsafe conditions of feed, grazing or water, since the stem cells are taken directly from a living cow. This was cleared up by explaining that these conditions would not affect the genetic make-up of the stem cells, even though it was agreed that concerns about such conditions could indeed be relevant, in general, to calling 'pure' any other food products derived from living cattle, such as milk or cheese. Also discussed was the possibility that the process of producing cultured meat might solve the problem of animal welfare, since there would be no need to slaughter livestock. However, they then began to question the viability of such a product in the market,[10] but no one thought that this *in vitro* meat could be considered appropriate for vegetarians. This is interesting in light of the findings by Bonny et al. (2015), who suggest that meat replacements of plant or mycoprotein origin, rather than cultured meat, would achieve the necessary environmental benefits. In fact, these are already being purchased more frequently in markets in place of meat as well as being considered suitable for vegetarians.

The students were sceptical about how much animal welfare would be improved by the method, stating that the livestock would still be kept penned-up. Yet, according to Bhat et al. (2015: 242), animal welfare most probably would benefit because tissue for the culture is removed from the cow with local anaesthetic, and there is no need for so much slaughter of livestock. Contamination in some way caused during the laboratory process of producing the cultured meat was a concern for some students. The eventual consensus was that it would be a long time before *in vitro* meat would be a feasible product on the market, with costs being viewed as the main problem. However, most thought that as far as the concept of pure food was concerned, this could be an example, since there would be no chemical contamination, such as fertilisers, insecticides, added hormones and antibiotics. But they did not discuss the topic of contemporary environmental conditions or the energy costs of production.

In conclusion, it is questionable how much of a notable change would in reality occur in food security or in improved environmental conditions with greater provision of *in vitro* meat, especially with its costs of production.

A Local Farmers' Market

The new trend in Guadalajara of elite famers' markets selling organic food can be seen in the expensive Andares Shopping Mall (Figure 9.1).

Figure 9.1. Farmers' market in the Plaza Andares, Zapopan, Jalisco, Mexico. © Daria Degara

This farmers' market is set up each Saturday from 11 am to 3 pm with a variety of products directed towards consumers of organic, vegetarian, vegan, health and natural foods. Along with packaged food merchandise, there are plants, herbs, household products and medicinal remedies for sale. This specialised market is very successful, due to the relatively recent preoccupation of some consumers about what they eat. Through social media, popular magazines, news reports and chat with friends, there is increasingly more awareness and criticism of food products. Most people cannot explain clearly why they choose what they choose, and are even less likely to give a scientific explanation for their choice, whether in favour of natural or organic or against transgenic foods or GMOs, but they believe it to be the right path to a healthier life. One male adult, when asked about the products on display, replied that he sometimes buys things from this farmers' market because 'people say' it is better, healthier food.

The main problem for consumers of the products offered in these elite farmers' markets is the high purchasing cost. For most people of the Guadalajara area, it would be out of the question to buy all their food at one of these markets, and so for many, only special products are sought out. Most probably it is primarily those following a strict vegan diet and people looking for an alternative to the general consumer's way of life who are more dependent on these markets. But apart from the high prices, the attraction is there, as people are becoming more concerned about the purity of food.

An Example of the New Trend

During a visit to a local artisanal fair in Guadalajara, dedicated to Mezcal[11] products and promoting artisanal, ecofriendly and sustainable methods of food production, I met and interviewed an adult male who produces organic bread in his private bakery. His products were included in a section of the fair dedicated to organic, natural and artisanal food, where there was also a section of special cooked dishes that are available for the visitors for consumption around midday. He explained how he spends time looking for people who sell organic ingredients for making his bread. Being organic, these initial cooking materials cost more than the equivalent products in the big commercial supermarkets. He stated that right from the beginning, the costs are higher for making his bread compared to the more common brands. When asked about how certain he was that the products he purchases can be truly considered organic, he said it was based on trust and believing what the producers claim. I asked about any special certificate verifying and stating the origin of ingredients, and he said there are some official organisations that inspect and declare the product organic if it meets the qualifications.[12] But he did not seem completely convinced. He had more trust in people he knew personally in the agricultural environment of natural, nontransgenic food products. Additionally, as was the case with the more radical pro-organic informants, when asked directly about transgenic foods, he simply lumped them all together as bad; there was no informed argument on the pros and cons.

Final Words

All the people interviewed in the studies used in this chapter were from the area of West Mexico, and most were opinionated on their choices of food they consumed, some being much more adamant than others. For most of them, the main access to information on food safety, transgenic foods, GMOs, organic and natural products was through popular magazines and other published information as well as groups of friends who discussed these products and exchange ideas. For students, the internet played an important role in acquiring information. A more scientific approach to research into transgenic plant and animal information was not apparent. The concept of the phrase 'pure food' in Spanish did not really stand out in the same way as it does in English. For most people, it simply meant food with nothing else mixed together with it. Where the idea of pure food did become apparent was during the discussions with students on the subject of cultured meat. In this case, they said it might be an example of pure food in the manner being discussed here because, as long as there were no added chemicals or hormones in its production process, it would be pure, being developed straight from the stem cells of the cattle.

What is really observable in West Mexico is the more recent concept of organic food products among a much more varied group of consumers; this is no longer limited to just a few, who in the past demonstrated their concern and then became dedicated to selective foods and healthy eating. Markets dedicated to organic products are springing up, and organisations to verify products as organic are now beginning to appear in Mexico. Through these interviews, which were done in an open, conversational way, I found an attitudinal change appearing, based on a greater degree of concern and selection of healthy food products being offered on the market by the younger generation of consumers in West Mexico. However, it is also observed that the older generations, and especially people from a more rural background, are still sceptical about the new trends related to food safety and food security.

Daria Deraga is a full-time researcher in biological anthropology at the National Institute of Anthropology and History, Centro INAH Jalisco, Guadalajara, Jalisco, Mexico.

Notes

1. https://www.who.int/health-topics/food-genetically-modified#tab=tab_1 (last accessed 6 October 2022).
2. https://www.fao.org/fileadmin/templates/faoitaly/documents/pdf/pdf_Food_Security_Cocept_Note.pdf (last accessed 7 October 2022).
3. https://www.fao.org/right-to-food/resources/resources-detail/ar/c/1035301/ (last accessed 6 October 2022).
4. https://www.ncbi.nlm.nih.gov/pmc/articles/PMC4648904/ (last accessed 6 October 2022).
5. https://www.who.int/emergencies/disease-outbreak-news/item/2013_11_13-en (last accessed 6 October 2022).
6. 'The use of clenbuterol to raise veal calves is illegal in the United States. Clenbuterol is not a hormone, but a growth-promoting drug in the beta-agonist class of compounds. Clenbuterol residues can affect lung and heart function in persons who have eaten liver or meat of animals given the drug. The United States Department of Agriculture considers any residue of clenbuterol in meat unacceptable because of this.' https://ask.usda.gov/s/article/Is-clenbuterol-used-in-veal-raising#:~:text=The%20use%20of%20Clenbuterol%20to,of%20animals%20given%20the%20drug (last accessed 6 October 2022).
7. https://pubmed.ncbi.nlm.nih.gov/7476054/ (last accessed 6 October 2022).
8. https://ecotec.unam.mx/organizaciones/red-mexicana-de-tianguis-y-mercados-organicos (last accessed 6 October 2022).
9. https://www.news-medical.net/health/Is-Lab-Grown-Meat-Healthy.aspx (last accessed 6 October 2022).
10. https://cellbasedtech.com/lab-grown-meat-companies (last accessed 6 October 2022).
11. Mezcal, very similar to tequila, is an alcoholic beverage made from the agave plant in Mexico.
12. Agreement provided to promote the national distinctive of organic products and establish the general rules for its use in the labeling of certified organic, https://www.gob.mx/cms/uploads/attachment/file/550718/Mexico_Official_Gazette_of_the_Federation_March_20_2020.pdf (last accessed 6 October 2022).

References

Bhat, Z.F., Kumar, S. and Fayaz, H. (2015) *In Vitro* Meat Production: Challenges and Benefits over Conventional Meat Production, *Journal of Integrative Agriculture*, 14(2): 241–48.

Bonny, S.P.F., Gardner, G.E., Pethick, D.W. and Hocquette, J.-F. (2015) What Is Artificial Meat and What Does It Mean for the Future of the Meat Industry? *Journal of Integrative Agriculture*, 15: 255–63.

Caucci, S. and Hettiarachchi, H. (2017) Wastewater Irrigation in the Mezquital Valley, Mexico: Solving a Century-Old Problem with the Nexus Approach. In *Proceedings of the International Capacity Development Workshop on Sustainable Management Options for Wastewater and Sludge, Mexico, 15–17 March 2017, Dresden*, United

Nations University Institute for Integrated Management of Material Fluxes and of Resources (UNU-FLORES).

Contreras, J.D., Trangucci, R., Felix-Arellano, E.E., Rodriguez-Dozal, S., Siebe, C., Riojas-Rodriguez, H., Meza, R., Zelner, J. and Eisenberg, J.H.S. (2020) Proximity of Untreated Wastewater Used for Irrigation in the Mezquital Valley, Mexico, *Environmental Health Perspectives*, 128(7): 770022.

Datar, I. and Betti, M. (2010) Possibilities for an *in Vitro* Meat Production System, *Innovative Food Science and Emerging Technologies*, 11: 13–22.

Deraga, D. (2008) *Sobre vacas y caballos en Jalisco. El saber especializado: un estudio en antropología cognitiva*, Instituto Nacional de Antropología e Historia, Colección Científica, Guadalajara.

Diaz-Quiñonez, J.A., Hernández-Monroy, I., Montes-Colima, N.A., Moreno-Pérez, M.A., Galicia-Nicolás, A.G., López-Martínez, I, Ruiz-Matus, C., Kuri-Morales, P., Ortiz-Alcántara, J.M., Garcés-Ayala, F. and Ramirez-González, J.E. (2016) Biochemical and Full Genome Sequence Analyses of Clinical *Vibrio Cholerae* Isolates in Mexico Reveals the Presence of Novel *V.Cholerae* Strains, *Microbes and Infections*, 18(5): 322–28.

Ford, B.J. (2010) Culturing Meat for the Future: Anti-Death versus Anti-Life. In Tandy, C. (ed.) *Death and Anti-Death*, Ria University Press, Palo Alto, pp. 1–26.

Gómez-Arroyo, S. and Infanzón, R.M. (2003) Persistent Organochlorine Pesticides in Mexican Butter, *Food Additives and Contaminants*, 20(4): 361–67.

Gutiérrez, G., Tapia-Conyer, T., Guiscafré, H., Reyes, H., Martínez, H. and Kumate, J. (1996) Impact of Oral Rehydration and Selected Public Health Interventions on Reduction of Mortality from Childhood Diarrhoeal Diseases in Mexico, *Bulletin of the World Health Organization*, 74(2): 189–97.

Hocquette, A., Lambert, C., Sinquin, C., Peterolff, L., Wagner, Z., Bonny, S.P.F., Lebert, A. and Hocquette, J.-F. (2015) Educated Consumers Don't Believe Artificial Meat Is the Solution to the Problems with the Meat Industry, *Journal of Integrative Agriculture*, 14(2): 273–84.

Hocquette, J.-F. (2015) Is It Possible to Save the Environment and Satisfy Consumers with Artificial Meat?, *Journal of Integrative Agriculture*, 14(2): 206–7.

Moore, S.M., Shannon, K.L., Zelaya, C.E., Azman, A.S. and Leasler, J. (2014) Epidemic Risk from cholera introductions into Mexico, *PLOS Currents*, 21: 6, published at https://www.ncbi.nlm.nih.gov/pmc/articles/PMC3933092/. Accessed on 4 February 2023.

Mora, A.M., Papoulias, D., Nava, I. and Buckler, D.R. (2001) A Comparative Assessment of Contaminants in Fish from Four Resacas of the Texas, USA – Tamaulipas, Mexico Border Region, *Environment International*, 27: 15–20.

Sepúlveda, J., Valdespino, J.L. and García-García, L. (2006) Cholera in Mexico: The Paradoxical Benefits of the Last Pandemic, *International Journal of Infectious Diseases*, 10(1): 4–13.

Sharma, S., Thin, S.S. and Kaur, A. (2015) *In Vitro* Meat Production System: Why and How?, *Journal of Food Science and Technology*, 54(12): 7599–607.

Waliszewski, S.M., Villalobos-Pietrini, R., Gómez-Arroyo, S. and Infanzón, R.M. (2003) Persistent Organochlorine Pesticides in Mexican Butter, *Food Additives and Contaminants*, 20(4): 361–67.

CHAPTER 10
THE LABEL 'ORGANIC' AS A REPRESENTATION OF FOOD PURITY: A STUDY OF AN ORGANIC BEEF FARM IN OXFORDSHIRE, ENGLAND

Helen Macbeth

Introduction

The word 'pure' has been discussed in previous chapters in this volume. It has a sense of the absolute, free from any additives or other mixture. It is also usually used to suggest something positive. The perspective on pure food in this chapter is based on the contemporary use of the word 'organic' as a classification of food and its production. I start with the observation that, in Western countries, consumers' interest in paying extra for so-called 'organic' foods is primarily based on their concepts of purity. However, a distinction needs to be made here between describing an item of food as 'pure' and relating 'organic' foods to concepts of purity. That the latter encourage the purchase of 'organic' foods is to a large extent rational, because of the avoidance of potentially harmful adulterations when the producer has to restrict the use of various products such as pesticides, weedkillers and fertilisers in the fields, and antibiotics, growth hormones, etc. in animals to achieve 'organic' certification. In this, it approximates the Latin *purus*[1] (see Lejavitzer, this volume) and can generally be perceived as a positive benefit (see MacClancy, this volume). As organic beef is the topic to be discussed here, a comparison of uses of the words 'pure' and 'organic' can be exemplified with reference to a packet of mince. Calling the contents 'pure beef' just means that the mince is entirely bovine, whether the animal was raised under the regulations of organic certification or not.

This chapter is centred on an ethnographic description of one farm producing 'organic beef' in Oxfordshire, England, originally studied from 2006 to 2011. I shall use the ethnographic present tense for the section describing that fieldwork and for that part of the discussion relevant to those years. The chapter will then continue with information since that fieldwork. First, however, I shall consider issues surrounding the certification of food as 'organic'. In this case, discussion of 'organic' relates primarily to what is needed for cattle rearing to produce 'organic beef', which includes all the restrictions that apply to maintaining the grass pasture and all the crops grown to feed these cattle, care of the cattle, the slaughter, butchery and all actions up to sale of the beef. The work involved is discussed in detail below, including the enormous load that it imposes on the lifestyle of the farmer and his wife.

In bringing information about this farm up to date during my later visits from 2015 to 2021, this chapter will go on to discuss the circumstances that led this farmer to discard his 'organic' classification for the benefit of his cattle and the resultant quality of the beef. I shall question whether some of the concepts on which 'organic' food classifications rest are always beneficial and whether they have kept up with modern molecular science.

Classifying and Certifying Food as 'Organic'

As indicated by my use above of quotation marks around the word 'organic', I am personally critical of this special use of the word in popular discourse, because the word *organic* suggests to a scientist all biological *organisms* in the biosphere, and, in chemical terms, that relates to their carbon content. However, a similar misuse of vocabulary exists in other languages that use either 'organic' or 'biological' for this specialised meaning: for example, *alimentos orgánicos* (Spanish), *Bio-lebensmittel* (German), *alimentation biologique* (French), *biopotraviny* (Czech), *βιολογικα τροφιμα* (Greek), etc.

In this chapter, I shall nevertheless use the word *organic* without quotation marks to convey this special meaning. Classification of food as organic is far more complex than I had thought before undertaking the research on which this chapter rests. I believe, too, that among the general public there is only a very vague understanding of what classification as organic means. Such uncertainty is understandable because the legal requirements vary to some extent from country to country, and even vary between some certifying bodies in the same country. I was astounded to learn, for example, that not all foods labelled as organic are necessarily pesticide-free in some classifications, as identified in the online article 'What Makes Produce "Organic"?':

> Contrary to what most people believe, 'organic' does *not* automatically mean 'pesticide-free' or 'chemical-free'. In fact, under the laws of most States [referring to the United States], organic farmers are allowed to use a wide variety of chemical sprays and powders on their crops. So, what *does* organic mean? It means that these pesticides, if used, must be derived from natural sources, not synthetically manufactured (Home n.d.).

In the quotation above, the 'derived from natural sources' is not a clear definition, for there is plenty of matter occurring naturally that is inorganic. Yet, an important point also lies in that clause: pure minerals are inorganic, but what about the minerals within an organism, which could thus be *derived from* organic sources? Biological organisms have chemical structures, which, depending on the organism, may contain inorganic components including minerals, i.e. components without carbon atoms within their complex chemical make-up. Consider the discussion of iron within the red blood cells of mammalian blood (discussed in Saucedo et al. this volume). While it is generally true that many synthetic substances containing inorganic chemicals cannot be used as fertilisers, pesticides or weedkillers on fields producing organic food, inorganic substances 'manufactured' from organic matter may well be allowed – for example, minerals derived from seaweed. This situation is even more interesting at the molecular level, where some molecules identical to those 'in nature' can now be synthesised in laboratories. Furthermore, when it comes to pesticides, there are many naturally occurring *organic* substances that are poisonous to some species, and many synthetic pesticides have been designed following molecular research into naturally occurring poisons. So, is a distinction in identical molecules between those produced in nature and those manufactured in a laboratory a scientifically significant difference between pesticides that are and that are not allowed in organic food production?

The above should not be taken as a refutation of the fact that fertilisers, pesticides and weedkillers have indeed been synthesised with ingredients, whether of organic or inorganic origin, that have passed into foods and have proved to be harmful to human health. Research literature on the carcinogenic effects of several pesticides has long existed (e.g. Dich et al. 1997; Dreiher and Kordish 2006; Grout et al. 2020), but it is beyond the scope of this chapter to examine whether that literature distinguishes how the molecular ingredients of the pesticides were formed. Research into carcinogenic risk falls into two general categories: those that attempt epidemiologically to correlate variables in case histories of a large number of cancer patients to seek a link between a specific variable and a specific cancer; and those drawn from laboratory experiments, in which nonhuman animals are exposed to specific chemicals. In the former, any correlation found may be hard to break down into precise elements, and for the latter, the origin of the molecular structure of the substances tested may not be discussed. What is consistently true is that food labelled organic must originate from producers, whose production methods from soil to sale have been certified as organic by some officially recognised certifying body and have followed the restrictions of that organic classification for a given period of time. Furthermore, neither genetic modification nor irradiation is allowed, even of totally organic cells.

Certification processes vary. For European Union (EU) countries, there has been EU legislation since 1992,[2] but each nation state supervises the certifying bodies in that nation. While there is now an EU-wide label and logo for organically certified foods, there is variation as to who is responsible for that certification. In the United Kingdom, for example, there are several certifying bodies. The five most common are: the Soil Association,[3] the Organic Farmers and Growers Ltd,[4] the Organic Food Federation,[5] the Biodynamic Agricultural Association[6] and Ascisco Ltd.[7] These not only certify but also assist and inspect the producers and their products regularly. They in turn are overseen by a government department and must comply with UK and EU regulations. Nevertheless, from the point of view of the producer, there are differences between these certifying organisations and reasons for a farmer to choose which certifying body they prefer, such as price of certification, the amount of help and advice given, the degree of rigour in the inspections or simply that one name is more familiar to the public and provides the sales benefit of its logo on the produce.

Under the policies of all these organisations, in order for a food product to be certified organic, there are restrictions at every step of its production: in the case of beef, from attention to the fertility of the soil, the planting and harvesting of feed crops, weed avoidance and responsibility for the grass pasture to the medical and dietary care of the animals themselves from insemination to slaughter. Then there are still more requirements at every stage of the butchering, packaging and labelling processes ... and finally for any repackaging and relabelling that occurs, right up to sale to the purchaser. That is why I used the phrase *from soil to sale* above, since the more common phrase *from farm to fork* incorrectly suggests further restrictions after sale to the consumer.

What I found on the farm in Oxfordshire that forms the case study for this chapter was how profound the implications of this certification process were for the life and work of the farmer and his wife. In their case it does not just refer to care of the cattle and the cultivation of all the feed of the cattle, which is nearly all grown on the farm; it also refers to their organising of the slaughter, butchery, packaging and labelling of the packs of beef that the farmer's wife sells at farmers' markets. From slaughter to packaging and labelling, this must all be done on premises certified for organic food production, and this includes a regulation against any work on foods not certified as organic being carried out on the same premises. This is to avoid any cross-contamination via machines or tools, or even confusion of produce.

An Ethnographic Study of One Organic Beef Form (2006–11)

This section concerns the original study of the farm from 2006 to 2011. The ethnographic present tense is used and regulations referred to and discussed were current at the time.

Crops, Feed and the Decision to Get the Farm Classified for Producing Organic Beef

The current farmer is the second generation on the farm. He and his father had always farmed beef cattle, fed primarily on the grass of traditional pasture fields and on its hay and silage in the winter, supplemented with a little barley mixed with peas grown on land in rotation with the pasture fields. Because of this, they were already essentially farming in an organic way when the British government offered financial subsidies for conversion to organic production. So, in 1999 they decided to convert to being *classified* as an organic producer; it takes two seasons to convert in order to ensure that the soil, plants and cattle are free of any previously added inorganic chemicals. After certification, initially the cattle feed remained little changed, although later on, the crops were further diversified (see below) with different grains grown organically on the farm. Some pasture fields are grazed, while on others the grass is left to grow to be cut once, sometimes twice, a year for hay to build up a large silage pile (see below).

In the later part of the summer, while the cattle are still out on the grass pastures, their feed is supplemented, partly with oat- or barley-straw laid out on the fields, and partly with grain put into special feed containers on the fields. Since 2002, this farmer has gradually diversified the arable feed crops grown on the farm, and has grown spring-sown and winter-sown oats and some barley for feed and straw; he tried growing beans, but after a particularly cold, wet summer, when the beans never matured before rotting, he stopped growing them. He also grows wheat in order to sell the grain at premium organic prices and use the straw for bedding. All are grown organically. Of course, all these feed crops have to be harvested and stored, and storing grain involves machines as well as space where the grain can be kept dry.

Growing organic crops has more risks than growing crops without restrictions on the use of inorganic fertilisers, pesticides, weedkillers, etc. Any weed infestation requires early removal of each seedling weed or else a later reduction in yield follows. The farmer told me that rearing organic livestock was inherently less risky than cultivating crops organically, but the risk increased in the case of his beef farm because they also grow the organic crops to feed the cattle. However, doing both at least provides a plentiful supply of manure for the fields. As inorganic chemical fertilisers are restricted, manure is used as the main fertiliser, primarily where dropped when the cattle are in the pastures, but also collected from the pens in the winter months, then loaded on to a tractor-drawn spreader and scattered on the pastures. The other traditional method to assist soil fertility while limiting unwanted infestations of pests and infections is crop rotation.

Around October, the cattle come in from the fields to pens under cover, which necessitates winter feeding, dry straw bedding and cleaning out the manure from the pens. For the winter feed, the dried grains (mostly oats,

Figure 10.1. Cattle in winter feeding on an organic mixture of silage and mashed grains. © Helen Macbeth

occasionally some barley) are first crushed. These crushed grains are then transferred to a large feed trailer, into which silage is added. The proportions of grains to silage vary depending on the needs of the cattle in each pen. Cows in calf are fed just silage, cows still feeding their calves have mostly silage and some grain, whereas weaned calves get more grain with the silage as they get older. The farmer referred a great deal to 'protein content' in what is given to each condition of cattle, but he was unspecific about amino acids. As shown in Figure 10.1, these troughs are outside the barrier rails of the cattle sheds, and the cattle feed with heads between the rails. The farmer told me that plenty of feed is deposited, so that there is enough left for the less dominant cattle when they at last can get forward to feed.

On one winter's day I observed fresh bedding straw being laid down in a pen, and I watched the cattle immediately put their heads down to feed on what they found edible in the bedding straw. This is an intriguing detail because, although on this farm the straw is homegrown, it is permissible for bedding straw on a farm with organic classification to be bought in from elsewhere and it need not be certified organic. So, although not on this farm, here was exemplified a permitted possibility for matter to be consumed off the bedding straw that was not classified as organic.

Cutting the Hay, Making Silage and Harvesting the Grain

Fields that have been left to grow for hay and silage get cut when the grass is of a suitable length and the weather is appropriate. Then, appropriate machinery is needed to cut and chop the grass ready for the dense packing down needed for silage, as well as appropriate trailers to carry it back to form one pile in the farmyard. This pile is then covered by black plastic sheeting weighted down by old tyres because compression is needed to remove air so that anaerobic fermentation takes place. It is left to mature initially for four months, but thereafter care is taken to let in as little air as possible during the whole period that the resultant silage, being fermented grass, is used for winter feed.

Harvesting the grain also requires large and expensive equipment, and it seems that farmers running traditional family farms can only survive financially by renting equipment or sharing equipment with neighbours. This farmer shares some equipment with a neighbour.

Registration and Care of the Cattle

Cattle in the United Kingdom, as throughout the European Union, have to be registered, as cattle identification and traceability are legal requirements for all cattle, whether organic or not. Referring still to the period of my field-work from 2006 to 2011, each calf is registered and tagged in each ear within twenty days of birth, and has a passport issued by the British Cattle Movement Service (BCMS). Movement to a new farm or death has to be notified to the BCMS; such recording of all movements registers the whereabouts of all individual cattle at all times. There are on-farm records and inspections. All this is important for disease control and even for maintaining consumer confidence, but it also allows for analysis of genetic relationships. Ear tags must not be removed without permission of the BCMS. In all EU countries, the registration systems have to conform to EU legislation and the protocols of a computerised tracking system. For cattle that may be moved internationally between EU countries, there are also EU passports – i.e. for the farmer, there is a great deal of paperwork and computer work to carry out. Such registration of cattle is especially important for organic cattle, as with the classification *organic* come further rules defined by legislation. Although EU legislation covers all nations in the EU, within that legislation there is also some diversity between areas leading to a complexity of legislation that is beyond the scope of this chapter.

An average of about a hundred breeding cows are kept on this farm and an average of about two hundred calves are being raised here until they are two years old. I learned that an individual beast can be treated, even with antibiotics, if a veterinary surgeon prescribes this. However, by law for all the United Kingdom, no animal may be slaughtered for human consumption within a given period, called the 'withdrawal period', which varies depending on certain variables, such as the antibiotic used. Under organic farming standards, this period may be doubled or even tripled. Also, there are precise rules about worming, which vary with the type of worm infestation and type of worm medicine used. Again, there is a withdrawal period afterwards. Not only is it illegal to let an unhealthy cow or bull suffer, but Soil Association standards also clearly state that organic animals *must be* treated 'conventionally'[8] *if* needed to prevent undue suffering or welfare issues. Poor animal welfare harms the reputation of any type of farming, including organic. Yet, with organic certification, one may only treat that individual animal for its condition and one may not treat a group of animals or use medicine prophylactically on the whole herd. Finally, of course, everything has to be recorded.

Slaughter, Butchery and Sale

Animals for slaughter have to be sent to a specialist abattoir, certified for slaughtering only organic livestock on its premises to avoid any possible cross-contamination. During this period of my research into the organic constraints, this farmer changed slaughterer three times, changing because of distance (e.g. one involved a three-hour drive each way) or because of the service received. Yet, there are few alternatives. One option is to sell live animals to the Organic Livestock Marketing Cooperative, an organisation that collects live animals off the farm, but this pays only for dead weight of the carcass in accordance with a quality grading by its own inspectors. This, as the farmer's wife told me, leaves the farmer totally in the Cooperative's hands as regards payment per animal. By organising the slaughtering, butchery and selling of the beef themselves, the farmer and his wife gain about one-third more price on each carcass than if selling to the Cooperative, but this also involves a great deal more work, long hours and, when selling the beef at a farmers' market, very early mornings.

The farmer usually takes two animals at a time in the farm's trailer to the specialist slaughterer every two weeks – that is, an average of four beasts a month. The cattle are slaughtered and hung at the abattoir for two weeks and then divided into large chunks of meat, which are vacuum-packed in plastic to be collected and brought back to the farm. Next comes the butchering, which again must be on certified premises where only organic meat is cut up. During the time of my fieldwork, the farmer and his wife converted a room in the farmhouse to the appropriately clean conditions required and started to employ a specialist butcher to come and carve up the meat into different cuts for steaks, roasts, stew and mince. The farmer's wife works with the butcher putting, for example, meat through the mincing machine and dividing the various cuts into appropriately sized packages for purchaser choices. Once packed, each bag is vacuum-sealed to become a consumer-friendly packet for sale. These packets are then taken to an outhouse with a large walk-in cold store. However, for the farmer's wife, there is still more work to do labelling each packet. She is often up until midnight the night before a farmers' market labelling the packets, and then she has to get up early the next morning to put them in large cool boxes and drive a van, often for several miles, to set up a stall at a market by 7 am. She stays at that stall, mostly on her feet, all morning until 1 pm, personally selling the beef to customers who are willing to pay the extra prices for this organic and local beef. The farmer summarised their dedication to the work as: 'One cannot go in for organic farming half-heartedly; one must be totally committed.' He gave me some figures for the mark-up in price at which their organic beef can be sold, which we, as purchasers, notice, but when these are balanced with the financial figures for the extra costs of maintaining the organic certification, it is clear that it is difficult to make organic beef farming profitable.

Information from My Returns to the Farm in 2014 and 2015

The first thing to report after the above descriptive part of this chapter is that in 2012 this farmer and his wife gave up the organic certification of their beef as not financially sustainable. There were several reasons behind this decision. A prime reason lay in the frustrations of the slaughtering and butchery options, and the poor recompense obtainable from the alternative of selling through the Organic Livestock Marketing Cooperative. Restrictions due to organic certification kept the slaughter and butchery firms small and their costs high without economies of scale. Then in 2008, there was the global financial downturn, which in the United Kingdom depressed demand for organic beef. Another element in the decision related to limited space for storage of the farmer's grain. When a neighbouring farmer built a new grain store in 2011, space was available for rent, but the organic grain could not be stored next to that farmer's conventional grain, without giving up its organic certification. As well as all that, a mineral deficiency in the soil of the farm was identified scientifically.

Restrictions for Organic Certification and Modern Science

As already discussed, at the time of my study of this farm, inorganic chemical fertilisers were restricted and manure collected from the pens fertilised the soil. The other traditional method used to limit unwanted infestations of pests, weeds, etc. was crop rotation. This farm has the acreage to allow this.

These traditional methods qualify as organic, but the soil on the farm was analysed using modern scientific methods, which indicated that the soil was inherently short of phosphate and low in magnesium; i.e. the mineral balance in the soil was not ideal, but an organic farmer is limited in terms of options to cure an inorganic imbalance. Science shows what is needed, but finding a certified organic remedy is a problem. Products accepted by the organic certifying body existed, but were expensive and of uncertain value; the farmer tried one such product based on seaweed, but it provided little benefit. Modern science was also used when a nutrition specialist tested the blood of the cattle and found minor mineral deficiencies – for example, on some occasions low magnesium, which if not addressed leads to hypomagnesemia in the cattle.[9] No chemical analyses were undertaken at the time to link these directly to the soil, but they were linked to mineral values in the feed that year, for example in the grass. This could hypothetically, and presumably, be linked to soil values, but no study was done.

Both of these modern scientific analyses exposed less than optimal conditions for the soil and for the cattle, and so presumably resulted in a less than perfect quality of meat. In other words, it can be argued that the very restrictions for keeping the farm organic were resulting in a less perfect quality of beef than might be achieved with inorganic improvement of the soil to improve the feed. Although I have not studied the subject myself, scientific knowledge has moved on greatly since the traditional rearing of cattle on which some of the organic food ideals are based. With the increase in knowledge of the environment, from soil chemistry to crop botany, as well as of animal biology, and with so much of this now at the molecular level, it would seem that a balance should be sought between the ideals of organic food production in avoiding harmful ingredients and an acceptable use of the most recent scientific developments, especially as organic molecules can now be mimicked in laboratories, which would allow for the *manufacture* of beneficial, mimicked organic supplements.

Three years after he gave up their organic certification, the farmer and his wife wondered how much the 'certified organic' label really had meant to their regular clientele at the local farmers' markets, or whether people returned to buy beef from this farm, due to its taste, or trust in its localism, or just loyalty to its stall.[10] Even today, when the farm is no longer certified as organic, the cattle have the same traditional feed, primarily the grass and silage from the farm's pastures, supplemented with grains all grown on the farm, but now they can address the mineral deficiencies in the soil and, where needed, supplement soil with safe fertilisers. The result is that the grain yield per acre has increased greatly and they can have fewer acres in grain and more in pasture, meaning more of the feed of the cattle is grass and silage. Furthermore, the cattle can now be provided with any minerals in which they were deficient, for example using a magnesium lick.[11] So, this farm is still producing cattle of high-quality beef, perhaps even higher quality than before, but no longer certified as organic. Their beef now goes to a well-known supermarket chain.

The farmer would like there to be a properly certified, different classification, supporting the traditional methods used on this farm, primarily grass-fed cattle and quality beef, still restricting chemicals with trace elements that are harmful to health, but allowing use of some of modern science's beneficial supplements. There are indeed all sorts of labels that people have created, such as 'natural', 'farm assured' and 'free range', but as there are no clear definitions or certifications of what these terms mean, or therefore proper recognition that they mean anything, public understanding of them varies. Some consumers may be persuaded, but I think most have become cynical. In the United Kingdom, as elsewhere, the publicity given to the worst food production methods has made many people more aware of risks, but also cynical of all methods. In this case study, doubt is at least thrown on whether the ideal option for highest-quality human food has yet been found in the current classification of food as organic.

There is another route to food 'purity' via recognition of quality and good production practices, which would include the absence of any harmful input, namely to buy food from the highest-quality retailers. There are two well-known retail food chains with stores all over the United Kingdom, enjoying a reputation for very high-quality food. Both of these maintain extremely close links with their farm producers, with strict inspections of production and quality from soil to sale, which underpin their 'guarantee of quality'. For one of these companies, I was informed in 2015 by a retired director that in their stores across the United Kingdom, organically certified foods never exceeded 5 percent of food bought, except in just two stores, both in affluent suburbs of London, and that, in his many years with the company, the proportion of organic food bought overall had never noticeably changed. In summary, it can be concluded that most customers of these stores are satisfied with the assurance and quality of their farm-produced foods and do not seek any added certification, such as organic.

Returning to the Farm in 2021 and 2022

On returning to the farm in both 2021 and 2022, I found that there had been changes. I had expected that a most significant set of changes would be due to the United Kingdom leaving the European Union, but although this has reduced some of the paperwork, the grants relevant to this farm are continuing, with the amount of money declining each year.

The biggest change that the farmer referred to was the change in UK government grants, in that those for activities that benefit the environment have increased. These include grants for wildlife areas, which this farmer supports and has little trouble in achieving. Furthermore, on one 11-hectare field of poor soil, he now has rows of photovoltaic solar panels for creating electricity (see Figure 10.2), under which a neighbour's sheep graze. At time of writing, planning permission for a second field is being sought. In the interview he agreed that whereas he was very much in favour of all actions benefiting the general environment, he wondered if at the same time, enough thought goes into where UK food will come from in the future.

Figure 10.2. Photovoltaic solar panels on a field of poor soil, providing renewable electricity to the local community. © Helen Macbeth

In summary, this farmer sees himself as striving for, as he puts it, 'a sustainable economic way of producing food in perpetuity, which will have no detrimental "side effects" to the consumer'. However, significantly, as our latest discussions have been during the spring of 2022, he qualified this that there may be times of need to produce more food nationally than is allowed under a sustainable system, for example, in adverse world circumstances such as war. As I write, the current war in Ukraine is affecting prices of fuel, wheat and fertiliser, which are all relevant to livestock farmers. The farmer argued that in reaction to food shortages after the Second World War, producing sufficient food for the population increasingly depended on environmentally unsustainable farming methods, excessive use of pesticides leading to pesticide resistance, excessive use of fertilisers leading to fresh water pollution, use of growth promoters in livestock (now banned), etc. Added to all this there was increasingly complex processing of the food, which is not discussed in this chapter. One objective of some of those promoting organic farming, he suggested, was an attempt to turn the clock back, while at the same time avoiding the now unacceptable levels of animal suffering and death that had occurred in those earlier periods. His personal aim is to seek ways 'to blend the old and the modern together' in the pursuit of sustainability. He suggests that some 'new system of production' should still be certified, but that 'organic' is not the right word for it.

Discussion

As is clear from the sections above, the research on which this chapter is based has continued over several years, but I now believe that the delays in publishing the ethnographic information have proved to be beneficial to the discussion.

Some of the changes on this farm have been described and meanwhile many changes are ongoing for the farming environment all around the United Kingdom. However, for me it was the situation in which the deficit of an inorganic mineral in the soil became a problem that has most affected my views in this discussion. Although the farmer tried using organically certified products, the problem was not resolved. Without the necessary scientific study, I can only make a prime assumption – that the reductions in mineral content in some feed and in the blood of the cattle are at least partially linked to the mineral deficiency in the soil. Whether or not this can be scientifically proven on this farm, it still becomes a useful hypothetical example, in which the limitations required for the production of food gaining organic certification do not necessarily lead to the highest-quality food nutritionally.

So, I turn to why consumers of organic food pay premium prices for organic food. From general conversations during my fieldwork, I learned that the perceived health benefits of organic food were the prime reason for paying the extra prices. Yet, at the time I found few academic journal articles on these issues, although the study by Pettinger et al. (2004) amused me, showing that, for the French sample studied, pleasure and taste were more important in their purchase of organic foods, while the English sample referred to health and ethical issues. Nevertheless, as shown by Fourmouzi et al. (2012), after comparing prices, the majority of people did not buy the more expensive organic options, so that only a relatively low proportion of all food sold had organic certification. This concurs with information I had received from the food retailer (discussed above). One can imagine that cost has been important in this, but other issues may be involved. Tandon et al. (2020), after mentioning growth worldwide in the demand for organic food (citing Sultan et al. 2020), make a distinction between the increasing interest in, plus positive attitude towards, organic food, and its generally low proportion of *all* food consumed, also pointing out that intentions may differ from actual behaviour.

When updating my literature search in 2022, the first thing to mention is the frequent reference in the press and in academic literature to increased consumer interest over the last decade in purchasing organic food. Relating this to land use, however, is not so straightforward. The statistics for the European Commission reported by Eurostat show that '[t]he total area under organic farming in the EU continues to increase, and in 2020 covered 14.7 million hectares of agricultural land'. [12] Yet, in the United Kingdom, whereas in 2011 there had been 656,000 hectares of land farmed organically – and that was a decrease by 9 percent from 2010[13] –, in 2020 there were only 489,000 hectares.[14] When this information was updated again in 2023, 507,000 hectares are shown for 2021;[15] so it has now increased. This may be partly due to an increased interest in buying organic food due to the COVID-19 pandemic, as suggested in the public media. The Statistica Research Department reported in January 2023: 'The UK is among the ten largest organic food markets worldwide, based on revenue generated.

However, it is not among the ten countries with the largest organic farm-land area.'[16] So, for the United Kingdom at least, the statistics for land used for farming organic food cannot be judged simply by rates of purchase of organic foods.

Considered from another angle, Hocquette et al. (2012), without reference to organic food, write on the complexity of measuring what meat 'quality' can be and they refer to the combination of considerations needed: sensory, nutritional, social, environmental, animal welfare and economic. Nevertheless, it would seem that the reasons for buying organic food primarily still relate to concepts of 'purity', based on avoidance of ingredients that might be harmful to health (examples of this can be found from Basha et al. 2015 to Lang and Rodrigues 2022; see also the Introduction to this volume). In parallel with these have been scientific studies of the health benefits, usually finding that organic diets had lower pesticide and other harmful residues than conventional diets (e.g. Vigar et al. 2019; Rebouillat et al. 2020; Rempelos et al. 2021). A consortium of French epidemiologists, toxicologists, nutritionists and economists studied the consumers of conventional foods and those of organic foods with attention to consumption, dietary patterns, health, the environment and monetary cost (Kesse-Gruyot et al. 2022), finding those following an organic diet to be healthier. Nevertheless, Ramakrishnan et al. (2021) reported on harmful residues remaining even in organic food, and Panseri et al. (2020) found evidence of pollutants even in organic honey (see the Epilogue to this volume).

In researching this literature, I have been intrigued to find references to other ethical issues in the motivations for consuming organic produce, and increasingly there has been a concern for the environment (e.g. Michaelidou and Hassan 2010; Basha et al. 2015; Tandon et al. 2020; Murphy et al. 2022). Although such consumers are equally interested in the avoidance of harmful residues in their organic diets, their concern for the environment would be of a different dimension having an interest in how farming practices affect the environment and being less relevant to the topic of pure food for the consumer[17]. Murphy et al.'s (2022) discussion of trust or lack of it in organic certification across Europe may be relevant to either dimension.

The regulations of all organic food certification schemes are designed to avoid pollutants and additives by restricting inputs that are not 'natural' or 'organic'. This concurs well with concepts of purity and the different English translations of the Latin word *purus*. Yet, if these pollutants are shown to be harmful for human consumption, why are they not illegal in *all* food? In fact, legislation banning the use of many substances in all food production does exist, but it is globally uneven. The other important issue is that by no means all dangerous substances that pollute are inorganic or synthetic in origin; organisms rot or gain fungi or other infections *organically*, some of which can be harmful, even fatal, if consumed by humans. As regards cattle, this can be exemplified by the prion protein causing bovine spongiform encephalopathy (BSE), which spread across cattle farms in Europe (Salman et al. 2012) and other parts of the world (Bradley and Liberski 2004) in the early years of this century. Although this exemplifies transmission of an organic prion, it was transferred through synthetic feed, including organically diseased meat and bone meal (Dagleish et al. 2008); such synthetic feed was avoided in certified organic farming.[18] Only after the spread of BSE did it become illegal to sell *any* feed for livestock that contained mammalian meat and bone meal.[19] So, in this case, the avoidance of a harmful substance became a legal requirement for *all* food for human consumption, which surely should always be the case.

Conclusion

Here I return to considering concepts of purity in the choice to buy organic foods. In that the English usage of the word *pure* includes the concept of the absolute, one could say that, by being consumed, all foods are 'absolutely food', but few would interpret it in this way (cf. Deraga, this volume). Instead, reflecting on MacClancy's demonstration (this volume) that concepts of purity are associated with the positive, one can argue that avoidance of what is harmful generally drives the positive attitudes to organic food. Returning to the different motivations for buying organic food, one can see the positive in the aims to avoid harm whether to the person or, more broadly, to the environment, although for the latter there is perhaps more sense of the effects of the organic processes *per se* on the environment than relevance to food. For whatever reason, this increasingly popular concern for the environment is welcome and it is very evident in the views (above) of the farmer. However, whether it is correctly directed at purchasing organic food is uncertain when reviewed scientifically. Since direct supplementation with the needed minerals is deemed to be *in*organic, the difficulties in ameliorating a mineral deficiency in the soil within the rules of organic certification suggest that the aims of organic certification may not have kept up with modern scientific options when these modern options can synthesise molecules identical to those in 'nature'. Also omitted in these concepts are additives – whether organic, inorganic or synthetic – that are beneficial or harmless to health. Surely, these too must reduce the *purity*!

This chapter, itself so firmly based on scientific principles, is fully cognisant of the range of reasons why people buy organic food, but the chapters in this book have helped me appreciate many more perspectives on pure food than I had understood in my original study of the farm. The greatest contribution to my understanding is how the original contribution to the topic by Mary Douglas (1966) can be encompassed within scientific thinking and should not be considered in opposition to it.

Acknowledgements

I wish to thank the farmer and his family, as well as Alex, Richard and Paul for help on other aspects.

Helen Macbeth is Honorary Research Fellow and retired Principal Lecturer in Anthropology at Oxford Brookes University. She is a former President of the International Commission on the Anthropology of Food and Nutrition with a strong interest in crossing the boundaries between traditional academic disciplines.

Notes

1. '*Purus, a, um* (adjective) I. pure, clear, free from dirt, filth, crime, etc. II. that is in its natural state, pure, simple, unadorned, inartificial, natural' (Riddle 1841: 306)
2. The fieldwork for the ethnographic part of this chapter and this part of the discussion on certification were carried out before United Kingdom left the European Union in 2020. Although the chapter continues beyond this time, this part of the discussion remains contemporary with the fieldwork. Below, this chapter will continue with changes since that time both on the farm and with discussion relevant to these later years. For example, relating to this one point about EU legislation made at the time is that later, in 2022, Murray et al., when discussing consumer trust in certifications of organic food, drew attention to the diversity between nation states in Europe and that respondents in Italy and Poland expressed higher trust in EU certification, whereas in the United Kingdom and Germany there was less trust in EU certification and a preference for their national certification boards.
3. See https://www.soilassociation.org/certification/ (last accessed 1 October 2022).
4. See https://ofgorganic.org/ (last accessed 1 October 2022).
5. See http://www.orgfoodfed.com/ (last accessed 1 October 2022).
6. See https://www.biodynamic.org.uk/ (last accessed 1 October 2022).
7. By 2021, this was registered as a dormant company with no website.
8. The farmer used the word 'conventionally' to refer to farming that was not organic but mainstream.
9. See https://medlineplus.gov/ency/article/000315.htm (last accessed 1 October 2022).
10. In the United States, research (e.g. Onozaka et al. 2010) has shown consumer motivation such as he suggested, as well as a campaign for 'Know your farmer'.
11. See https://www.fas.scot/news/magnesium-supplementation-for-cows/ (last accessed 1 October 2022).
12. See https://ec.europa.eu/eurostat/statistics-explained/index.php?title=Organic_farming_statistics (last accessed 4 February 2023)
13. See https://assets.publishing.service.gov.uk/government/uploads/system/uploads/attachment_data/file/137832/defra-stats-foodfarm-environ-organics-statsnotice-120605.pdf (last accessed 4 February 2023).

14. See https://assets.publishing.service.gov.uk/government/uploads/system/uploads/attachment_data/file/996197/Organic_Farming_2020_stats_notice-24jun21.pdf (last accessed 4 February 2023).
15. See https://www.gov.uk/government/statistics/organic-farming-statistics-2021 (last accessed on 4 February 2023)
16. See https://www.statista.com/topics/7117/organic-farming-in-the-uk/#topicOverview (last accessed 4 February 2023).
17. See also the discussion of this in the Epilogue to this volume.
18. See https://www.soilassociation.org/ (last accessed 2 October 2022).
19. See https://www.legislation.gov.uk/uksi/2002/843/part/III/crossheading/mammalian-protein-and-mammalian-meat-and-bone-meal/made) (last accessed 2 October 2022).

References

Basha, M.B. and Mason, C. (2015) Consumers' Attitude towards Organic Food, *International Accounting and Business Conference 2015*, 31: 444–52.

Bradley, R. and Liberski, P.P. (2004) Bovine Spongiform Encephalopathy (BSE): The End of the Beginning or the Beginning of the End? *Folia Neuropathologica,* 42 (Supplement A): 55–68.

Dagleish, M.P., Martin, S., Steele, P., Finlayson, J., Sisó, S., Hamilton, S., Chianini, F., Reid, H.W., González, L. and Jeffrey, M. (2008) Experimental Transmission of Bovine Spongiform Encephalopathy to European Red Deer (*Cervus elaphus elaphus*), *BMC Veterinary Research*, 4: 17. Published at: https://doi.org/10.1186/1746-6148-4-17. Accessed on 17 January 2022.

Dich, J., Zahm, S.H., Hanberg, A. and Adami, H.O. (1997) Pesticides and Cancer, *Cancer Causes Control*, 8(3): 420–43. Published at: https://link.springer.com/article/10.1023/A:1018413522959. Accessed on 17 January 2022.

Douglas, M. (1966) *Purity and Danger: An Analysis of Concepts of Pollution and Taboo*, Routledge & Kegan Paul, London.

Dreiher, J., and Kordysh, E. (2006) Non-Hodgkin Lymphoma and Pesticide Exposure: 25 Years of Research, *Acta Haematologica*, 116(3): 153–64.

Fourmouzi, V., Genius, M. and Midmore, P. (2012) The Demand for Organic and Conventional Produce in London, UK: A System Approach, *Journal of Agricultural Economics*, 63(3): 677–93.

Grout, L., Baker, M.G., French, N. and Hales, S.A. (2020) Review of Potential Public Health Impacts Associated with the Global Dairy Sector, *Geohealth*, 4(2): e2019GH000213. Published at: https://www.ncbi.nlm.nih.gov/pmc/articles/PMC7017588/. Accessed on 12 February 2022.

Hocquette, J.F., Botreau, R., Picard, B., Jacquet, A., Pethick, D.W. and Scollan, N.D. (2012) Opportunities for Predicting and Manipulating Beef Quality, *Meat Science*, 92(3): 197–209.

Home, L. (n.d.) About Organic Produce. Published at: https://www.ocf.berkeley.edu/~lhom/organictext.html. Accessed on 1 February 2022.

Kesse-Guyot, E., Lairon, D., Allès, B., Seconda, L., Rebouillat, P., Brunin, J., Vidal, R., Taupier-Letage, B., Galan, P., Amiot, M-J., Péneau, S., Touvier, M., Boizot-Santai, C., Ducros, V., Soler, L.-J., Cravedi, J.-P., Debrauwer, L., Hercberg, S., Langevin,

B., Pointereau, P. and Baudry, J. (2022) Key Findings of the French BioNutriNet Project on Organic Food-Based Diets: Description, Determinants, and Relationships to Health and the Environment, *Advances in Nutrition*, 13(1): 208–24. Published at: https://doi.org/10.1093/advances/nmab105. Accessed on 17 April 2022.

Lang, M. and Rodrigues, A.C. (2022) A Comparison of Organic-Certified versus Non-certified Natural Foods: Perceptions and Motives and Their Influence on Purchase Behaviors, *Appetite*, 168: 105698. Published at: https://doi.org/10.1016/j.appet.2021.105698. Accessed on 13 March 2022.

Michaelidou, N. and Hassan, L.M. (2010) Modelling the Factors Affecting Rural Consumers' Purchase of Organic and Free-Range Produce. A Case Study from the Island of Arran in Scotland, UK, *Food Policy*, 35(2): 130–39.

Murphy, B., Martini, M., Fedi, A., Loera, B.L. and Elliott, C.T. (2022) Consumer Trust in Organic Food and Organic Certifications in Four European Countries, *Food Control*, 133: 108484. Published at: https://doi.org/10.1016/j.foodcont.2021.108484. Accessed on 13 March 2022.

Onozaka, Y., Nurse, G. and McFadden, D.T. (2010) Local Food Consumers: How Motivations and Perceptions Translate to Buying Behavior, *Choices*, 25(1). Published at: https://www.choicesmagazine.org/UserFiles/file/article_109.pdf. Accessed on 24 December 2022.

Panseri, S., Bonerba, E., Nobile, M., Di Cesare, F., Mosconi, G., Cecati, F., Arioli, F., Tantillo, G. and Chiesa, L. (2020) Pesticides and Environmental Contaminants in Organic Honeys According to Their Different Productive Areas toward Food Safety Protection, *Foods*, 9(12): 1863. https://www.ncbi.nlm.nih.gov/pmc/articles/PMC7764946/pdf/foods-09-01863.pdf. Accessed on 13 March 2022.

Pettinger, C., Holdsworth, M. and Gerber, M. (2004) Psycho-social Influences on Food Choice in Southern France and Central England, *Appetite*, 42(3): 307–16.

Ramakrishnan, B., Maddela, N.R., Venkateswarlu, K. and Megharaj, M. (2021) Organic Farming: Does It Contribute to Contaminant-Free Produce and Ensure Food Safety?, *Science of the Total Environment*, 769: 145079. Published at: https://doi.org/10.1016/j.scitotenv.2021.145079. Accessed on 17 April 2022.

Rebouillat, P., Vidal, R., Cravedi, J-P., Taupier-Letage, B., Debrauwer, L., Garnet-Payrastre, L., Touvier, M., Hercberg, S., Lairon, D., Daudry, J. and Kesse-Guyot, E. (2020) Estimated Dietary Pesticide Exposure from Plant-Based Foods Using MF-Derived Profiles in a Large Sample of French Adults, *European Journal of Nutrition*, 60: 1475–88.

Rempelos, L., Wang, J. Berański, M., Watson, A., Volakakis, N., Hoppe, H.W., Kühn-Velten, W.N., Hadall, C., Hasanaliyeva, G., Chatzidimitriou, E., Magistrali, A., Davis, H., Vigar, V., Srednicka-Tober, D., Rushton, S., Seal, C.J. and Leifert, C. (2021) Diet and Food Type Affect Urinary Pesticide Residue Excretion Profiles in Healthy Individuals: Results of a Randomized Controlled Dietary Intervention Trial, *American Journal of Clinical Nutrition*, 115(2): 364–77.

Riddle, J.E. (1841) *The Young Scholar's English-Latin and Latin-English Dictionary*, Longman, Orme, Brown, Green and Longmans, and John Murray, London.

Salman, M., Silano, V., Heim, D. and Kreysa, J. (2012) Geographical BSE Risk Assessment and Its Impact on Disease Detection and Dissemination, *Preventive Veterinary Medicine*, 105(4): 255–64.

Sultan, T., Tarafder, T., Pearson, J. and Henryks, J. (2020) Intention-Behaviour Gap and Perceived Behavioural Control-Behaviour Gap in Theory of Planned

Behaviour: Moderating Roles of Communication, Satisfaction and Trust in Organic Food Consumption, *Food Quality and Preference*, 81: 103838. Published at: https://doi.org/10.1016/j.foodqual.2019.103838. Accessed on 14 April 2022.

Tandon, A., Dhir, A., Kaur, P., Kushwah, S. and Salo, J. (2020) Why Do People Buy Organic Food? The Moderating Role of Environmental Concerns and Trust, *Journal of Retailing and Consumer Services*, 57: 102247. Published at: https://doi.org/10.1016/j.jretconser.2020.102247. Accessed on 17 April 2022.

Vigar, V., Myers, S., Oliver, C., Arellano, J., Robinson, S. and Leiferts, C. (2019) A Systematic Review of Organic versus Conventional Food Consumption: Is There a Measurable Benefit on Human Health? *Nutrients*, 12(1): 7. Published at: https://doi.org/10.3390/nu12010007. Accessed on 15 April 2022.

EPILOGUE
FROM PURE FOOD TO PURIFICATION: A REVIEW OF PERSPECTIVES

....

Helen Macbeth and Paul Collinson

Introduction

What is pure food? Honey straight from the hive perhaps or a mother's breast milk? In the preceding chapters of this cross-disciplinary volume, different perspectives on pure food have been identified and discussed. The purpose of this concluding chapter is to review the ways in which the contributions have approached the subject and to draw together some of the linking themes between them. Following a review of definitions of the word 'pure', we use this to inform a discussion of how concepts of 'pure food' are considered in previous chapters. We then go on to explore the relationship between pure food and purification pertaining both to individuals and to the environment, noting how some foods are considered purifying whereas others may be a source of pollution. A final section offers some tentative thoughts on the future of pure food in the light of social, societal and economic trends.

The Meanings of 'Pure'

The word 'pure' in the English language primarily has the sense of the absolute, something free from any additives. 'Pure gold' is gold without any adulteration with other metals; it is pure in its entirety. 'Pure nonsense' is entirely nonsense. Should 'pure water', then, be just H_2O? Yet, when calling water in a glass 'pure', one is saying neither that the glass contains nothing but water nor that its contents are chemically 100 percent H_2O. Some might *believe* that, but it is most unlikely to be true. In the case of that glass of water, the use of the word 'pure' is to convey something positive about the water; usually the intended meaning is that it is unmixed with anything harmful for humans to drink, not that there is no admixture to the H_2O at all. It is interesting to note that 'spring water' is often marketed as 'pure water', but it certainly would never be just H_2O, because it is likely to contain acquired minerals and, if derived straight from a rural spring, will almost certainly have acquired some organic matter too.

Several chapters refer to different meanings of 'pure', some referring to a dictionary source. For example, MacClancy discusses the variety of meanings given to the word, noting that 'its most common thread of meaning appears to be "unmixed"' (p. 47), but he then points out that the *Oxford English Dictionary* lists thirty-one further meanings. It is an interesting and easy exercise to compare the definitions of 'pure' given in the different online English dictionaries, in which 'unmixed' is regularly the first definition: for example, for the *Merriam Webster Dictionary*[1] 'unmixed with any other matter', and for the *Cambridge Dictionary*[2] and the *Collins Online Dictionary*[3] 'not mixed with anything else'. Then in each case a variety of meanings follows, which only to some extent overlap, including 'free from dust, dirt or taint', 'spotless, stainless', 'free from harmful substances', 'complete, only', 'sheer, unmitigated', 'of unmixed ancestry' and (regarding sound or colour) 'clear and represents a perfect example of its type'. Also, there are always a number of definitions regarding morality, such as 'free from moral fault or guilt', 'marked by chastity' and 'morally good, especially because they have no sexual experience or sexual thoughts'. This range of definitions supports MacClancy's view of purity being referred to as something positive, but in a diversity of ways.

As the word 'pure' is derived from the Latin word *purus*, it is interesting also to consider definitions in Latin-English dictionaries. *The Young Scholar's English-Latin and Latin-English Dictionary* (Riddle 1841: 306) states:

I.   Pure, clear, free from dirt, filth, crime, etc.

II. That is in its natural state, pure, simple, unadorned, inartificial, unsophisticated

     Hence: 1. bright or clear
                2. holy, virtuous, pure, incorrupt, faultless; pure, unstained
                3. (*of gain*): clear after all deductions
                4. that which purifies[4]
                5. pure, unmixed

III. That is without any condition or exception, free from conditions or exceptions.

For a contemporary version, the *Online Latin Dictionary* gives the following definition:

Purus – pure, clean, unsoiled; free from defilement, taboo, stain; blame-
less, innocent; chaste, unpolluted by sex; plain and unadulterated; genuine;
absolute; refined; clear, limpid, free of mist and cloud; ... net; simple.[5]

From these two examples, it is clear that a diversity of meanings was already
present in the meaning of the word *purus* in Latin. Again, there is the fundamental meaning of unmixed or absolute, plus a clear bias towards the positive and particularly towards definitions concerning morality, even holiness.

Differing Conceptions of Pure Food

In our Introduction to this book, we explored the development of the English
words 'pure' and 'impure' provided in the online etymological dictionary *etymonline*,[6] emphasising their changes in meaning over the centuries in relation
to their positive and negative associations (p. 2); this in turn concurs well with
the diversity of meanings in Latin, including those that can be considered positive and moral. This is a theme taken up by Lejavitzer, who starts her chapter
with a discussion of meanings of *purus*, with quoted sections from Lewis and
Short's *A Latin Dictionary* (1991: 494). She then goes on to contend that the
'idea of "pure" is linked to the sacred, the order, the cosmos, representing
that which has no stain or defect, which has not been altered or adulterated
by any fault and which presents no anomaly' (p. 95). It is important to note
that her chapter strongly emphasises the meanings of 'pure' that are related
to morality and she refers to examples of translation of the word from Latin
into French and the links with religious language, which in turn correspond to
the Greek word καθαρός.

Meanwhile, MacClancy's discussion of the concepts of 'pure' and 'purity'
in relation to food is concerned above all with their malleability through time,
between different communities and according to context. His chapter emphasises a *discontinuity* of meanings and the way in which these can change
according to who is doing the defining; as he evocatively puts it, 'purity is
more a shapeshifter than a statue' (p. 68). His chapter reminds us of Humpty
Dumpty's contention in *Through the Looking Glass and What Alice Found
There* (Carroll 1872): 'When I use a word ... it means just what I choose it to
mean – neither more nor less.'

Referring to human sociocultural and biophysical reactions to the acceptance or rejection of different foods in different cultures, Schiefenhövel
explores the relevance of people's concepts about which foods are 'pure' or
'impure' in terms of their cultural categories, sometimes causing very physical reactions to different foods. His interest lies in his informants' views on,
selection or avoidance of and even physical reactions to culturally identified foods, and how these interact so strongly with beliefs of what is 'pure'

(and thus proper) or 'impure' (and thus improper). Again, the importance of cultural context is highlighted, strongly echoing MacClancy's perspective.

The Introduction to this volume discusses the significance of Mary Douglas' (1966) work as well as later criticisms of it, which are also referred to in a number of other chapters. In Carter's chapter, Douglas' view of the importance of order and classification is central to his discussion of 'purity' as in 'ordered relations and where contravention is disorder or "dirt"' (p. 86). Based on this premise, his chapter is about the resonance between structuralist ideas and contemporary research in psychology and neuroscience, exemplified through a psychoanalytical case study in which the significance to a child patient of the fairytale of The Gingerbread Man is interpreted in Douglasian terms as a form of pure food. In overview, the message in Carter's chapter parallels that in Schiefenhövel's chapter in terms of highlighting the psychological efficacy of purity in relation to food and the way in which this dovetails with cultural categories and symbols.

The diversity of meaning of 'pure' is also evident in Saucedo et al.'s chapter on the differing cultural concepts about blood and its uses as food. The authors contrast the way in which blood is seen as both inherently 'pure' in some contexts as well as potentially dangerous and a source of possible contamination and pollution, i.e. 'impure', in others. These observations are projected in the chapter in differing attitudes to blood as a food source, with ethnographic evidence from rural areas in Mexico being used to illustrate these themes. They conclude by arguing that consumption of blood could improve nutrition in contemporary Mexico if different public attitudes were to be adopted, particularly in urban areas. Blood in this chapter can be viewed as a microcosmic reflection of the way in which conceptions of what is 'pure', 'impure' or polluting alter across time and space.

With an interest in bioethics, Deraga's chapter is directly concerned with people's concepts of what might be considered 'pure food'. Among the poorest in the rural communities she studied, their concerns were in acquiring enough food to eat, their foods were local and traditional, and the 'purity' of such foods was barely questioned. Thus the concept had little reality for them. However, she found that with less impoverished and more educated interviewees, she was able to discuss attitudes to genetically modified organisms, vegetarianism, organic food and finally *in vitro* meat, with issues such as food safety, food labelling and certification also being significant. Her chapter is backed up with information on cases of food contamination in Mexico and disease due to such contamination. She suggests that these have only recently had any real effect on people's attitudes to food safety, and therefore on their conceptions of 'pure food'. Her inclusion of *in vitro* meat within the context of what might be considered 'pure food' is particularly interesting and should stimulate debate beyond this volume.

In her chapter, Macbeth limits her discussion of 'pure food' to organic food. Although public perceptions of organic food are briefly considered, the chapter is primarily about the reality of producing food that can qualify for certification as 'organic', including relevant biological and biochemical issues that raise questions about the bases for contemporary certification of the production of such foods. Once greater biochemical precision is considered, she argues that only some risks of adulteration are avoided by the ideals of organic farming and the regulations for its production, since living organisms can also adulterate food, whether these are harmful to health or not.

Honey provides an interesting example in this respect. The diversity in flavour of different varieties of honey depends on the blossoms (heather, lavender, acacia, manuka, rosemary, local wild flowers and so many more) within the range of the bees and thus the biochemical differences that are incorporated into the honey that affect the flavour. In response to this point, one could decide that all honey is 'pure' if straight from the hive with no *later* adulteration, but what of honey from bees that have been deliberately fed other sugars through human intervention? Is that still a 'pure food'? Furthermore, Panseri et al. (2020) found residues of diverse unhealthy pollutants in samples of certified organic honey in different proportions, depending on the environmental conditions of the areas over which the bees roamed. So, when can even 'organic' honey be thought of as assuredly 'pure' in the sense of without any component harmful to health?

As for olive oil, the other 'divine' food in Lejavitzer's chapter, today there are scientific methods for detecting fraudulent admixtures of cheaper oils in 'virgin' olive oil (and of course that prefix is a classic example of the type of 'purity marketing' referred to in the Introduction, with a direct parallel with the etymology of the word 'pure' itself). Biochemical studies have also shown alkyl and ethyl esters occurring organically in some virgin olive oils due to fermentation occurring in some of the olives used (e.g. Conte et al. 2014). It is unknown whether the gods of the ancient Greeks were able to avoid these admixtures in the gifts they bestowed of honey and olive oil(!). Finally, what is often considered to be the ultimate pure food – breast milk – may not be as pure as we think. Concerns over the presence of microplastics in the environment were heightened further in 2022 when a study in Italy found them in breast milk for the first time, a discovery that was widely reported in the media (Ragusa et al. 2022).[7] And what about the case in which a mother's consumption of a ready meal containing soya caused her infant's eczema through her breast milk (personal communication)? As Macbeth's chapter makes clear, when one applies detailed chemical analyses to some foods considered 'pure', it becomes almost impossible to define any food as wholly 'pure' in objective, scientific terms.

Deraga's and Macbeth's informants have a modern scientific approach to information, the validity of which is often assumed but not questioned. Also based on an unexpressed acceptance of modern scientific concepts is the discussion of 'pure food' in Antal's chapter. In her chapter, reporting on efforts in Liverpool, England, to provide 'pure food' in public institutions, the objective of the initiatives she describes is to improve the health of the consumers and thus the health of the local population. For her, the concept of 'pure food' can be interpreted as that which is 'free from preservatives, colouring or other additives' and 'cultivated without the use of chemical fertilizers' (p. 125) (a definition taken from the online dictionary Lexico.com)[8] – in other words, food that avoids admixtures, while presuming negative properties of these admixtures. She gives examples of formal attempts to create identifiable standards of purity for the foods provided to patients in hospitals and to schoolchildren, such as the 'Balanced Scorecard' approach, and the Soil Association's certification of organic foods and its catering mark, 'Food for Life', as well as the UK government's Government Buying Standards. She concludes by welcoming the wider local and national concerns for providing 'purer' food and lifestyles as a way to promote better health of the population.

From Pure Food to Purification

A key theme that links several chapters in the book is the potentially purifying effects of pure food. As suggested in the Introduction, Mariano and Medina's exploration of the culture of fitness adherents has intriguing parallels with concepts of purity in South Asian communities (considered in the Introduction) and in ancient Greece and Rome (a central theme in Lejavitzer's chapter), in terms of foods that are considered to 'purify' or pollute. For Mariano and Medina's informants, choosing the correct foods in a regime that includes other aspects of lifestyle is geared towards achieving an ideal that goes beyond our concepts of health into metaphysical realms. Yet Mariano and Medina refer to evidence suggesting that their informants' food choices in their quest for 'purification' may in some cases be in reality detrimental to health. This is also paralleled by the research referred to in the Introduction concerning the sometimes less-than-healthy 'alternative' (e.g. meat-free) processed foods, as well as the potentially harmful effects of restrictive diets (also mentioned by MacClancy).

Similar to points made by Lejavitzer regarding ancient Rome, many of the new dietary regimes promoted today across the internet and social media, in multitudinous popular books and advocated by celebrities in recent years have at their heart the purification of the individual, with foods consumed, lifestyle and spiritual wellbeing all being seen as intrinsically interrelated. It is not difficult to see the appeal of this in the context of the postmodern, risk society, with its inhabitants navigating an increasingly fast-paced, and often alienating and stressful social landscape. The abundance of yoga studios in the modern Western city and the plethora of health-food shops, organic cafes, vegan restaurants, sugar-free bakeries and so on have much in common with this same aim. Collinson's chapter picks up this theme, but ties it in with the ways in which the supposedly purifying effects of tourism, particularly in the case of environmental, cultural and, importantly, food tourism, are promoted. In western Ireland, traditional, local foods are often marketed to outsiders through an interlacing with depictions of the environment and culture of the region as a pristine rural idyll, with the power to cleanse both the body and the mind. This has echoes in the way in which western Ireland has long been portrayed in literature and art, with explicit or implicit contrasts drawn between the ashramic qualities of the locale and that which lies outside it.

As well as the purification of the individual, we can also talk about the purification of the environment. As we pointed out in the Introduction, the early organicists were the first to promote this concept in the West, but they had imported their ideas from South Asia, where the indivisibility of 'the health of the soil, plant, animal and man', to quote Albert Howard,[9] was long established and central to farming methods. The farmer described in the chapter by Macbeth embodies the continuation of this ideal. In farming without polluting chemicals, in creating woodlands, in erecting photovoltaic solar panels to create electricity and in attempting to balance out any effects of methane production from raising beef cattle, concerns for the environment are central to his philosophy of farming. Nevertheless, the attempts at purification of the environment stem from his farming methods rather than from the food that he produces. Deraga's discussion about *in vitro* meat is couched in terms of the potential it might offer in relation again to its production minimising the environmental impact when compared to producing real meat. However, the case is far from proven, and, as argued by Bonny et al. (2015), producing plant and mycoprotein meat substitutes may be less harmful for the environment than producing *in vitro* meat. Yet, in both of these cases, the production methods are complex; thus, the energy use and other costs for the whole production process should also be considered when assessing environmental impacts, not just limiting that assessment to terms of some potential benefits such as a reduction in the emission of methane.

In the situations considered above and in many other ways, the production of foods can be considered in terms of whether their production is beneficial or harmful for the environment, and the crucial role of farmers in protecting the environment is increasingly enshrined in public policy in many (and probably most) countries in the world. For example, the UK's Department for Environment, Food and Department for Environment, Food and Rural Affairs stated in 2022:

> Farmers also play a crucial role in protecting and enhancing the natural environment. If we want farming and food production to be resilient and sustainable over the long term, then farming and nature can and must go hand in hand. (Department for Environment, Food and Rural Affairs 2022: 4)

Below this, the document lists ways in which the UK government will assist farmers in England, one of which is by:

Providing regular income for farmers to improve the environment, as part of their farm business. (Department for Environment, Food and Rural Affairs 2022: 5)

Many environmental concerns, such as those aimed at minimising the impact of human activities on the environment and ultimately improving the quality of land, water and air, fit well within the diverse meanings of the word 'purification'. However, other ecological objectives are geared towards the maintenance and often enhancement of biodiversity, which, in recent years, has also come to be viewed as a very important aspect of environmental health. Examples include increasing the diversity of local wildlife, encouraging mixed species hedgerows, leaving areas of farmland fallow for wild flowers to grow for the benefit of insects, and establishing appropriate niches for wild birds, along with many others. As was argued at the beginning of this chapter, in all the English dictionaries studied the prime meaning of pure given is that which is 'not mixed with anything else'. Yet the central attribute of biodiversity is that the environment should be mixed; a healthy environment is defined partly by the extent of its diversity, in that such an environment also encourages a 'natural' mixture and interaction of many species in a virtuous ecological feedback loop. It follows from this that not all that benefits the environment can be associated with the word 'purification'. Positive images of the environment are a product not only of what we interpret as pure air, water and land, but also of whether or not each is teeming with desirable biodiversity. In this respect, and as MacClancy's chapter highlights, the concept of 'purity' reflects what is positive, even if this is based on diversity and admixture. These concepts are well established and increasingly part of our culture, and governmental support to encourage the nurturing of the environment in agricultural practices reflects this.

Among the definitions of *purus* in Riddle's (1841) Latin dictionary is 'that which purifies', and that concept of 'pure food' purifying recurs in the preceding chapters. However, the question arises as to whether the food resulting from agricultural and production methods that are environmentally benign can itself be considered a 'pure food' simply on that basis? If one chooses to be vegetarian for the benefit of the environment, are the plants eaten thereby 'purer' by definition – even inasmuch as they stand in contrast to meat, the production of which is often considered more environmentally harmful? As our survey of attitudinal research towards pure food in the Introduction demonstrates, it is highly likely that consumers themselves feel that way. Such complexities exemplify the malleability of the concepts of 'pure' in relation to food, as the chapters in this book have shown.

The above discussions on the effects of food production on the environment, just like those on the precise biochemistry of food ingredients or the effects of pathogens on the human body, are today firmly based on scientific principles in most countries. Whether understood with precision by scientists or only partially understood by the majority, one can say that in our contemporary culture, our sense of order usually stems from a scientific explanation for phenomena. Science thus fulfils a desire for order in things, just like any other belief system, and as such is perfectly compatible with Douglas' framework.

Looking to the Future

So, what of the future of pure food? As was highlighted in the Introduction, among Western (and increasingly non-Western) populations, the consumption of what are considered to be 'purer' forms of food has become a central trend in recent years, manifested variously in the growth of vegetarianism and veganism, the emergence of new dietary regimes, an emphasis on 'clean eating' with all its physical, psychological and often quasi-spiritual associations, and the rise of organic food. Modernity and the 'risk society' have brought with them a new emphasis on food safety and regulation, which is driving both the behaviour of consumers and their expectations of public institutions and governments in relation to the quality of food available. This is reified in a multitude of different ways, from the rules governing food production, through food labelling and hygiene ratings for food outlets, to the serving of food in public institutions. We can fully expect these trends to deepen going forward.

At the same time, the atomisation of familial and social life in much of the Western world has also led to a striving for 'tradition' and 'authenticity' in all their myriad forms. This has had a profound effect on food consumption patterns, with the marketing of food (and culture) a key part of this – along with new lifestyle trends such as the seeking out of 'food experiences' and food and environmental tourism. The dovetailing of physical, psychological and spiritual health, central both to our ancestors and to many contemporary cultures around the world, has been rediscovered in many Western countries and so has become an intrinsic aspect of the different ways in which foods are promoted and, in response, chosen and consumed. Based on the profound changes that have occurred in recent years in these areas and others, we can say with some certainty that among a significant proportion of the world's population, particularly in richer countries, a demand for 'pure food' – however this is defined – is likely to remain a central driver of the way in which food is produced, distributed, marketed and consumed. The relationship between lifestyle and diet is also likely to become ever closer in the coming decades.

Yet, it is also evident that a profound bifurcation of food consumption patterns is underway. At the time of writing, the effects of the COVID-19 pandemic, Russia's invasion of Ukraine in 2022, rising food price inflation and climate change-induced disruptions to food production have led to a rise in food insecurity in many areas of the world. For far too many people, the reality of life is not having enough to eat; from their perspective, as exemplified by Deraga for the rural poor in West Mexico, considerations of whether food is pure or not is an indulgent luxury with little meaning in their everyday lives. Meanwhile, the obesity epidemic in many countries in the West is also related partly to economic trends, with the rise of cheap, 'fast' and too often unhealthy convenience foods becoming another key element of contemporary foodscapes. 'Food purity', by almost any definition, comes at a cost. It follows that global economic trends over the coming years are likely to be a significant determining factor in the future consumption of 'pure food'. Growing levels of inequality in many countries are potentially important here too. Food consumption patterns are likely to become increasingly polarised between different groups of people, with a widening gap between those who can afford to eat (and produce) food according to their ideals of 'purity', and those who cannot. Finally, the expected deepening of climate change over the coming decades is likely to lead to increasingly profound changes in the ways in which food is produced and consumed. Together with increases in the world's population – expected to reach 9.7 billion by 2050[10] – the need to create a more sustainable global food system is likely to push ideals about how to minimise the environmental impacts of food production, distribution, consumption and waste further into the mainstream.

Nevertheless, as expounded so eloquently by Mary Douglas over fifty years ago and emphasised in many of the preceding chapters here, the categorisation of food is related to systems of classification that are fundamental to all societies and have profound psychological and cultural resonance for all human beings. As such, the distinction between what is considered 'pure' and what is not, in all the multitudinously variable forms that have been described in this book, is a key aspect of what it is to be human – and as such, 'pure food' will always be with us, however we choose to interpret it to be.

Helen Macbeth is an Honorary Research Fellow and retired Principal Lecturer in Anthropology at Oxford Brookes University. She is a former President of the International Commission on the Anthropology of Food and Nutrition with a strong interest in crossing the boundaries between traditional academic disciplines.

Paul Collinson is a social anthropologist with interests in the anthropologies of food, conflict and development in Europe and Africa. He is a Visiting Research Fellow and former lecturer at Oxford Brookes University. He also works as a senior conflict analyst for the UK government.

Notes

1. See https://www.merriam-webster.com/ (last accessed 29 September 2022).
2. See https://dictionary.cambridge.org/ (last accessed 29 September 2022).
3. See https://www.collinsdictionary.com/ (last accessed 29 September 2022).
4. This meaning is referred to again below.
5. See https://www.online-latin-dictionary.com/ (last accessed 17 September 2022).
6. See https://www.etymonline.com (last accessed 17 September 2022).
7. See https://www.theguardian.com/environment/2022/oct/07/microplastics-human-breast-milk-first-time (last accessed 8 October 2022).
8. Quoting from www.lexico.com/definition/pure_food (last accessed 14 April 2022).
9. See https://www.thelandgardeners.com/siralbert (last accessed 2 October 2022).
10. See https://www.un.org/en/global-issues/population (last accessed 28 January 2023).

References

Bonny, S.P.F., Gardner, G.E., Pethick, D.W. and Hocquette, J.-F. (2015) What Is Artificial Meat and What Does It Mean for the Future of the Meat Industry?, *Journal of Integrative Agriculture*, 15: 255–63.

Carroll, L. (1872) *Through the Looking Glass and What Alice Found There*, Macmillan, London.

Conte, L., Mariani, C., Gallina Toschi, T. and Tagliabue, S. (2014) Alkyl Esters and Related Compounds in Virgin Olive Oils: Their Evolution over Time, *Rivista Italiana delle Sostanze Grasse*, 91: 21–29.

Department for Environment, Food and Rural Affairs (2022) *New Farming Policies and Payments in England (Updated in July 2022)*. Published at: https://www.gov.uk/guidance/funding-for-farmers. Accessed on 21 September 2022.

Douglas, M. (1966) *Purity and Danger: An Analysis of Concepts of Pollution and Taboo*, Routledge & Kegan Paul, London.

Lewis, C.T., and Short, C. (1991) *A Latin Dictionary*, Clarendon Press, Oxford.

Panseri, S., Bonerba, E., Nobile, M., Di Cesare, F., Mosconi, G., Cecati, F., Arioli, F., Tantillo, G. and Chiesa, L. (2020) Pesticides and Environmental Contaminants in Organic Honeys According to Their Different Productive Areas toward Food Safety Protection, *Foods*, 9(12): 1863. Published at: https://www.ncbi.nlm.nih.gov/pmc/articles/PMC7764946/pdf/foods-09-01863.pdf. Accessed on 13 March 2022.

Ragusa, A., Notarstefano, V., Svelato, A., Belloni, A., Gioacchini, G., Blondeel, C., Zucchelli, E., De Luca, C., D'Avino, S., Gulotta, A., Carnevali, O. and Giorgini, E. (2022) Raman Microspectroscopy Detection and Characterisation of Microplastics in Human Breastmilk, *Polymers*, 14(13): 2700. Published at doi: 10.3390/polym14132700. PMID: 35808745; PMCID: PMC9269371. Accessed on 4 February 2023.

Riddle, J.E. (1841) *The Young Scholar's English-Latin and Latin-English Dictionary*, Longman, Orme, Brown, Green and Longmans, and John Murray, London.

INDEX